# Walking the Via de la Plata

### The Camino de Santiago
### from Sevilla to Santiago de Compostela

## Ben Cole &
## Bethan Davies

## Pili Pala Press
### www.pilipalapress.com

Walking the Via de la Plata

Published by Pili Pala Press, 2934 Woodland Drive, Vancouver, BC V5N 3R1 Canada
www.pilipalapress.com

© Ben Cole and Bethan Davies, 2004
Editor: Michael Harling

cover photo: grape truck at Torremegía
back cover photo: detail from Puerta del Perdón, Santiago cathedral

Printed in Canada on 100% post-consumer recycled paper, processed chlorine-free

**National Library of Canada Cataloguing in Publication**

Cole, Ben, 1970-
Walking the Via de la Plata : the Camino de Santiago from Sevilla to Santiago de Compostela /
Ben Cole and Bethan Davies.

Includes index.
ISBN 0-9731698-1-8

1. Christian pilgrims and pilgrimages--Spain--Santiago de Compostela. 2. Spain--Description
and travel--Guidebooks. 3. Hiking--Spain--Guidebooks. I. Davies, Bethan, 1970- II. Title.

DP43.2.C64 2004            914.6'2              C2004-900924-9

## About the Authors

**Ben Cole** has worked in travel bookshops for longer than he cares to remember,
after gaining a degree in archaeology and ancient history. Ben fell in love with Iberia
in 1993 while exploring the mountains of Portugal, and a chance encounter with the
camino a few years later led to a fascination with the various routes to Santiago. He
finds it hard to start the day without a *café solo, grande*.

**Bethan Davies** has been dreaming of Spain ever since her first glass of Rioja,
and is now marked out as a lunatic supporter of the Spanish national football team
(especially Raúl) in bars up and down Spain. A librarian and former editor, she
co-authored Pili Pala Press' *Walking in Portugal* and *Walking the Camino de Santiago*
with Ben Cole.

# Walking the Via de la Plata

## Thank you

Thanks to everyone who helped put *Walking the Via de la Plata* together.

Our fellow pilgrims, especially Bernard, Eneko, Manolo and Virginia. The people along the Vía de la Plata who point pilgrims the right way, unlock town halls and schools, provide meals and beds, and make walking the route a fabulous experience.

Bar Fonda, still the best bar in the world. And we're still not telling you where it is.

Sophia Wege for keeping things ticking along at HQ while we were off gallivanting.

Geoff Hancock for detailed comments on accommodation, and Lucy Kenward for a welcome smile in Zamora, insights into cycling the route and editorial comments.

Michael Harling for proofreading and editorial work; all the mistakes is his fault.

Ed Luciano and Alison Roy for not burning down the homestead.

Tony McCurdy for encouragement, enthusiasm and generous leave-granting.

To our families for love and support, and to Idris, who came along for the ride.


## About Pili Pala Press

Founded in 1993, Pili Pala Press publishes walking guides to Spain and Portugal. Pili Pala is Welsh for butterfly (the clue's in the logo); we could say that we chose the name to reflect our love of nature and our restless desire for travel, but really we just like the way it sounds. We donate 4% of the cover price of each book to environmental organizations in Iberia; past recipients include Iberian Lynx conservation and clean up from the *Prestige* oil disaster. Look for *Walking in Portugal*, our invaluable guide to this forgotten walking destination and *Walking the Camino de Santiago*, our comprehensive guide to the *camino francés*. To order these titles, and for more on the Vía de la Plata, visit our web site at www.pilipalapress.com.

Trails become overgrown, quiet lanes become main roads, and *albergues* open up and close down. Drop us a line if you find something new or different, and check out www.pilipalapress.com for updates.

# Contents

# How This Guide Works

## Glimpse of the Vía de la Plata (page 2)

Background information about the Vía de la Plata, walking, geography, food & drink, history and the arts.

## Flora (page 19) & Fauna (page 21)

English, Spanish and Latin names of birds, mammals, reptiles, amphibians and trees. Includes detailed identification tips, quirky facts and illustrations.

## Tourist Information (page 30)

Practical information to ease your pilgrimage. What to do before you leave, what to bring, how to get there, where to stay, how much things cost, and what to if things go wrong.

# Regional chapters

regional map →

weather

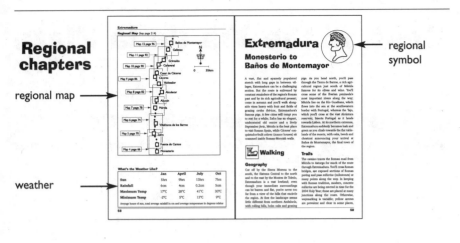

← regional symbol

# Regional Information

regional flora & fauna, people & culture, food & drink and tourist information

# Walk Description

camino sketch map includes distances & at-a-glance symbols

camino profile chart

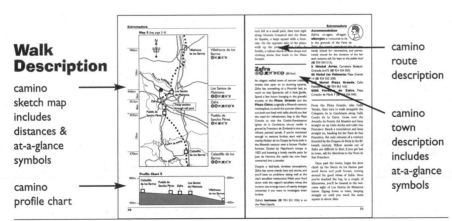

camino route description

camino town description includes at-a-glance symbols

# Best of the Vía de la Plata

 **best bread celebration**

In early July the town of Cea in Galicia (page 171) honours *pan de Cea*, a dense, heavy and delicious loaf.

 **most spectacular mass**

At the pilgrims' mass in Santiago's cathedral (page 179), the *botafumeiro*, a massive incense burner, is swung across the transept in a huge, head-skimming arc.

 **best place to stay in a castle**

Well worth a splurge, the Parador de Zafra (page 71) is a sumptuous hotel in a converted fourteenth-century castle.

 **strangest place to see a cow**

At Galisteo's La Vaquilla festival (page 94), cows are let loose inside the town walls. One year, a cow climbed the steep stone steps to the top of the walls.

 **best place to ease aches and pains**

Follow the robed hordes into the spa at Baños de Montemayor (page 105), where the thermal waters will soothe tired limbs.

 **best place for pork lovers**

Visit Monesterio (page 65), the self-styled sausage and ham capital of Spain, particularly during the El Día del Jamón (day of ham) festival in September.

 **best place to spot a frog**

If you find the carved frog in the façade of Salamanca university (page 112), you'll be blessed with good luck. The unwed will also be married within a year!

 **best place to drink sherry**

Spend a night in Sevilla (page 44) on a *tapas* crawl of the city's intoxicating sherry bars.

# best place to act prehistoric

Watch the sunrise from the overgrown Dolmen de la Cabra (page 67), a megalithic corridor grave made from huge stone slabs.

# oddest-looking bird

On the *meseta*, listen out for the pooo-pooo-pooo call of the hoopoe (page 25), and look for its distinctive coral and black mohican.

# best place to get hit on the head

At Laza's Carnaval (page 142), Peliqueiros, dressed in crazy frilled costumes with oversized grinning masks, have license to hit onlookers with sticks.

# best way to eat cheese

Casar de Cáceres (page 88) is known across Spain for torta de Casar, a round sheep cheese with a centre so creamy that you'll need to eat it with a spoon.

# most spectacular town entrance

The Vía de la Plata enters Mérida (page 77) across the city's 60-arch Puente Romana, one of the largest bridges ever built by the Romans.

# best place to get your feet wet

End the camino in feet-soothing style at the sea in Finisterre (page 192), where you can pick up a scallop shell and visit the end of the world.

# best place to hang out with monks

Pilgrims who stay at the *albergue* in Alcuéscar's monastery (page 83) spend a night in a cell after being treated to a delicious meal by the hospitable monks.

# most essential equipment

Don't go anywhere without your *credencial* (page 31), the pilgrims' passport that lets you stay in *albergues* along the camino.

# best source of up-to-date information on the Vía de la Plata

Visit our web site at www.pilipalapress.com for photos, updates & links.

# The Vía de la Plata

(key page 214)

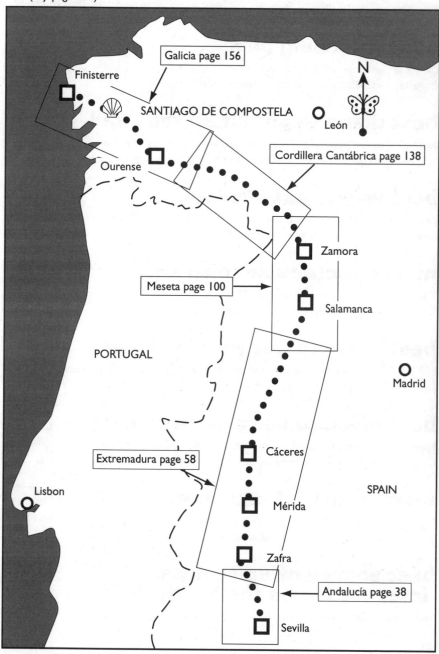

Galicia page 156

Finisterre

SANTIAGO DE COMPOSTELA

León

N

Cordillera Cantábrica page 138

Ourense

Zamora

Meseta page 100

Salamanca

PORTUGAL

Madrid

Extremadura page 58

Cáceres

Lisbon

Mérida

SPAIN

Zafra

Andalucía page 38

Sevilla

# An Introduction to the Vía de la Plata

A spectacular 1000km walk, the Vía de la Plata is an ancient pilgrimage route from Sevilla in southern Spain to the country's northwest corner, where St James is entombed at Santiago de Compostela. Christians weren't the first to make this journey; by medieval times the route was already a well-trodden trade and cultural highway used to spread Roman and Muslim culture to Iberia's heathen north.

Today, pilgrims walk the Vía de la Plata for many different reasons. For some, the pilgrimage to the Holy City is a lifelong dream borne out of religious faith. Others seek a break from daily routines or wish for a simpler way of living, and some want to immerse themselves in Spanish history and culture. Many have already walked the *camino francés* and can't get the pilgrimage out of their system. The Vía de la Plata is a more varied trip than the more popular northern route, passing through stunning landscapes and cultural treasures, and with only 2000 pilgrims making the trip each year, you'll have more chances to meet with local people. Still, it's a tougher, more isolated trip, with fewer facilities and less of a pilgrim infrastructure.

This guide leads you step-by-step along the Vía de la Plata, from Sevilla to Santiago de Compostela and on to Finisterre. Begin your journey in Andalucía, home to *flamenco*, *tapas* and splendid Moorish architecture, and bask in a sunny climate ideal for cork oaks, cacti and cotton. Then head north on a Roman road, crossing glorious arched bridges, and passing hippodromes, amphitheatres and fabulous mosaics. You'll pass through places made famous by rampaging Christian knights and wander through grand houses built by the *conquistadores* who overran the Americas. Finally, you'll cross into northwest Spain, green as Ireland and damp as can be, where thick stone houses and splendid rural architecture dot isolated mountainsides.

While you walk, we'll point out wildlife found nowhere else in the world, such as the Iberian lynx, the most endangered wild cat in the world. We'll introduce you to bizarre festivals where cows clamber up town walls or masked men batter spectators with large sticks. We'll help you sort out your *fino* from your *amontillado*, discover unique local wines, and try (or avoid) regional dishes from deep-fried rooster comb to spicy snails. And we'll smooth your journey with practical information, from places to stay to useful phrases in *Castellano* (Spanish) and *Galego* (Galician).

# A Glimpse of the Vía de la Plata

 **El Camino**

## The story of Santiago

Just how Santiago ended up in the remote northwestern corner of Iberia is a strange and marvellous tale.

Santiago, or St James as he's known in English, was one of Jesus' apostles, and after the crucifixion, he headed to Spain to spread the gospel. Though he preached as far north as Galicia, he didn't have much luck with the native peoples, and attracted a mere seven converts before turning around to head home to Jerusalem.

Although there's no biblical basis for Santiago's visit to Spain, it's clear that Herod Agrippa had him beheaded in AD44 in Jerusalem, making him the first apostle to be martyred. Santiago's friends managed to sneak his body out from under Herod's nose and put him on a stone boat headed for northwest Spain without oars, sails or crew. After a week-long journey, the body arrived in Padrón on the Galician coast, where his disciples were waiting. They buried Santiago 20km inland in Compostela, after the local queen witnessed a series of miracles and converted to Christianity.

Santiago lay forgotten for a good few centuries, while all around him Spain became Christian through rather gradual, more conventional means. The move to Christianity ended abruptly at the start of the eighth century, when Muslim armies crossed over from North Africa, soon conquering most of the Iberian Peninsula and pushing up into central France. Still, persistent pockets of Christianity remained, notably in northwestern Spain.

In 813, a curious Christian hermit followed sweet music and twinkling stars to a remote hillside in Galicia. The bones he found at Campus Stellae (Compostela) were quickly identified as those of Santiago, and the bishop of nearby Iria Flavia sanctified the discovery. Within a few years, Alfonso II, King of Asturias, visited the site, built a chapel and declared Santiago the patron saint of Spain.

Visions of Santiago multiplied, and the saint became instrumental in the fight against the Muslims. His most famous appearance was at the battle of Clavijo in northern Spain, where he rode high above the battle on a white charger, and personally scythed his way through tens of thousands of Moors. This kind of behaviour earned him the name Santiago Matamoros (Moor-slayer), to go with his more pacific image as Santiago Peregrino (pilgrim).

## The history of the camino

By the ninth century, Christian authorities had seized on the pilgrimage to Santiago as a way to drive out Muslim invaders and to prevent the peoples of northern Spain from falling back on their pagan ways. Local churchmen were also keen on the cash that a stream of pilgrims would bring, and their promotion of Santiago de Compostela as a pilgrimage destination was a masterful piece of medieval marketing.

The number of pilgrims rose over the next couple of hundred years, particularly after the Turkish capture of the Holy Sepulchre made Jerusalem unsafe for pilgrims. The French were particularly eager, so much so that the main route over the Pyrenees from St-Jean-Pied-de-Port and across Spain is called the *camino francés*.

In 1189, Pope Alexander III declared Santiago de Compostela a Holy City, along with Rome and Jerusalem. Under his edict, pilgrims who arrive during Holy Years (when the Día de Santiago, July 25, falls on a Sunday) can bypass purgatory entirely, whereas those arriving in other years get half their time off.

It wasn't all voluntary penitence. Sometimes people were sentenced to walk to Santiago as punishment for a crime, although wealthy convicts could get around this by paying someone else to walk the pilgrimage. Other pilgrims went on behalf of their villages in an effort to get rid of plagues, floods or locusts, or as an excuse to see the world in the days before package holidays.

The flow of pilgrims peaked in the eleventh and twelfth centuries, when about half a million people made the pilgrimage. Churches and pilgrim hospices sprung up along the various routes to Santiago, often built on the site of miracles. Their walls provided havens from a dangerous and arduous outside world, where wolves and bandits thwarted the faithful.

## The Vía de la Plata

Although northern Europeans made up the bulk of pilgrims, people arrived in Santiago de Compostela from all over the world. Pilgrims from southern Spain journeyed north along a road known as the Vía de la Plata.

Even though the route follows an old Roman road towards the precious metal mines of northern Spain, the name Vía de la Plata (silver route) has nothing to do with the precious metal. Instead, the name is possibly a corruption of the Latin *Platea* (wide road) or *Lapidata* (stone road) or, most likely, the Arabic *al-Balath* or *Balatta*, both terms used for roads throughout Iberia, but which for some reason stuck here.

Well before anyone had thought up a name for the route, paleolithic man hunted migrating beasts up and down the natural corridor between the north and south of the peninsula. When prehistoric peoples began to make the transition from hunter-gatherers to farmers, the route was used to move domesticated animals from the summer pastures of the northern *meseta* to the more benign climate of the Tajo and Guadiana valleys. Commerce flowed backwards and forwards too, as Egyptians, Phoenicians and Greeks arriving in southern ports traded ceramics and glass for gold and silver from northern mines. Hannibal brought his elephants this way, and local hero Viriatus used it to flee to his northern strongholds, but it was the Romans who really etched the route on to the map of Iberia.

In 25BC, Augustus founded Emerita Augusta (Mérida) as a home for veterans of the Iberian wars. The city became the capital of Lusitania, and Augustus soon commissioned a road to link his new capital with the city of Asturica (Astorga), allowing for easy transport of gold and other precious metals to southern ports and for rapid deployment of troops should unruly northerners cause trouble. The Calzada Romana was divided into *mansiones* (stages) of 20 to 25 Roman miles (a Roman mile was equivalent to 1000 Roman steps or about 1472m) along its 465km length. Each mile was marked by a *miliario* (milestone) and each *mansio* ended with a *mansion*, where soldiers and travellers could rest, eat and hire horses. There are traces of original road along the Vía de la Plata, most notably around Baños de Montemayor, and fabulous Roman bridges straddle the rivers at Mérida and Salamanca. The route was improved by successive emperors, and although Tiberius and Nero's milestones line the way, it was under the Spanish-born Trajan and Hadrian that it became one of the principal means of Romanizing the Iberian peninsula.

As Roman power waned, the Vía de la Plata was used as an invasion route for Suevi, Vandals and Visigoths, and in the eighth century the route allowed Moors to quickly advance into northern Spain from their power base in the south of the peninsula. The Moors expanded the route into an impressive road, wide enough to take four carriages side by side. Reconquering Christian armies came the other way a few centuries later, and the route was used by the opposing sides to traverse the no man's land of Extremadura, between southern Moorish Andalucía and the northern Christian kingdoms.

But the Vía de la Plata wasn't entirely a military route. Moorish Spain was extremely tolerant of Christianity, and *mozarabes* (Mozarabic Christians) were making the pilgrimage to Santiago de Compostela as early as the tenth century. In 1062, the body of San Isidro of Sevilla was taken towards León along the Vía de la Plata, and the bells of Santiago cathedral, which had been captured by Al-Mansur and installed in the mosque at Córdoba, were returned to Santiago some two centuries later.

Meanwhile, Alfonso X *El Sabio* (the Wise) was expanding the peninsula's network of drove roads: the Cañada Real, 75m wide along much of its way, was a Royal drove road that largely followed the existing Vía de la Plata.

Even at the height of medieval piety, the Vía de la Plata wasn't nearly as popular as the northern routes to Santiago. As with the *camino francés*, the number of pilgrims dropped off once the *reconquista* was complete, and by the twentieth century the route was all but forgotten.

## The Vía de la Plata today

It wasn't until the 1980s, by which time the *camino francés* was gaining in popularity, that the revival of the Vía de la Plata began. In 1982, Pope John Paul II became the first pontiff to visit Santiago de Compostela, then in 1987 the European Union declared the camino Europe's first Cultural Itinerary, and UNESCO followed suit in 1993, adding the camino to its World Heritage list.

Meticulous documentation of the Roman road, using aerial photographs as well as more traditional excavation of *miliarios* and bridges, began to fuel interest, as did the revival of the *transhumancia*, the mass movement of herds of cattle and sheep along the old Cañada Real. Meanwhile, interested individuals and Amigos del Camino (friends of the camino) associations began marking the route to Santiago with yellow arrows. The Amigos in Sevilla, particularly José Luis Salvador Salvador, were instrumental in waymarking the route and in establishing a network of basic accommodation along the way; in 1992, 50 pioneers walked the length of the Vía de la Plata. The work is being continued by many others, including Don Blas, parish priest at Fuenterroble de Salvatierra, a modern-day camino evangelist who pesters local mayors and priests into providing accommodation and other facilities.

Today's pilgrims rarely make the complete journey from their homes to Santiago and back, and the vast majority begin the *camino francés* at some point between France and Santiago. Of the 70,000 or so pilgrims who arrive in Santiago de Compostela each year, only 2000 travel the Vía de la Plata. The number of pilgrims travelling the camino peaks during Holy Years: 150,000 people reached Santiago in 1999, and future Holy Years are likely to see even more pilgrims.

Any pilgrim who walks the last 100km to Santiago can apply for a *compostela* (a certificate recognizing the completion of the pilgrimage) from the authorities in Santiago de Compostela. Some pilgrim traditions have survived into the modern era. Many pilgrims walk with the aid of a tall staff and wear a scallop shell attached to their pack or person, mimicking statues of Santiago Peregrino. The beaches of Galicia are awash with scallop shells, and medieval pilgrims would often collect one as a souvenir of their journey; scallop symbols are also ubiquitous, adorning concrete camino markers, churches and houses along the way.

The Vía de la Plata has two main variations, which split just north of Zamora. The first heads due north to Astorga to join with the *camino francés*, a transition that can be a bit of a jolt for pilgrims accustomed to the solitude of the Vía de la Plata. Instead, we describe the route that goes northwest to Santiago de Compostela via Ourense and rural Galicia.

# Walking

Hiking is gaining popularity in Spain, particularly amongst southern city dwellers who escape to cooler mountain regions like the Picos de Europa on sticky summer weekends. You'll see some signs for day walks along the camino, particularly close to cities, but most urbanites prefer the civilized tradition of the evening stroll, browsing in shop windows, sipping Rioja and nibbling *tapas*.

In places like rural Extremadura and

Galicia, walking is an integral part of life, whether heading to work in the fields or making for a post-farming glass of wine, and exercise for its own sake can be seen as rather ridiculous.

Of course, the Vía de la Plata's Christian origins make it much more than a multi-week walking holiday, and locals won't consider walking pilgrims the least bit strange. A smattering of *Castellano* (Spanish) and a willingness to stop and chat will make a big difference to the welcome you receive.

There's a certain snooty hierarchy amongst pilgrims. Many walkers look down on cyclists, often called *peregrinos descafeinados* (decaffeinated pilgrims), and *albergues* (pilgrim hostels) may ask cycling pilgrims to wait until early evening before deciding if there's room. Self-propelled pilgrims, even non-religious ones, often dismiss car-pilgrims as "tourists." Pilgrims on horses or donkeys are now a rarity: fewer than one percent of pilgrims travel this way.

 **Trails**

The camino heads up through Spain on a variety of different surfaces, from narrow paths to wide tracks to tarmac (paved) roads. It's mostly easy walking with very few rough or uneven surfaces, although stone and mud tracks can become slippery after rain. Occasionally, trails can become overgrown, particularly in spring. Road walking can be unpleasant, and the odd stretch can be dangerous due to narrow shoulders, busy roads, and blind corners; walk on the left-hand side

of the road, facing oncoming traffic, if possible.

Along much of the Vía de la Plata there are an abundance of yellow arrows, painted on everything from sidewalks to trees to the sides of houses. Markers vary from modern concrete *miliarios* (milestones) in Extremadura to beautiful carved stones in Galicia. You'll see ancient *miliarios* too, as the route traces the Roman road that ran from Mérida to Astorga; there are restored stretches of Roman road just after Baños de Montemayor and before Cáceres.

The camino also follows broad tracks used to move thousands of sheep, goats and cows from winter to summer pastures. One estimate has the total length of these green corridors at 125,000km, and the partial revival of the practice at the end of the twentieth century means that some of the Vía de la Plata is marked with white arrows both towards and away from Santiago.

Navigating through cities can be difficult, and local authorities in places like Salamanca, Cáceres and Zafra seem reluctant to despoil their attractive old centres with yellow arrows; *turismos* (tourist offices) can be helpful in showing you the route through town. Elsewhere, navigating through towns can be tricky, as new building work or industrial development can obliterate arrows and paths.

In places, there can be long, remote stretches between villages and towns, in one case 38km. Summers can be particularly tough, as there's often little or no shade or water. The wind on the plains of Extremadura and the *meseta* can be strong and quickly sap your energy;

you'll need to eat plenty and drink lots of water, even if it isn't very hot.

# Maps

The sketch maps in this book will give you a general idea of the villages, terrain and sights you'll encounter, along with distances and facilities along the way. And, as the camino is generally well-marked and easy to follow, most pilgrims don't bother with detailed additional maps. Where trail marking is poor, people you meet along the way will be able to direct you back to the camino if you should stray from the route; see our language section on page 197 for helpful walking phrases.

Michelin road maps are good for a general overview of the camino, and although they're next to useless for walking, they do mark most of the towns and villages you'll pass through. You'll need four of these 1:400,000 maps if you start in Sevilla: 578 (Andalucía), 576 (Extremadura, Castilla–La Mancha, Madrid), 575 (Castilla y León, Madrid) and 571 (Galicia).

If you're determined to weigh down your backpack with walking maps, the Spanish Instituto Geográfico Nacional (www.mfom.es/ign/) publishes up-to-date 1:25,000 maps, and the Servicio Geográfico del Ejército publishes the most current 1:50,000 maps.

Walking maps are difficult to find along the camino, but can be ordered from the UK before you go. Try the following: Stanfords (☎ 020 7836 1321; www.stanfords.co.uk) in London, The Map Centre (☎ 01432 266322;

www.themapcentre.com) in Hereford or The Map Shop (☎ 0800 0854080; www.themapshop.co.uk), located in Upton upon Severn.

# Geography

The most stunning aspect of walking the Vía de la Plata is the gradual unravelling of the landscape in front of you. As the camino snakes its way north through Europe's third-largest country, the walker traverses everything from high mountain passes to wide river valleys. Although Spain is the second most mountainous country in Europe (after Switzerland), your route follows the line of least resistance across gently undulating terrain.

From Sevilla, the Vía de la Plata leaves the Guadalquivir river basin and heads up into the Sierra Norte de Sevilla, passing through the massive *latifundias* (large estates) that characterize much of Andalucía. It's an agricultural region where vines, olives and cork oaks grow in river valleys but the scorching summers are also suitable for cacti and cotton. As you pass into Extremadura, you'll find yourself in a hot, dry basin surrounded by mountains and covered with holm oak forests, vines and cereal fields. The landscape of northern Extremadura is barren, but around Galisteo it gets hillier and more fertile, until the climb out of the Extremadura basin at Baños de Montemayor brings you through the damp, green pass at Puerto de Béjar and on to the *meseta*.

The *meseta* is a vast, 800m-high plateau that dominates central Spain, covering almost two-fifths of the country. Treeless for the most part, the *meseta*'s horizon seems to stretch endlessly across yellow wheat fields, broken only by views of the spectacular surrounding mountains that dictate the *meseta*'s climate. In winter, a strong, cold wind howls down from the snowy peaks, freezing the land for eight months of the year. In summer, temperatures soar as the same mountains block cool breezes from the ocean and trap the baking heat.

From Mombuey, you'll enter a mountainous region and the toughest climbs of the Vía de la Plata. It's also the wettest section: the Gulf Stream of the Atlantic Ocean brings soggy warm air from the Caribbean that clings to northwestern Spain for weeks on end. The mountains have also protected the indigenous people from successive waves of invaders; consequently, this isolated corner of Spain often seems to have more in common with northern Celtic nations than with the rest of Spain.

Water dominates the coastal province of Galicia, which gets an average of 2m of rain each year. Deep river valleys have been carved by all that precipitation, and water-loving oak forests cover the land. From Santiago, it's downhill to the ocean at Finisterre, a slim finger of a peninsula that reaches out into the Atlantic towards the setting sun.

 **Environment**

**Hunting** is a big part of Spanish culture, and Spain gives over much of its land to *reservas nacionales de caza* (hunting reserves). In summer, you'll often hear staccato bursts of noise, although these are just as likely to be from *fiesta* firecrackers as from hunters' rifles. Since Franco's demise, regional governments have converted many of the *reservas nacionales* into environmentally protected spaces. Hunting has eliminated some of Spain's rarer creatures, and the **Iberian lynx**, the most endangered wild cat in the world, barely clings to existence, mostly in the southwest of the country. Although the **wolf** is also a protected species, local farmers put their rifles away with gritted teeth, as compensation from the government for lost livestock arrives at glacial speed.

Although it's hard to believe when you're getting soaked by a Galician rainstorm, **water** is one of Spain's major environmental problems. Not only does the country get less rainfall than it did a few years ago, Spain's *per capita* water consumption is one of the highest in the world. River flow is decreasing at an alarming rate as water is siphoned off to satisfy thirsty industries and agriculture. Tourism, destructive in its own right in Spain's coastal region, is also causing water problems as foreign visitors demand emerald-green golf courses, even in water-starved areas.

As in much of the rest of Europe, modern **development** has had environmental consequences. Flush with European Union cash, Spain embarked on a frenzy of road building, and at times along the camino you'll be surrounded by underused, multi-lane roads. In tourist areas and city edges there's a building boom too, and in a country where planning permission is seen as a nicety rather than a legal requirement, ugly, poorly built construction is often the norm. In Galicia, indigenous forests have been torn down to make way for fast-growing **eucalyptus**. Very few birds and other animals can live in these monocultural stands because the acidic leaves sterilize the soil.

The **green movement** in Spain is much younger than those of most northern European countries, but it has become much more organized and high-profile in the last few years. For more information about environmental issues in Spain, contact Amigos de la Tierra (www.tierra.org) or Adena, now affiliated with the World Wildlife Fund (www.wwf.es). For links to environmental organizations, see our web site at www.pilipalapress.com.

 # When to Go

Pilgrims traditionally timed their journey to arrive in Compostela for the Día de Santiago. Now a Galician holiday, July 25 is still the liveliest time to be in the city, when the Plaza de Obradoiro in front of the cathedral is illuminated by a magnificent fireworks display.

**Summer** weather can be brutally hot as daytime temperatures in Andalucía, Extremadura and the *meseta* rocket to 45°C for weeks at a time, with little respite at night. There are long stretches of the camino where there's no shade or water, and walking in these conditions is difficult, if not dangerous. If you do travel in the heat, make sure that you acclimatize gradually and carry lots of water.

Many regions along the Vía de la Plata come alive in August and September with traditional festivals. This time of year also marks the start of the **harvest**, when food-based *fiestas* celebrating everything from sausages to cheese pop up everywhere. Early autumn is the perfect time for wine buffs and olive fans, as the harvest gets into swing. In and around Galicia, it's wild mushroom season and the traditional *hórreos* (granaries) are packed to the gills with bright yellow corn. The Vía de la Plata follows a natural migratory route, and autumn is an excellent time to see birds heading south for the winter. It can still be very hot, particularly in the south, although the weather tends to break towards the end of September.

After this time, nights will cool considerably and daylight hours become much shorter, making very early starts next to impossible. The weather worsens throughout the winter. You'll need to carry more equipment to cope with rain at any time, and to deal with snow on the mountain passes. It can be an inconvenient and chilly time to travel, as churches and tourist sights may be closed and those hotels and *albergues* that stay open in the winter months often lack heating. Despite this, travelling the Vía de la Plata in winter can be a fabulous, solitary experience; you may not see another pilgrim on the whole route and there's a definite camaraderie amongst any hardy souls you do encounter.

Come **spring**, the weather improves, although there's still a chance of snow at higher elevations. You'll probably be rained on for at least a few days of your trip and may get bogged down in the sticky red mud of Extremadura. Spring is the best time to see wild flowers, which bloom much earlier in the warmer southern regions than in chillier, damper Galicia, and it's also an ideal time to spot migrating birds heading back north.

The Vía de la Plata is always busier during **Holy Years** such as 2004 and 2010, when the Día de Santiago falls on a Sunday. Pilgrims who walk the camino in Holy Years get more time off purgatory, and special ceremonies are performed in Santiago and in churches and cathedrals along the way. The number of pilgrims quadrupled in the 1993 and 1999 Holy Years, so space in *albergues* and hotels will be at a premium.

## How long will the pilgrimage take?

If you're fit and healthy and don't want to stay for more than one night in any of the places along the way, you can walk the camino from Sevilla to Santiago de Compostela in about six weeks. It's a good idea to allow for extra time in case of any unforeseen injuries, an occasional lazy day or a whimsical decision to linger in one of the lovely towns along the way. Pilgrims who have already walked the *camino francés* should not underestimate the physical challenge of the Vía de la Plata; as well as being a longer route, there are also fewer facilities, waymarking is poor in sections and there are some very isolated stretches. Cyclists should set aside four weeks for a leisurely trip, although the Vía de la Plata can be pedalled in three weeks.

## Where should I start?

If you have less time, or if you're not used to walking long distances, consider starting somewhere closer to your destination; you only need to walk the last 100km to Santiago to earn a *compostela*. Many pilgrims walk the camino in stages, and returning every year or so to walk another two-week stretch is particularly popular with Spanish pilgrims.

Begin in Sevilla for a stunning trip through a variety of Spains. It can be very hot in Andalucía, but places to stay are spaced some 20 to 25km apart for the first couple of days, allowing pilgrims to break themselves in gradually. If you choose to begin your pilgrimage in Mérida, be prepared for some long initial stages; after passing through Alcuéscar, the gaps between towns increase, and you'll soon find yourself walking for more than 30km a day just to get to the next accommodation. From Cáceres, it's about four weeks to Santiago, but you'll still be faced with some long, empty days. Salamanca and Zamora, some three weeks from Santiago, are both lovely cities and easy to get to. You'll also find that places to stay are spaced closer together from here on. Those who start in Puebla de Sanabria will head straight into the mountains, making for some tough and likely wet days. Ourense is a popular starting point; it's easy to get to and a little more than the magic 100km point from Santiago, and you'll still get a good idea of Galician landscape and culture.

# People & Culture

## History

Neolithic peoples arrived in Spain in about 5000BC and built some splendid dolmens and menhirs, including the Dolmen de la Cabra near Monesterio. The Celts came south across the Pyrenees in about 800BC, leaving a string of *castros* (hill forts) and a lasting influence on Galicia's culture and architecture.

By the sixth century BC, Spain was largely controlled by Carthage, a rule that lasted until the Second Punic War, when the Roman Empire took advantage of Hannibal's march-with-elephants across the Alps to invade Spain from the southern coast. Although the **Romans** struggled to control the wayward Celtic and Iberian tribes of northern Spain, Baetica, as Andalucía was named, was prospering. Emperors Trajan, Hadrian and Theodosius were born here, and at one point it was governed by none other than Julius Caesar. The best Roman remains, including some spectacular mosaics and a phenomenal amphitheatre that sat 15,000 people, can be seen when the Vía de la Plata passes Italica, a town just outside Sevilla, and when the route arrives at Mérida, some 200km further north. The Romans, as always, chose the shortest, most logical routes for their roads: the Vía de la Plata follows a Roman road that linked Italica and Astorga for much of its length.

As Roman power waned, northern armies poured into Spain. The Vandals, Suevi and Visigoths made little impact on the country, although a couple of lovely Visigothic chapels remain, and others lie buried underneath the foundations of later, grander churches.

In the eighth century, a small band of **Moors** arrived in Andalucía and quickly moved north, controlling much of the peninsula in a few short years. This conquest, one of the fastest in medieval Europe, was a high point of Muslim expansion and was celebrated in Damascus with a parade of captured Visigothic nobles. The emirate of Al-Andalus was proclaimed in 756 and, although it covered most of modern Spain, its power and riches were concentrated in Andalucía.

The Muslims introduced oranges, cotton, rice and sugar to Andalucía and turned the area into a rich agricultural region by adapting and perfecting Roman irrigation techniques. The Moors also left spectacular architecture, particularly Sevilla's La Giralda and Alcázar. Meanwhile, the Christian kingdoms of northern Spain were growing in power. Although the notorious Al-Mansur spent the end of the tenth century ransacking Christian towns such as León and Barcelona and even stole the bells from the cathedral at Santiago de Compostela, the Moors never really got a grip on Spain's unruly northerners. After Al-Mansur died, everything began to fall apart. Infighting split Al-Andalus into largely powerless states, and Christian armies began to push south.

The camino's popularity peaked in the Middle Ages, when some of the grandest and most glorious churches and cathedrals along the *camino francés* were built. Meanwhile, Spain's disparate Christian kingdoms were drawing closer together: León, Castilla and Navarra joined forces in 1212 to defeat the Moors at Las Navas de Tolosa, and a more concrete union was cemented in 1479, when Fernando V of Aragón married Isabel I of Castilla.

Fernando and Isabel's reign began a flurry of Spanish **exploration** and conquest; Christopher Columbus left Sevilla to discover the New World in their names, while Francisco Pizarro set about dominating South America. Back home, the invidious Inquisition was driving almost half a million Jews from the country and was also systematically rooting out Muslims, gypsies and witches.

New World gold and silver swelled Spain's coffers in the sixteenth century, and Sevilla's population leapt from 20,000 to 100,000. Much of this money was squandered by a corrupt monarchy, a large chunk being spent by Carlos I (Charles V) in his bid to become Holy Roman Emperor. By the seventeenth century, the country's power base was in Madrid. Many northern towns went into gradual decline, and Andalucía's agricultural base collapsed without the upkeep of its Moorish irrigation systems.

In 1808, **Napoleon** crossed the Pyrenees via the *camino francés*, and soon installed his brother on the Spanish throne. Spain called for help from the British, who were spectacularly unsuccessful at first, and Sir John Moore's troops speedily retreated to A Coruña on the northern coast. It took Wellington's army to drive the French out of Spain, although his soldiers were just as apt to destroy the Spanish towns they liberated.

The rest of the nineteenth century was a muddle of coups and counter coups as Spain swung from a monarchy to a liberal constitution and back again. By the early twentieth century, politics had splintered into factions, and regionalism, anarchism, communism and fascism all gained ground. Almost inevitably, **civil war** broke out in 1936. The province of Castilla was firmly on Franco's side, and the Nationalists made Burgos their wartime capital. Galicia was also largely Nationalist, partly because Franco was a local boy from Ferrol and partly because of the region's inherent conservatism. Andalucía had split loyalties, but quickly fell to the Nationalists in the first months of the war.

When Franco came to power at the end of the civil war in January 1939, he set about rewarding friendly cities like Salamanca, which was showered with money from the dictator. Economically, however, the country suffered from the costly fighting and the isolation of Franco's fascist regime, so much so that the late 1940s were known as the *años de hambre* (years of hunger).

Franco finally died in 1975, wielding influence beyond the grave by nominating King Juan Carlos as his successor. Spain flirted with dictatorship and military coups in the late 1970s, but by 1982 the country was flinging herself into democracy and capitalism with abandon under the leadership of Felipe González, a native *Sevillano*. Spain's economic development in the last 20 years has been largely due to its enthusiastic membership in the **European Union**, which it joined in 1986. European money has flooded into the country, leading to industrial development, agricultural modernization and an unstoppable orgy of road building. In keeping with European Union philosophy, Spain's modern era has seen a devolution of power to the regions, and the Galicians in particular have gained a large measure of autonomy.

## Spain Today

Spain is not so much a single country as a *paella* of diverse and disparate cultures.

Many Galicians don't consider themselves Spanish at all, and even less autonomous regions are intensely proud of their homelands. Having said this, foreign visitors will notice certain things that are distinctly, and often uniquely, Spanish.

The country might be in the same time zone as many of her European neighbours, but the Spanish day is unrecognizable to those from more northern climates. For a start, things happen later in Spain. A lot later in the case of meals, as restaurant lunches aren't usually served until 2pm, and Spaniards rarely eat dinner before 10pm. Nights out in Spain aren't for the faint-hearted, as bars don't get going until midnight and clubs rarely open before 4am. It's no wonder that the Spanish need a long *siesta*, and you'll find that even in the cities, life will grind to a halt from 2pm to 5pm for the practice that's become known as *yoga ibérico*.

Life in Spain seems to revolve around eating and drinking. Sunday lunches, in particular, are vast, communal affairs, which stretch well into the afternoon and involve all members of the family from the oldest to the youngest. Children are universally adored, and more puritanical northern Europeans may be shocked at the extent to which Spanish kids are heard as well as seen in public. Children are positively welcomed in restaurants, and you'll often see youngsters along for a late-night stroll or *tapas* crawl.

There's very little English spoken along the camino, and even a smattering of *Castellano* (Spanish) will help with communication and hunting out elusive *albergues*. In the north, *Galego* (Galician) is undergoing a literary and linguistic revival and 90% of locals speak the language.

Spain is still an inherently **Catholic** country 500 years after the Inquisition drove out Jews and Muslims. Since the 1978 constitution, Spaniards have enjoyed official religious freedom, but there are still fewer than a million non-Catholic souls in the country. In practice, however, secularism is taking hold as church attendance plummets; regular churchgoers are likely to be older, poorer, rural Spaniards. The country's Catholic leanings don't prevent extensive **gambling**; the Spanish spend more money than any other Europeans on lotteries, slot machines and other games of chance. The national lottery, established in 1812, is hugely popular. It culminates with the Christmas El Gordo (the fat one) draw, thought to be the world's single biggest lottery prize, when about 98% of Spaniards buy either a ticket or a share in a ticket.

The Vía de la Plata passes through some of Spain's most important bullfighting regions. The culture — Spaniards insist that **bullfighting** is an art form, not a sport — has its origins in Andalucía, and the southern region is still one of the best places in the country to see a *corrida*. Further north, the area around Salamanca breeds Spain's fiercest bulls for the ring, although many of these *toros bravos* are handicapped by shaved horns, not to mention the vast array of weaponry available to the bullfighters. For more on bullfighting, see the Andalucía section.

Bullfighting may be emblematic of Spain, but **football** is far more important to most Spaniards. Sevilla is the only place on the Vía de la Plata that's home to a major football team, but this scarcely seems to dim support for the beautiful game in other camino towns. Almost all Spanish football fans support both their local club and either Barcelona or Real Madrid, and matches between the two giants of Spanish football pack bars and cafés throughout Spain. Galicians are excited by the recent successes of Deportivo La Coruña, and care much more about the fate of their adopted provincial club than that of the national side.

## Arts

The Vía de la Plata is a journey through changing architectural styles. You'll constantly be reminded of the route's **Roman** origins as you walk along a Roman road and cross Roman bridges, but you'll also pass through three major Roman cities. In Italica, just north of Sevilla, an entire Roman city has been preserved, including a magnificent, massive amphitheatre. Mérida's Roman remains are even more spectacular, particularly the restored theatre, and the city's gorgeous Museo de Arte Romano preserves stunning mosaics. Further north, the Vía de la Plata passes under the squat, rectangular arch that dominates the archaeological site at Arco de Cáparra, where you can also see foundations of the forum and baths.

Most of Spain's **Muslim** masterpieces are in southern Andalucía away from the camino, but you can visit Sevilla's beautiful Alcázar palace and La Giralda, the minaret of the city's mosque that now forms part of the cathedral. More common is a blend of religious styles, whether the Mudéjar style of Muslims in Christian areas or the Mozarabic architecture of Christians in Muslim parts of Spain.

The northern section of the camino boasts some wonderful examples of **Romanesque** architecture, particularly in Zamora's old town, which is replete with elegant, simple stone churches. In eighteenth-century Spain a new, fantastical building style emerged from the work of José Churriguera and his brothers. Partly a reaction against the austerity of Renaissance style, **Churrigueresque** architecture is characterized by intricate carving, bold reliefs and huge gilt *retablos*. It's best seen in the Plaza Mayor and cathedral at Salamanca.

Spanish **art** has very few important schools and movements but some amazing peaks of individual creativity. In the sixteenth and seventeenth centuries, **El Greco**, a native Greek who lived most of his life in his adopted Spain, painted passionate and deliberate canvasses of elongated figures and intense contrasts of light and colour.

A few decades later, Diego de **Velázquez** created intricate, life-like portraits and landscapes with such meticulous care that he left fewer than 200 works. A native of Sevilla, Velázquez left the city early in his life to become the court painter, and most of his paintings are in Madrid. Francisco de **Goya** was contrastingly prolific. He was a late starter who began with fairly conventional paintings before spiralling towards embittered and imaginative works as his health declined and the Napoleonic war sent him into depression. Along the Vía de la Plata, you'll pass through Fuente de Cantos, the small home town of Francisco de **Zurbarán**, who painted brilliant, light-filled portraits and still lifes, and whose magnificent *retablo* graces Zafra's cathedral.

Born in Andalucía, Pablo **Picasso** is probably Spain's best-known artist, although he spent much of his long life in neighbouring France. With Georges Braque, he developed Cubism, a style also adopted by his countryman, Juan Gris. Politicized by the civil war, Picasso's most famous painting, *Guernica*, portrays the Basque town's decimation by Nazi bombers in 1937. Salvador **Dalí** put the fish in surrealism, and was as talented at self-promotion as he was at his bizarre, dream-like art. Alongside him, Spain's other noted surrealist, Joan Miró, seems positively normal.

Spanish **film** is well-respected internationally, but only a handful of directors are household names. Luis Buñuel and Salvador Dalí made many of their films in France, where Buñuel was exiled after the civil war. Carlos Maura's bleak, allegorical films subtly disparaged the Franco dictatorship during the 1960s and 1970s. In common with many of Spain's younger generation, Pedro Almodóvar sees the Franco years as irrelevant to his work, and instead makes quirky, controversial and commercially successful films about desire and sexuality.

Spain's **music** is firmly regionalized. *Flamenco*, the closest Spain has to a national music, is rooted in Andalucía and rarely heard outside the south, Madrid and Barcelona. Outside Spain, however, its dramatic, melancholy melodies are hugely popular, and performers such as Paco de Lucia, Enrique Morente and Tomatito are familiar to *aficionados* worldwide. Galician tunes have much in common with the Celtic music

of northern Europe, and the province even has its own version of the bagpipes.

For more about history, culture and the arts, see the People & Culture sections in the regional chapters.

# Food

The cuisine of Spain is as varied as the country, but as a rule of thumb it's tasty, substantial and lacking in all vegetables other than potatoes. It's also very cheap by northern European standards.

Traditionally, Spaniards have adopted the southern European custom of a large main meal at lunchtime followed by a much-needed *siesta*. Although a heavy lunch is becoming less popular with city workers, it's still the norm in rural areas. Sunday lunch is the meal of the week, and the whole day is taken up with preparing, eating and digesting the midday meal.

Hungry pilgrims may find Spanish mealtimes hard to stomach. Restaurants open for lunch at 2pm, and dinner doesn't begin until 9pm or 10pm. The best value comes from the *menú del día*, a three-course set meal with bread and wine, and an excellent deal at between €6 and €9. The tastiest food is often found in restaurants that serve *comida casera* (home cooking).

On most *menús* there's a choice of dishes for each course. The **primero plato** (first course) can be anything from salad to spaghetti, but you'll often get a hefty serving. Soups are fabulous, and often meals in themselves. In

Andalucía, this will likely be *gazpacho*, the region's tomato-based chilled soup.

You'll have to wait until Galicia to eat authentic *caldo gallego*, a thick soup made of shredded *gallego* (a dark green cabbage), beans and potatoes. Vegetarians be warned: the soups are usually made using a tasty meat stock, and *caldo gallego* often includes a few slices of *chorizo* (spicy sausage). *Fabada* is a hearty dish made from slowly stewed fava beans, *chorizo* and ham; choose this as a starter and you'll barely have room for the main course. *Ensalada mixta* (mixed salad) usually comes with tuna, olives and white asparagus, a delicacy that's dropped limply on top. The salad is usually padded out with insipid iceberg lettuce, although you'll be offered tastier greens as you near Galicia.

The **segundo plato** (second course) is a plate of either fried or roasted lumps of meat served with fries or boiled potatoes. Pork is almost always served, but you'll also see chicken, beef and fish, usually trout, on offer.

If you still have room, **postre** (dessert) is mercifully small. Usually you'll be offered a piece of fruit or ice cream or yoghurt served in its plastic container. *Flan* (egg custard) can come out of a plastic container, but *flan casero* (home-made *flan*) is an excellent choice. *La cuenta* (the bill) usually includes service, although it's common to add a small tip; many Spaniards just round up the bill to the nearest euro.

Most cafés and bars will serve **bocadillos**, sandwiches made from half a baguette stuffed with a range of fillings. *Bocadillos* are often filled with whatever happens to be in the kitchen,

usually cheese, *chorizo* or *jamón serrano* (a *prosciutto*-like ham); one of the most fiendishly tasty and satisfying versions is *tortilla con chorizo* (*chorizo* omelette sandwich). In some cafés you'll also see *sándwiches*; these are usually and disappointingly made from sliced white bread and can be grilled or fried.

**Breakfast** can be tricky. In summer, early starts mean that pilgrims can often begin walking hours before any of the cafés or bars open. Even then, many cafés can't serve food until the daily *pan* (bread) has been delivered. To avoid starving, it's best to purchase breakfast the night before or to pop into a café or *panadería* (bakery) for a mid-morning refuelling stop. In southern Spain, particularly in Andalucía, this will likely be either *churros* (long doughnuts) and thick, sweet hot chocolate, or *tostada* (toast), an innocuous sounding choice that often comes smeared with *manteca* (pork lard), mixed with paprika or tomato, and topped with a sliver of delicious *jamón serrano*. One of the most common breakfasts in northern Spain is *tortilla*, a deliciously thick omelette made with potatoes, then left to cool and served by the slice with a hunk of bread. Most bars also have an assortment of synthetic packaged pastries and packets of crisps. In larger towns, small rolls with a variety of fillings will also be on offer in the morning.

**Vegetarians** will have a hard time eating out. The *menú del día* is unlikely to offer a vegetarian option, and your culinary options are usually limited to a *bocadillo con queso* (cheese sandwich), variously prepared *huevos* (eggs) such as *tortilla francés* (omelette) or potato-based *tapas* treats such as *patatas bravas* (potatoes in spicy tomatoes sauce) and *patatas al alioli* (potatoes in garlic mayonnaise). Vegetarianism is defined very broadly in Spain and often includes tuna or other fish; be sure to ask if you don't eat any living creatures.

The best way to eat well and meet fellow pilgrims is to join in the evening meal at the *albergues*. Some have a sociable kitchen where people of different nationalities gather to cook, generating a fantastic hum as pots boil and bottles of wine are uncorked and shared. There's usually a shop nearby to pick up supplies, and most kitchens are stocked with basics such as salt, oil, pots and pans.

When out shopping, look out for staples such as *jamón serrano* (*prosciutto*-like ham) and *chorizo* (smoked sausage) at most *carnicerías* (butchers). Try the varied local cheeses, too. Save a fish dinner for short walking days, as most *pescaderías* (fishmongers) open only in the morning. Spain's varied climate means that there's a wide selection of fruits and vegetables available year-round. In most shops, you'll need to ask for what you want rather than picking up and squeezing the fruit yourself. Try not to get caught short of food on Sundays, when most shops close.

At least once during the camino, head out for an evening of **tapas** grazing. At its most basic, a *tapa* is just a little snack to go with a glass of wine, often offered free by the bartender. In other places, you'll need to order what you like: *pinchos* are small tasters, whereas *raciones* are bigger portions. The best way to sample the delights of *tapas* is to embark on a *tapeo* (*tapas* crawl) with a large group of friends, hopping from one bar to another. Here, you'll rub shoulders with local bankers and road sweepers sharing a glass of wine and debating the shortcomings of Real Madrid's latest striker.

For more culinary information, see the regional Food & Drink sections.

# Drink

Spanish people spend a lot of time in cafés, and even the smallest village café will boast a big, shiny espresso machine. Days in Spain rarely begin without a caffeine hit from the excellent, supercharged **coffee**, known as *torrefacto*, which is double roasted and extra finely ground for extra oomph. Coffee comes in many variations, but essentially you have two options: the strong and espresso-like *café solo*, or the long and milky *café con leche*.

**Hot chocolate** in southern Spain is sweet, delicious and so thick that you can stand your spoon up in it. As you head further north hot chocolate can be hard to find, and you're more likely to be offered Cola Cao, a sickly, powdery substitute. There's a wide array of soft drinks available, from the usual imports to Spanish sparkling fruity drinks. Fruit juice tends to be sweet and thick, but it's delightfully refreshing when diluted with sparkling water.

Get used to drinking **wine** with your meal. The Spanish, who have an abundance of intoxicating proverbs, say, *"comer sin vino es miseria y desatino,"* which loosely translates as "a meal without wine is a mean and foolish one." Even teetotalling Spaniards will drink wine with food: it's so much a part of the meal that it's not even thought of as an alcoholic drink. You'll pass hundreds of vineyards along the camino, particularly around Almendralejo in Extremadura and the Tierra del Vino near Zamora. Both regions' reds are well worth sampling as they are rarely found in other parts of Spain, let alone shipped overseas.

In Andalucía, you're likely to be offered **sherry**. *Tapas* are best washed down with crisp, dry *fino*, served chilled as an aperitif and as far away from the sickly Bristol Cream that your granny brought out at Christmas as you can imagine. *Oloroso* is darker, sweeter and more potent, and goes well with red meat; between the two extremes are amber-coloured *amontillado* and straw-coloured *manzanilla*.

Galicia's cooler climate is ideal for producing white wines that perfectly complement the region's wonderful seafood. Albariño is unoaked and crisp with flavours of peach and apricot, and the cloudy Ribeiro rarely makes it outside the province. Less sophisticated palates may enjoy *tinto de verano* (*sangria*), a refreshing option in southern tourist bars, but pilgrims should steer clear of *calimocho*, a particularly vile mixture of red wine and Coca Cola popular with teenagers and young men.

For more about wine, see the Food & Drink section in the regional chapters.

Spanish **beer** is rather bland and tasteless, although brands like San Miguel, Cruz Campo and Estrella de Galicia can be refreshing on a hot evening. Ask for a *caña* if you want a small draught beer.

**Bars** and cafés in Spain are mostly interchangeable and you can get a great *café solo* at a late-night bar. It's a bit more of a shock the first time you see locals waking up with a glass of red or a shot of something stronger alongside their morning *café con leche*. Bars are an integral part of Spanish culture, and a 1990s survey found that Spain had 138,200 bars, slightly fewer than the rest of the European Union put together. Despite this glut, identikit Irish and Belgian bars are opening up in larger towns.

Alcohol in bars is very cheap, with wine and beer usually costing less than €1 a glass, although the glasses may be smaller than you're used to. As always in Europe, bars on main squares will be more expensive than those tucked down a side street. It often costs more to drink at a table, particularly one outside, than standing at the bar.

Long, afternoon-consuming lunches aren't complete without a stiff drink. Northern and rural Spain's favourite tipple is **orujo**, a ridiculously strong spirit made, like Italian *grappa*, from grape husks. Despite the pretty bottles, manufactured *orujo* isn't as good as the rough-and-ready homemade version, known as *orujo casero*. Most people you meet will have their own version of *orujo casero*, and you'll see unmarked bottles under the counter in bars, restaurants and even bakeries. Spanish pilgrims may even bring their own from home. *Orujo* can be *blanco* (clear, tastes like alcohol) or *con hierbas* (often green, with more of a flavour from added herbs). Avoid spirits such as gin and whisky, which are likely to have been gathering dust on a high shelf for a long while, and stay well away from the dodgy brands of Scotch made for mainland European tastes.

 # Flora

Spain is one of Europe's richest botanical regions. The mix of Mediterranean, Atlantic and Continental climates makes for a diverse collection of flowers, shrubs and trees. Isolated from the rest of Europe by the Pyrenees, the Iberian peninsula's plant life developed at its own pace, helped by windblown seeds from North Africa. The results are spectacular, with more than 8000 species of flora, about a quarter of which are indigenous to the region and occur nowhere else in the world.

Northern Spain was once covered by deciduous forest, dominated by Pyrenean oak and beech. Frequent forest fires, clear-cutting and the introduction of faster-growing imported species, such as pine and eucalyptus, are rapidly destroying what little forest survived into the twentieth century.

In the unforested areas that cover much of the central part of the country, the landscape is dominated by dense patches of brambles and wild herbs such as lavender, sage and thyme. At higher altitudes gorse, broom and heather cover the ground and hardy plants such as St Patrick's cabbage, mat grass and sphagnum moss cope with strong winds, deep snow cover and extreme temperature change.

Southern Spain is largely agricultural, and Andalucía and Extremadura are dotted with cork oak and holm oak forests, vines, olives and cereals. Little land is wasted, and even barren areas scented with cistus bushes are used to graze animals.

For more about Spain's varied plant life, see the regional Flora & Fauna sections.

| English name | Latin name | Spanish name |
|---|---|---|
| **Holm Oak** | **Quercus Ilex** | **Encina** |

**Leaves** 7cm long, 5cm across, dark glossy green on top, grey and hairy underneath, shape varies from tree to tree
**Bark** Craggy and almost black
**Fruit** Acorn, 2cm long
**Habitat** Hills, scrubland. Well adapted to Iberian climate
**Height** Up to 25m
**Did you know?** This tree was eulogized by the Roman poets Virgil and Horace

| English name | Latin name | Spanish name |
|---|---|---|

## Sweet chestnut  Castanea sativa  Castaño dulce

**Leaves** 10–25cm long, oblong with pointed tip and sharp-toothed edges
**Bark** Grey ridges that seem to spiral around trunk
**Fruit** Edible chestnut
**Habitat** Farmland, plains and mixed woodlands
**Height** Up to 30m
**Did you know?** Chestnuts are a staple food in parts of Spain, used as a stuffing for meat or to thicken hearty soups

## Beech  Fagus sylvatica  Haya

**Leaves** 4–9cm long, oval, with 7–8 parallel veins, silky hairs underneath
**Bark** Smooth grey
**Fruit** Triangular brown nuts
**Habitat** Farmland
**Height** Up to 40m
**Did you know?** Planted for timber because it grows tall and straight without knots

## Cork oak  Quercus suber  Alcornoque

**Leaves** 7cm long, 4cm wide, deep lobes, dark green on top
**Bark** Gnarly, pale grey with thick ridges; smooth, vivid brownish-red when stripped
**Fruit** Acorn 3cm long
**Habitat** Rolling hills, mainly in the south of the country
**Height** Up to 20m
**Did you know?**Stripping the bark does not damage trees; bark harvested every decade or so

## Olive  Olea europaea  Olivo

**Leaves** 2–8 cm long, narrow, grey-green above with delicate silver hairs underneath
**Bark** Pale grey
**Fruit** 1–4cm long
**Habitat** Farmland
**Height** Up to 15m
**Did you know?** Fruit is green the first year then turns black when ripe in second year

# Fauna

Spain is home to an assortment of rare animals. Nooks and crannies hide fire salamanders, genets and wild boar, and large tracts of remote wilderness, especially in the mountains on the Galician border, offer animals such as the wolf and brown bear the space to roam unhindered. Agricultural underdevelopment in these areas has preserved unique ecosystems that are only now being studied for the first time. Spain is also a major refuelling stop on the north-south bird migration route and these passages make spring and autumn a great time to visit.

Wildlife is most active, and easiest to see, at dawn and dusk. There's also a greater chance of spotting animals when you're on the edge of two habitats, such as the fringes of a wood near a river or open woodland. As you walk along, stop every now and then to sit quietly for a few minutes. The animals will become accustomed to your presence and, as they resume their normal routines, previously undetected creatures will emerge.

There's more information about local animals in the regional Flora & Fauna sections.

| English name | Latin name | Spanish name |
| --- | --- | --- |
| **Brown bear** | **Ursus arctos** | **Oso pardo** |

**Length** 230cm **Tail** 1.5cm **Height** 120cm
**Description** Very large, heavy build, beige to dark brown
**Habitat** Mixed woods in the Cordillera Cantábrica
**Voice** Occasional grunts or howls when angry or frightened
**Diet** Berries, roots, carrion, insects. Occasionally mammals
**Viewing tips** Very difficult to see, mainly nocturnal
**Did you know?** Brown bears have an excellent sense of smell and hearing, but poor eyesight

| **Wolf** | **Canis lupus** | **Lobo** |
| --- | --- | --- |

**Length** 130cm **Tail** 40cm **Height** 80cm
**Description** Grey, bushy tail, alert ears
**Habitat** Woods and open country in mountains
**Voice** Silent when hunting; growls, yelps and long howls
**Diet** Large and small mammals
**Viewing tips** Dog-like footprint; visible at dawn and dusk
**Did you know?** Wolves mate for life. Travel up to 40km per day with a maximum speed of 50km per hour

| English name | Latin name | Spanish name |
|---|---|---|

## Iberian lynx — Lynx pardinus — Lince Ibérico

**Length** 100cm **Tail** 25cm **Height** 70cm
**Description** Large and small black spots, black tip on tail, distinctive feathery tufts on head
**Habitat** Holm oak woods in rocky mountains
**Voice** Hisses and howls
**Diet** Birds, young deer, fish, small mammals and reptiles
**Viewing tips** Very rare and difficult to spot; vast territory
**Did you know?** Most endangered carnivore in Europe

## Wild cat — Felis silvestris — Gato montés

**Length** 50cm **Tail** 30cm **Height** 35cm
**Description** Yellow-grey fur with black ringed tail
**Habitat** Woodland and scrubland
**Voice** Purrs and meows
**Diet** Mice, birds, fish and insects
**Viewing tips** Active in late afternoon, often sunning itself
**Did you know?** Persecution of cats in medieval times led to spread of black death as rat population exploded

## Genet — Genetta genetta — Gineta

**Length** 50cm **Tail** 40cm **Height** 20cm
**Description** Pale fur with defined dark spots & tail rings
**Habitat** Dark woods close to streams
**Voice** Purrs loudly
**Diet** Small birds, mammals, insects
**Viewing tips** Nocturnal, look for footprints near water
**Did you know?** Lives up to 21 years. Strong swimmer and climber; found at altitudes up to 2500m

## Badger — Meles meles — Tejón

**Length** 60cm **Tail** 15cm **Height** 30cm
**Description** Silver-grey back; black & white striped face
**Habitat** Scrubland, farmland, woods
**Voice** Growls
**Diet** Small rodents, reptiles and plants
**Viewing tips** Nocturnal; listen for the sound of it digging
**Did you know?** Foxes and birds of prey often follow badgers to catch animals they disturb while digging for food

| English name | Latin name | Spanish name |
|---|---|---|

## Wild boar  Sus scrofa  Jabalí

**Length** 150cm **Tail** 15cm **Height** 90cm
**Description** Pale grey to black; tusks up to 30cm
**Habitat** Mixed, deciduous woodland; scrubland
**Voice** Snorts. Female barks and chatters teeth when angry
**Diet** Roots, vegetables, small mammals, insects
**Viewing tips** Mainly nocturnal but also active in mornings
**Did you know?** Litters of 4 to 12 piglets common, independent after 6 months and can live up to 25 years

## Otter  Lutra lutra  Nutria

**Length** 80cm **Tail** 40cm **Height** 30cm
**Description** Brown fur; long, slender body with short legs
**Habitat** Rivers, lakes, marshes, estuaries and sea
**Voice** Clear whistle, sometimes growls
**Diet** Fish, birds, frogs and aquatic mammals
**Viewing tips** Look for remains of meals along riverbanks
**Did you know?** Good climber and jumper, can walk on land for long distances

## European tree frog  Hyla arborea  Rana de San Antón

**Length** 4cm
**Description** Usually green but changes to grey or brown as temperature fluctuates
**Habitat** Marshland, damp meadows, reed beds
**Voice** Croaks
**Diet** Insects and spiders
**Viewing tips** Easily spotted, active by day and twilight
**Did you know?** Female lays up to 1000 eggs

## Natterjack  Bufo calamita  Sapo corredor

**Length** 8cm
**Description** Brown-grey back with huge warts, belly white
**Habitat** Varied, especially dry sandy soil, up to 1200m
**Voice** Loud croak
**Diet** Insects, worms and spiders
**Viewing tips** Mainly nocturnal, occasionally active in day
**Did you know?** When the natterjack becomes alarmed, it inflates its body, lowers its head and sticks its bum in the air

| English name | Latin name | Spanish name |
|---|---|---|

## Fire salamander — Salamander salamander — Salamandra común

**Length** 20cm
**Description** Shiny black; yellow, orange or red markings
**Habitat** Damp woodlands, streams, meadows up to 1000m
**Diet** Insects and worms
**Viewing tips** Emerges at night or in bad weather
**Did you know?** Don't touch, as the oily slime that covers the body is poisonous. Can live for up to 42 years

## Iberian wall lizard — Podarcis hispanica — Lagartija ibérica

**Length** 18cm
**Description** Flat head, long tail, upper parts grey to brown
**Habitat** Dry, stony places, especially walls and ruins
**Diet** Small insects and worms
**Viewing tips** Look and listen for them scuttling away as you approach
**Did you know?** Lays eggs in holes; lives up to 15 years

## Green lizard — Lacerta viridis — Lagarto verde

**Length** 40cm
**Description** Males vivid green with tiny black dots; sky blue throat during mating. Females duller and brownish
**Habitat** Dry, sunny locations with shrubs, especially near walls and along roads
**Diet** Insects and fruit
**Viewing tips** Again, look and listen for scuttling!
**Did you know?** When threatened opens mouth and bites

## White stork — Ciconia ciconia — Cigüeña común

**Description** 100cm, long bill and legs, white with black flight feathers, red bill and legs
**Habitat** Marshes, grassy plains
**Voice** Hisses and claps bill
**Diet** Fish, insects
**Viewing tips** Flies at high altitude, neck straight ahead
**Did you know?** Nests on buildings and churches along the Vía de la Plata

| English name | Latin name | Spanish name |
| --- | --- | --- |

## Black stork   Ciconia nigra   Cigüeña negra

**Description** 100cm, black body, white belly, red bill & legs
**Habitat** Marshy land near forests
**Voice** Noisy, claps bill, random notes
**Diet** Fish, insects
**Viewing tips** Flies like white stork, only more gracefully as less reliant on thermals
**Did you know?** Nests high in the tops of trees. More solitary than white stork

## Bee-eater   Merops apiaster   Abejaruco común

**Description** 30cm, bright blue belly, yellow throat and shoulders, black eyeband
**Habitat** Open scrubland with some trees
**Voice** Prruep prruep prruep
**Diet** Insects
**Viewing tips** Sociable, likes to perch & watch the world go by. Good flier, with sudden acceleration and graceful glides
**Did you know?** Breeds in big groups in holes in the ground

## Hoopoe   Upupa epops   Abubilla

**Description** 30cm, crest on head, pinkish body, barred white and black wings, long bill
**Habitat** Farmland, open woodland
**Voice** Pooo pooo pooo
**Diet** Insects
**Viewing tips** Undulating flight as it opens & closes wings
**Did you know?** One of our favourite birds. Nests in ruins and hollows of old trees

## Black woodpecker   Dryocopus martius   Pito negro

**Description** 45cm, almost all black, red crown, yellow eyes
**Habitat** Old coniferous and beech forests
**Voice** Manic laugh: kwick-wick-wick-wick
**Diet** Ants and wood-boring beetle larvae, tree sap
**Viewing Tips** Found in mature forests, listen for call and loud drumming
**Did you know?** Three separate, isolated populations in Spain

| English name | Latin name | Spanish name |
|---|---|---|
| **Chough** | **Pyrrhocorax pyrrhocorax** | **Chova piquirroja** |

**Description** 40cm, red legs and long, thin, curved red bill
**Habitat** Rolling hills and mountains
**Voice** High-pitched cheeeaaah and chuff
**Diet** Mainly insects
**Viewing tips** Good flier, tumbles and twists during flight, also frequently seen hopping on ground
**Did you know?** Nest in caves and on crags

| **Great bustard** | **Otis tarda** | **Avutarda** |
|---|---|---|

**Description** 100cm, pale grey head and upper neck, rufous upper parts. Breeding males have pale fluffy feathers on lower face and fan white tails out in a spectacular display
**Habitat** Open treeless plains
**Voice** Not often heard. Low bark in breeding season
**Diet** Mainly insects
**Viewing tips** Usually in small flocks on the ground
**Did you know?** Heaviest bird in Europe

| **Golden eagle** | **Aquila chrysaetos** | **Águila real** |
|---|---|---|

**Description** 90cm, golden feathers on head, white patches on wings and tail
**Habitat** Mountains, forests, sea cliffs
**Voice** Seldom-heard kya
**Diet** Rabbits, reptiles
**Viewing tips** Soars with wings in shallow V, solitary
**Did you know?** The largest eagle in the world

| **Short-toed eagle** | **Circaetus gallicus** | **Culebrera europea** |
|---|---|---|

**Description** 65cm, long wings and tail, white underneath except for brown chest
**Habitat** Mountain slopes, plains and coastal dunes
**Voice** Noisy; jee or peak-oh
**Diet** Snakes, lizards and frogs
**Viewing tips** Resembles osprey but without dark stripes
**Did you know?** Frequently hovers with legs dangling

| English name | Latin name | Spanish name |
|---|---|---|

## Booted eagle  Hieraaetus pennatus  Águila calzada

**Description** 50cm. Two different varieties; can have either dark or white body with black wing edges
**Habitat** Forest clearings
**Voice** Keeee
**Diet** Small birds and reptiles
**Viewing tips** Always seen near trees; six obvious feathers at end of wings
**Did you know?** Smallest eagle in Europe

## Bonelli's eagle  Hieraaetus fasciatus  Águila perdicera

**Description** 70cm, white body underneath, except dark tail band and wing
**Habitat** Rocky mountains, plains and wetlands
**Voice** Fast or slow kai kai kai
**Diet** Rabbits, birds up to heron size
**Viewing tips** Look for acrobatic courtship display in spring
**Did you know?** Pairs stay together even when not breeding

## Goshawk  Accipter gentilis  Azor

**Description** 60cm, barred, grey belly, some white near tail and around eye
**Habitat** Woods on edge of open country
**Voice** Pee-lay or kik kik
**Diet** Wood pigeons and other forest-dwelling birds
**Viewing tips** Great flier, zooms 2–3m above the ground between and around trees
**Did you know?** Persistent; chases prey even if ends in crash

## Buzzard  Buteo buteo  Busardo ratonero

**Description** 50cm, dark with barred underside, broad wings and fat, round tail
**Habitat** Mountains, plains, farmland
**Voice** Peee-aah
**Diet** Birds, small mammals, insects
**Viewing tips** Common over most habitats
**Did you know?** Seen as the laziest raptor, it rarely chases prey and refuses to fly in the rain

| English name | Latin name | Spanish name |
|---|---|---|

## Sparrohawk — Accipiter nisus — Gavilán común

**Description** 35cm, long tail, barred underparts, grey above
**Habitat** Woodland and farmland
**Voice** Varies. Lots of noise especially in breeding season
**Diet** Small mammals and birds
**Viewing tips** The sparrowhawk is a common sight hovering over fields looking for food
**Did you know?** Young birds and captive adults frequently resort to cannibalism

## Red kite — Milvus milvus — Milano real

**Description** 60cm, white head, red brown upper body, tri-coloured wings, black wing tips and clear white base
**Habitat** Wooded hills, open country with scattered trees
**Voice** Hi-hi-heeea
**Diet** Small vertebrates, insects and sometimes scavenges
**Viewing Tips** Long, deep wing beats, noticeable forked tail which constantly twists during flight
**Did you know?** Iberia has the most red kites in the world

## Kestrel — Falco tinnunculus — Cernícalo vulgar

**Description** 35cm, pointed wings, black band at tail base
**Habitat** Coast, farmland, woodland, cities
**Voice** Kee kee kee in breeding season
**Diet** Mainly rodents, but also lizards and small birds
**Viewing tips** Often seen hovering patiently over fields checking the ground for prey
**Did you know?** Breeds in old nests of other birds, on cliffs or even buildings

## Peregrine falcon — Falco peregrinus — Halcón común

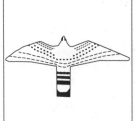

**Description** 45cm, slate colour, thick black moustache, white speckled belly. Female larger and darker than male
**Habitat** Open country, mountains, cliffs
**Voice** Hek hek hek or airk airk airk
**Diet** Small and medium-sized birds and mammals
**Viewing tips** Graceful flier, languid at rest but dramatic dive-bomb as attacks prey
**Did you know?** Dives at up to 100km/hr

| English name | Latin name | Spanish name |
|---|---|---|

## Montagu's harrier  Circus pygargus  Aguila perdicera

**Description** 45cm, dark wing tips, male grey, female brown with black bars underneath
**Habitat** Marshes, farmland, plains
**Voice** Chattering kek kek kek
**Diet** Frogs, small mammals
**Viewing tips** Acrobatic flier as it patrols territory
**Did you know?** Winters in Africa and returns to same territory each year to breed

## Griffon vulture  Gyps fulvus  Buitre común

**Description** 100cm, long broad wings, short stumpy tail, pale lines under wings
**Habitat** All types of landscape but usually mountains
**Voice** Croaks and whistles
**Diet** Carrion
**Viewing tips** Flies gracefully by soaring, with only an occasional flap of wings
**Did you know?** Often breeds in caves

## Egyptian vulture  Neophron percnopterus  Alimoche común

**Description** 60cm, long wings with black edges, white body, wedge-shaped tail
**Habitat** Mountains and open country
**Voice** Largely silent
**Diet** Carrion
**Viewing tips** Easily confused with high-flying storks
**Did you know?** Often seen at rubbish dumps

## Eagle owl  Bubo bubo  Búho real

**Description** 65cm, rust colour with streaks and bars, big feathers on top of head look like ears
**Habitat** Rocky ledges on crags and mountains
**Voice** Ooo hoo
**Diet** Small mammals, birds up to game bird size
**Viewing tips** Active at dawn and dusk
**Did you know?** Easily mistaken for buzzard from a distance; uses other birds' abandoned nests

# Tourist Information

## Getting There & Back

Many discount airlines fly to various airports in Spain, and the most convenient airport for you will depend on where you choose to begin the camino. Scheduled flights also serve Spain, and both British Airways (www.britishairways.com) and Iberia (www.iberia.com) offer flights to many destinations, including Santiago de Compostela. Pilgrims from outside Europe will probably land in Madrid, which is also served by dozens of flights daily from the UK, and from where it's easy to get bus or train connections to all the starting points along the camino. If you're starting at Sevilla, you can take advantage of cheap charter flights to Málaga; Jerez is even more convenient and some airlines also fly to Sevilla's tiny airport. If you're travelling with a bicycle, your options are more limited. Most scheduled flights will take your bike free of charge, but many of the cheaper charter airlines don't provide this service.

International buses and trains will get you from northern Europe to most major towns along the camino. They're unlikely to be any cheaper than flying, however, and will take considerably more time. Bicycles aren't allowed on most trains, but can be carried on some buses; you may need to reserve a space and/or pay a surcharge. For UK bus information, see Eurolines (www.eurolines.co.uk), and for selected train schedules, visit SNCF's web site at www.raileurope.co.uk.

## Getting back

Iberia offer a 50% pilgrim discount on one-way tickets out of Santiago within Spain; there's an Iberia desk in the pilgrim office. Daily trains link Santiago to Madrid via Ourense, Puebla de Sanabria and Zamora. You'll need to change trains at Avila to make the trip back to Salamanca or at Madrid to return to Mérida or Sevilla. Alternatively, rent a car in Santiago and drop it off in Madrid or another major city or airport; rates are cheap compared to the rest of Europe.

## Red Tape

EU nationals can stay in Spain indefinitely, and you don't need a visa if you're from Australia, Canada, USA or New Zealand for stays of less than 90 days. EU nationals are covered by reciprocal health care arrangements; UK residents should pick up an E111 form at a post office before they leave. Travel insurance will give you extra health protection and also cover your baggage. Be sure to read the fine print, as some policies classify walking as a dangerous activity.

In order to stay at an *albergue* (pilgrim hostel), you must show a *credencial*, a pilgrim passport that gets stamped with a *sello* (stamp), which can usually be obtained from whoever has the key to the *albergue*. It's best to get a *credencial* from your local Camino de Santiago organization before you go (see page 194 for a list of these), but you can also pick one up in certain spots along the camino. To qualify for the *compostela* (certificate of completing the camino), you must show your stamped *credencial* to prove that you have walked the last 100km or cycled the last 200km to Santiago.

 # Money & Costs

Spain is a member of the European Monetary Union, and like the other members its currency is the euro (€). You'll still occasionally see prices marked in *pesetas*, mostly for cars, houses and other very expensive items.

The most convenient way to get cash is to use your debit or credit card in a cashpoint or ATM. Banks charge high commission fees on travellers' cheques and cash exchanges, and often close for the day at 2pm. *Bureau de change* rates are generally unfavourable. We list bank and cashpoint locations at the beginning of each regional chapter. Cashpoints frequently dispense €50 notes, which can be hard to change in small towns and villages. Visa and Mastercard are widely accepted in restaurants, hotels and larger shops; American Express is less common.

Your cultural and transport costs can

go down significantly if you're under 26, over 60 or a student. Students should pick up an ISIC (International Student Identity Card) before leaving, for discounts at certain museums. The Euro<26 card, available for about €10 from youth and student travel agencies throughout Europe, is more widely accepted and gets you a 20% discount on train travel. Spain is a very child-friendly country; as well as being the centre of attention wherever they go, your little ones will get generous discounts on hotels and transport.

If you stay in *albergues*, eat the *menú del día* once a day and picnic on bread and cheese in the meantime, you can get by on €20 a day. To eat all your meals in cafés or restaurants, and to splurge on a hotel every now and then, allow about €40 a day.

## How much does it cost?

| | |
|---|---|
| *Albergue* | €3–€7 |
| Cheap hotel, double room | €25–€35 |
| *Menú* (three-course meal) | €6–€9 |
| Cheap bottle of wine | €2–€3 |

 Transport

At some point along the way, you may need to recover from injury, catch up time or simply miss out a section. Spanish trains are generally good value, and one of the most useful lines for pilgrims is the one from Santiago to Madrid, which passes through Ourense, A Gudiña, Puebla de Sanabria and Zamora. You can get information and book tickets online at www.renfe.es.

Buses are usually a more flexible option, particularly to get to and from towns south of Zamora. In smaller places the bus stop can be just a street corner, and a café may act as the ticket office; ask a few locals where the bus stops and when it leaves.

Hitching long distances can be a frustrating experience, as foreign visitors are loathe to pick up hitchhikers and locals may only be travelling as far as the next village. For shorter distances, hitching may be a useful option, particularly on weekends when bus services are limited. Hitching does, of course, involve risk, so take care.

Car hire is cheap compared to the rest of Europe and can be a good way of visiting sites on rest days, or of getting from Santiago to airports like Madrid.

All the *albergues* on the Vía de la Plata allow cyclists to stay, although in high season some will only do so in late evening, after walkers have arrived for the day, which makes for a frustrating wait to find a bed. Road conditions are generally good, and most of the off-road tracks can be ridden on a mountain bike. Some airlines will transport bikes for free, but find out in advance about any restrictions and requirements.

 **Accommodation**

## Albergues

*Albergues*, also known as *refugios*, provide cheap or free places to stay at regular points along the Vía de la Plata. They are restricted to self-powered pilgrims, and most insist on seeing your *credencial* before giving you a bed. Although all the *albergues* take cyclists, walking pilgrims often have priority, and pedal-pushers may have to wait until the evening before being given a space.

The *albergues* along the Vía de la Plata run the complete gamut from a corner of a cold draughty hall to über-modern design classics with heating and kitchen facilities. At their most basic, sleeping space is organized by a local village or parish, in a public building like an *ayuntamiento* (town hall), swimming pool or school. Mattresses are often provided, and there's usually, but not always, access to a shower and toilet; a sleeping bag is a must. In more modern *albergues*, accommodation is mostly in mixed bunk-bed dormitories, where beds can be crammed into every available space and are often laid out side-by-side, letting you have a close relationship with the person in the next bed. Toilets and shower facilities are usually mixed, too, and you'll often have to provide your own toilet paper. Some *albergues*, particularly those in Galicia, have kitchens, and these are usually equipped with pots, plates and cutlery.

Most *albergues*, whether basic or sophisticated, aren't staffed by a *hospitalero* (*albergue* warden) and are locked. Often, the first thing you'll need to do on arrival at a village or town is find out who has the key to the *albergue*. Although we list this information for each place, things change, and a smattering of Spanish can make all the difference between an early bed and a frustrating wait. Cleaning and maintenance of the *albergues* can be sporadic; it's your responsibility to make sure that the *albergue* is in an excellent condition for future pilgrims.

Unlike *albergues* on the *camino francés*, most places on the Vía de la Plata do not have a curfew. Even so, mornings tend to begin early and, even if you fancy a lie-in, the noise of other pilgrims packing up and leaving is likely to wake you up. Earplugs are useful, not only to block out early risers but also to try to muffle the noise of *roncadores* (snorers). Very few *albergues* along the Vía de la Plata charge a fixed price (expect to pay between €3 and €7 in those that do); many have a box to leave donations instead. Most *albergues* are open year-round, and all will be busiest from June to September.

The Spanish call pilgrim hostels *albergues* or *refugios*; we use *albergue* in this book, and attempt to list every one along the way.

## Casas, hotels & paradors

On the Vía de la Plata *albergues* are often long distances apart and very few of the main cities have *albergues*; at times you'll need alternative accommodation. There are places to stay in most villages, and even if there isn't a hotel someone in the village may rent out rooms; local café-bars are generally the best place to ask about somewhere to stay. At the other end of the price scale, *paradors* are government-run luxury hotels, often in sumptuously converted historic buildings; they're well worth the splurge.

In each town and village, we include accommodation suggestions for a range of budgets. Accommodation is divided

into the price categories listed below. The price is given for a double room in high season; rates drop at other times and may be open to negotiation.

| | |
|---|---|
| **$** | up to €30 |
| **$$** | €30–€50 |
| **$$$** | €50–€75 |
| **$$$$** | more than €75 |

## Camping

Most campsites are inconveniently located a few kilometres off the camino or a fair way out of town. They often have excellent facilities, but are set up for car campers and can be noisy, particularly on weekends. There's no camping in urban areas or within 1km of an official campsite, but camping wild elsewhere is possible. Make sure you ask permission locally, particularly if you're camping on private land.

 # Equipment

Bring as little as possible. Spain is a modern European country and the camino passes through many towns and cities where you can shop to your heart's content. Remember that you'll need to carry everything you bring, and every luxury in your backpack leaves you more vulnerable to blisters and other injuries. Once you start walking, it's easy enough to ditch non-essentials and send them on to Santiago or post them home.

Good, lightweight walking shoes, or even running shoes, are the best bet for your feet; some pilgrims suggest buying shoes a size too big to account for swelling feet in hot weather. Walking boots are probably overkill on the camino's good tracks and can be uncomfortable in hot weather, though you may be glad of them in winter. Take a pair of sandals or other shoes to pad about towns, villages and *albergues* in the evening.

Even in summer, it's a good idea to bring rain gear. A good quality rain poncho will keep you and your equipment dry, but avoid the cheap versions found in supermarkets as these can shred in high winds. Although lightweight waterproofs will be fine for summer rain, bring something more substantial to protect against winter downpours. Other clothes should be comfortable and fast-drying: bring lightweight layers rather than bulky sweaters. You'll be washing clothes most nights, so pack some laundry soap or travel wash and bring pegs or safety pins to hang things out to dry.

Bring a sun hat, sunglasses and sunscreen from spring to autumn, and a warm hat and gloves from autumn to spring. It's important to drink plenty of fluids throughout the year, and a collapsible bladder holds more water for long, dry stretches and takes up less room than a rigid water bottle. Try to find one that will carry at least three litres.

A lightweight sleeping bag is a must if you're planning to stay in *albergues*. Most *albergues* do not provide blankets and some, especially the more basic ones in schools, swimming pools, and other public buildings, can be chilly at night. A foam sleeping pad can make some of these floors warmer and more comfortable, although most *albergues* will provide mattresses. A small torch can be useful at night and for poking around churches, and an alarm clock can get you up in the morning. Plastic bags are useful for keeping clothes and other equipment dry. Keep toiletries and first aid to a minimum, but bring something for blisters, and consider packing earplugs if you're a light sleeper.

Even though we list useful Spanish phrases in our Reference section (page 197), a phrasebook is a good idea as many people along the way won't speak English; choose one with a menu reader to avoid nasty surprises when eating out. Binoculars can help you identify soaring birds of prey; they're also ideal for viewing lofty cathedral ceilings and, of course, for spotting yellow arrows.

A walking stick is a matter of personal choice; some pilgrims swear by them, and others find them awkward. Unless you bring a telescopic hiking pole, it's best to pick up a stick in Spain, as airlines are wary of carrying weapon-like objects. Many pilgrims hang a scallop shell from their pack or round their neck to distinguish themselves from ordinary tourists.

# Health & Safety

Pharmacies are generally open from 9am to 2pm and from 5pm to 8pm. There should be at least one pharmacy open outside these times too; look at the notice posted outside each one for contact information. Spanish Pharmacists speak English, usually offer more medical advice than in other European countries and are able to dispense some drugs without a doctor's prescription.

In an emergency, dial 091 or ask for Cruz Roja (Red Cross), which runs a national ambulance service. EU nationals are covered by reciprocal health care arrangements; UK residents should pick up an E111 form at a post office before they leave, but it's a good idea to supplement this coverage with private health insurance.

## Walking Hazards

Although the pilgrimage presents few natural hazards, walking every day will inevitably take a toll on your body — see Training & Fitness for more information. Read the description of your day's route before setting out each morning, and make sure you are equipped to deal with any problems that may arise.

Ask local people about the weather forecast before heading over the mountain passes, and be prepared to delay your start or to detour via an easier route in case of fog or snow. On uninhabited stretches, make sure that you have enough warm and waterproof clothes, and always take more food and water than you think you'll need.

Route-finding is mostly easy along the camino and there will often be someone around to point you in the right direction. If you do get lost, look around for obvious landmarks and use these to pinpoint your whereabouts. Better still, return to the last yellow arrow or camino marker that you passed. If you're not sure where you are, if it's getting dark or if visibility is poor, stay put.

Cyclists will find that most drivers are courteous but may not expect bikes; be visible, wear a helmet and obey the rules of the road. Thorns can be a problem in southern cactus country and there are lots of metal nails elsewhere; carry spare inner tubes and patches and know how to use them. Theft of bicycles is rarely a problem, but don't tempt anyone by leaving your bike unattended, and use a good quality lock in cities.

## Specific Health Risks

Blisters are the most common health problem you'll encounter. You're more likely to get blisters if your feet are hot, wet or tired, so be sensible about the distance you cover and the speed you walk at. Change your socks often, at least once a day. Vaseline may help prevent blisters, and sheep's wool (readily available on barbed wire fences) can help cushion sore feet. If you do get blisters, try the following treatment: sterilize a needle and thread (or use dental floss), poke it through the blister, leaving the string in place, then cover the pierced blister with a non-padded plaster.

Other common problems are related to the heat. Wear a wide-brimmed sun hat, take good sunglasses and use plenty of suntan lotion with a high sun-protection factor. Treat mild sunburn with cold water, ice or calamine lotion, and consult a doctor in more serious cases. The Spanish *siesta* for a reason: it can be uncomfortably hot in the afternoon, and many pilgrims finish their day by 2pm. Rest often, drink lots of fluid and acclimatize gradually to hot conditions to stave off heat exhaustion and the more serious heatstroke. Symptoms of heat exhaustion include cold and clammy skin, nausea and dizziness. Move to a shady place and sip plenty of water. With heatstroke, there may be some early sensation of feeling unwell, but symptoms of flushed skin, dizziness, lack of sweating and restlessness usually occur suddenly. Move the sufferer to a cool place, cover them with wet clothes and fan constantly. Get medical help immediately, as the condition can be fatal.

There's very little water in the southern part of the Vía de la Plata, so make sure that you carry plenty of fluids. Further north, water from local springs is delicious and most villages have a village fountain; use your common sense before drinking from streams and purify or boil it if there are villages or farms nearby.

Most Spanish snakes are harmless, but the latastes viper, which has a distinctive horn on its head, is venomous. Avoid poking around in holes or sitting on piles of rocks, and make slow, deliberate movements if you spot a snake. If you do get bitten, secure and support the affected limb. Seek medical help, armed with a description of the snake, if possible. You're more likely to encounter dogs along the route. These can be intimidating, but the cliché holds true and their bark is generally worse than their bite. Cyclists in particular should move slowly, and be prepared to dismount, keeping the bike between you and the animal.

## Training & Fitness

The most important thing you can do is to wear comfortable, sturdy shoes and walk them in thoroughly before leaving home. A couple of months before you leave, start walking. Try to walk every day, even for a short time, as this mimics the routine of the camino. Gradually build up the distance walked over the next few weeks, then once you start to get fitter, take your pack along with you. A few times before you leave, pack everything you plan to take and go for a long walk; you'll get used to carrying a load, and perhaps be encouraged to leave non-essentials behind. Cyclists should ride a solid, dependable mountain bike and know how to repair it; build up your fitness before you leave and bring your panniers with you on at least a couple of training trips.

If you've left things until the last minute or if you plan to get fit along the way, don't make your first day too tough. Begin at Ourense to avoid the climb over the mountains from Puebla de Sanabria, for example. Be sensible distance-wise for the first few days too, and walk at a gentle pace. Even after you've been walking for a while, there will be days when you'll be lacking in energy. Try to be flexible about how far you travel each day and be prepared to stop if you're flagging. Consider doing shorter days in wet weather, as you're more likely to get tired if you're soaking and you'll also give your pack and shoes more time to dry out.

 **Communication**

## Post Offices

*Correos* (post offices) in smaller towns often close at 2pm, though some city *correos* re-open after the *siesta* from 5pm to 8pm. It's faster and more convenient to buy stamps at *estancos*, state-run tobacconists. It's easy to send packages overseas, but if you're simply trying to lighten your load, then it's cheaper to send items on to Santiago. Label the package with your name (surname first and in capitals), and address it to *Lista de Correos*, Santiago, Galicia. At the post office, if nothing's found under your last name, ask the staff to check under any other names too.

## Phones

Most public phones will take both coins and *tarjetas de telefónica* (phonecards). If a phone booth posts international dialling codes, then you can make overseas calls: dial 00, then the country code (44 for UK; 1 for Canada and USA; 61 for Australia; 64 for New Zealand). Mobile phones are ubiquitous on the camino as many companies provide Europe-wide coverage, and *albergue* bathrooms can be sacrilegiously crowded with recharging phones. The international dialling code for Spain is 34.

## Internet

Internet cafés are springing up in cities and bigger towns along the camino. They may be closed in the morning but are frequently open late into the evening, and they are a sociable place to hang out and check e-mail. Most charge very low hourly rates; ask at the *turismo* (tourist office) for a list. Don't forget to check out www.pilipalapress.com for up-to-date information and useful links.

 **Opening Hours & Public Holidays**

The Spanish take the *siesta* seriously. Most shops open at 10am, firmly close their doors at 2pm, then open again for the evening from 5pm to 8pm. Museums often stay open through the *siesta* and close for the day at 4pm; most also close on Mondays. Mealtimes are later than in northern Europe. Lunch starts at 2pm, and the evening meal is eaten from 10pm. It's often possible to ask for dinner to be served early in rural restaurants, but remember early in Spain is 8pm onwards. For more on Spanish eating habits, see the Food and Drink sections earlier in the book.

## Public Holidays

Most shops and banks close on public holidays, and public transport is limited, although restaurants and café-bars can be packed. If you're low on cash, take some money out a few days before the holiday, as bank machines can empty fast. The following public holidays are celebrated in most of Spain. For local festivals and holidays, see the Events & Festivals section in each regional chapter.

| | |
|---|---|
| January 1 | *Año Nuevo* (New Year's Day) |
| January 6 | *Día de los Reyes* (Epiphany) |
| March/April | *Jueves Santo, Viernes Santo* (Maundy Thursday, Good Friday) |
| May 1 | *Fiesta del Trabajo* (May Day) |
| August 15 | *Asunción* (Feast of the Assumption) |
| October 12 | *Día de la Hispanidad* (National Day) |
| November 1 | *Todos Santos* (All Saints' Day) |
| December 6 | *Día de la Constitución* (Constitution Day) |
| December 8 | *Inmaculada Concepción* (Immaculate Conception) |
| December 25 | *Navidad* (Christmas Day) |

**Regional Map** (key page 214)

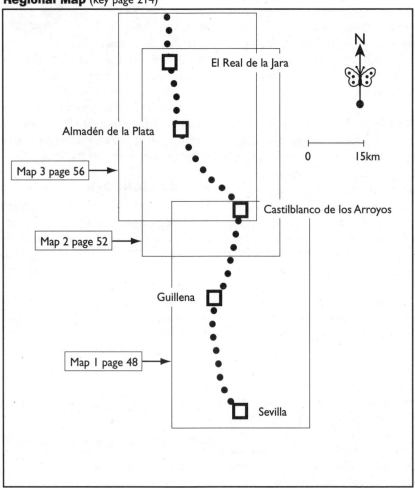

El Real de la Jara

Almadén de la Plata

Map 3 page 56

Castilblanco de los Arroyos

Map 2 page 52

Guillena

Map 1 page 48

Sevilla

N

0    15km

## What's the Weather Like?

|  | Jan | April | July | Oct |
|---|---|---|---|---|
| **Sun** | 6hrs | 8hrs | 12hrs | 7hrs |
| **Rainfall** | 6cm | 4cm | 0.1cm | 6cm |
| **Maximum Temp** | 21°C | 27°C | 38°C | 28°C |
| **Minimum Temp** | 4°C | 9°C | 18°C | 12°C |

Average hours of sun, total average rainfall in cm and average temperature in degrees celsius

# Andalucía

## Sevilla to Monesterio

Picture a Spanish stereotype, and you're probably thinking of Andalucía. Home of bullfighting, *flamenco*, whitewashed villages and sherry, the baking hot province was also the first region of Spain to embrace package tourism when it developed the resorts along the Costa del Sol in the 1950s.

 **Walking**

## Geography

Leaving Sevilla, the Vía de la Plata follows the Rio Guadalquivir. The Moors called this 560km-long river Wadi al-Kebir and harnessed its waters to irrigate the surrounding plains. In more modern times, ancient problems of flooding and silting up of the river have been conquered by the building of the Guadalquivir Canal.

Heading gradually up into the rounded hills of the Sierra Morena, the Vía de la Plata passes through the western edge of the Parque Natural de la Sierra Norte de Sevilla. Although the highest peak, Banuelo, is only 1320m, these mountains are a natural barrier between the fertile coastal plain and the more arid plains.

## Trails

For the most part, the way is well marked and navigation isn't a problem. The route leaves Sevilla via the abandoned Expo '92 lands and there are long stretches of industrial wasteland as the camino heads through Camas towards Santiponce. The hills of the Sierra Morena, although not particularly high, have some steep climbs on good dirt tracks. In the mountains, isolated stretches with no shade and water can pose problems if you're not prepared; it's important to carry enough water and not to over-exert yourself in the heat.

## When to go

Searing temperatures can make the summer uncomfortable even for locals, so much so that July and August are the low season in Sevilla, when the city empties and hotel prices drop considerably.

Spring and autumn offer the most pleasant climate for walking, and migration of birds through the region at these times is another good reason to come. Sevilla is famous for its solemn, macabre *Semana Santa* (Holy or Easter Week) processions, when it's impossible to find a bed in the city unless you've booked ahead, and hotel prices can double or even triple. Winter can bring rain but is mainly a good time to walk as the temperature is very pleasant.

 # Flora & Fauna

The remote corners of the Sierra Morena are one of the best places in Europe to spot the **black vulture**. Today, only an estimated 365 pairs live in Spain, and their numbers have been in gradual decline over the last hundred years as foreign trees usurp native forests. You're most likely to see immature birds as they fly solo high over the ground looking for carrion. The endangered **Iberian lynx** also has a tenuous paw hold in this area, with about 30 breeding pairs calling the Sierra Morena home. There are rumours of wolves in the mountains too, but there's no proof yet that this fierce carnivore has permanently returned.

The **eagle owl** is a massive bird with distinctive ear tufts that's strong enough to take on prey the size of a hare or large bird. At dawn and dusk, listen for its hoot, a continuous oooohu-oooohu-oooohu that can be heard up to 4km away on a still night. Easier to see are the many deer, pheasant and hares that keep local hunters occupied every Sunday.

The landscape is a mix of oak woodland and large clearings, where the scent of lavender, rosemary and thyme waft in the air. Agriculture dominates the more fertile valley bottoms, with large fields of olives, oranges, corn and cotton. Keep an eye out, because lurking in fields are **toros bravos**, fighting bulls waiting to take on the *matadores* of Spain. It's

unlikely that you'll be confronted with a bull in the open, but should you be so unlucky, make sure you leave a wide berth between yourself and the animal, and plan your escape route in advance. The wild boars of the region may also pose a hazard to pilgrims, as they can charge when they feel threatened.

You're unlikely to come across the peculiar **amphibisbaenia**, a subterranean reptile that's somewhere in between a snake and a lizard. Look instead for plentiful wall lizards and geckoes, and avoid the latastes viper, Spain's only venomous snake, recognizable by a distinctive horn on its head.

 # People & Culture

Although scribblings on Andalucían cave walls are more than 25,000 years old, the region's prehistoric past remains murky and uncertain. One of the first civilizations historians mention is the mysterious Kingdom of **Tartessos**, which flourished from the eighth to sixth centuries BC. Legend tells of two separate dynasties, the first headed by Geryon, a three-headed titan killed by Hercules as part of his twelve labours, and the second founded by Habis, said to be the inventor of agriculture. Modern archaeologists believe that the kingdom evolved from the megalithic culture of southern Iberia, and though it's clear that the people introduced grapes and olives to the area, had written laws and an excellent knowledge of metallurgy — Arganthonios, a seventh century BC ruler was known by Herodotus as the silver one — the exact location of the ancient capital remains one of the great unsolved mysteries of archaeology.

Andalucía prospered under **Roman** rule too. Baetica, as the Roman province became known, continued to trade in metals, and added olive oil, dodgy wine and dancing girls to its list of exports. The best Roman remains in Andalucía, including some spectacular mosaics, are in Italica, on the camino just outside Sevilla.

In the eighth century, a small Arab force arrived in Andalucía and, helped by peasants disgruntled with authoritarian Visigothic rule, quickly overran much of the peninsula. The emirate of **Al-Andalus**, proclaimed in 756, covered most of modern Spain, although its power and riches were concentrated in Andalucía. The Arabs perfected Roman irrigation techniques, developed a rich agricultural region and introduced oranges, cotton, rice and sugar.

The Christian **reconquista** finally reached Andalucía in the thirteenth century, and a couple of centuries later, Fernando and Isabel set about changing the face of the region. Sevilla became a wealthy and powerful port, sending Columbus off to the New World and receiving the gold and silver that swelled Spain's coffers in the sixteenth century, when it controlled much of the shipping traffic between Europe and the Americas. At the same time, the Inquisition was driving out and massacring Andalucía's large Muslim and Jewish populations, and the region suffered as Muslim agricultural expertise was lost.

Andalucía was sharply divided and quickly conquered by the Nationalists during the Civil War in the 1930s. The renowned poet Federico García Lorca was one of 150,000 Andalucians murdered by Franco. The economy plummeted during the first years of fascist rule, and Andalucía came close to famine. A decade later saw considerable Spanish and US investment and the birth of mass tourism on the Costa del Sol.

The influence of the Moors can still be seen in the the **architecture** of Andalucía. Many of Sevilla's metropolitan buildings were built by the Muslims, and smaller towns and villages along the camino often boast well-preserved Moorish legacies. Churches and houses of the region are often built in Mudéjar style, a mix of Almohad, Gothic and Renaissance influences. Andalucian Muslims were without a mosque for 500 years, but thanks to public pressure and the recent Spanish policy of *convivencia*, which encourages the peaceful co-existence of faiths and cultures, a mosque was built in Granada in 2003.

**Bullfighting** is a peculiar part of Spanish life, and stands closer to opera and literature than to football on Spain's cultural horizon. Echoing Roman gladiatorial battles, Moorish contests and medieval jousting, modern bullfighting emerged in Ronda in 1800 and the Royal School of Bullfighting was founded in Sevilla soon afterwards. It's a controversial spectacle, and hardly a fair fight, as the bull is softened up by *picadores* and *banderilleros* who pierce the animal with spears and darts before the cape-wielding *matador* arrives to take all the glory. After a good fight, the *matador* is given a bull's ear; exceptional performances yield both ears or, rarely, the bull's tail. Despite bullfighting's iconic status, there

are only 500 or so bull-fights a year in Spain; these *corridas* take place between April and October and usually coincide with *ferias* (holidays).

Romanies first brought **flamenco** to Andalucía in the fifteenth century, although its eclectic roots stretch to India, Greece and Egypt. As Arabs and Jews fled to rural Andalucía to escape the Inquisition, the refugees' musical traditions were incorporated, and *flamenco* emerged as a rhythmic, improvisational paean to despair. In *flamenco*, the guitarist and singer play off each other, grounded by the *jaleo*, a rhythmic combination of hand-clapping, finger-snapping and shouts of encouragement, and usually accompanied by foot-clacking dancers. Late nineteenth-century Spaniards found *flamenco* a bit depressing, and invented the *Sevillana*, a lighter, fluffier version now danced at *ferias* across Andalucía. Every *flamenco* musician and *aficionado* hopes to experience *duende*, the peak of *flamenco* artistry, when performers and audience merge in impromptu melancholy. If you're looking for your own *duende*, avoid the tourist *flamenco* shows and trawl the late-night streets, listening at the doors of dingy, smoke-filled bars.

Andalucía is still poor compared to the rest of the country; unemployment can reach as high as 40% and the average working Andalucían earns half that of his Barcelonan compatriot. Most of the region's farming takes place on *latifundias*, vast estates owned by filthy rich landlords and largely worked by casual labourers whose employment and income is seasonal.

Throughout the region, life is still lived at a slow pace. The *siesta* is taken very seriously and in summer months can stretch from 2pm until 6pm. Once the heat of the day has gone, people move chairs outside and chat until the early hours of the morning.

# Food & Drink

The fabulous Spanish tradition of **tapas** originated in Sevilla, where small portions of food were served on a *tapa* (small plate) placed on top of a glass of wine or sherry. The best way to join in is to graze with the locals in a *tapas* crawl, bar-hopping around town.

Seafood lovers are spoilt for choice throughout the region, particularly in Sevilla, which is famous for *pescaíto frito*, fried fish marinated in *adobo*, a paste made from garlic, salt, vinegar, herbs and spices.

Chilled **gazpacho** is a refreshing soup traditionally made with tomatoes, cucumber, peppers, oil, vinegar, garlic and salt; there are enough local variations on the basic recipe to see you all the way through the region. Andalucía is also famous for its hearty *guisos* (stews), *embutidos* (cured sausages), *morcón* (blood pudding) and the well-named *revollitos* (tripe).

You'll need a strong stomach to eat the traditional Andalucían **breakfast** of toast smeared with *manteca colorá* (lard coloured with paprika or tomato), and sweet-toothed pilgrims may prefer *churros* (long doughnuts) with thick hot chocolate.

You'll see olive groves everywhere in Andalucía and you shouldn't leave

Sevilla without trying its famous, monstrously fat green **manzanilla olives**.

As in the rest of Spain, the *menú del día* is the cheapest way to eat out; in Andalucía, try to eat at *ventas*, family-run places that are at their best at Sunday lunchtime. In the evening, *menú del día* may be hard to find because *tapas* dominate the local tastes, particularly before 9pm.

Moorish-inspired Andalucían desserts are renowned throughout Spain. Try the Christmas *polvorones* (shortcake) and *mantecados* (made with almonds), and the delightfully named *tocinos de cielo* (bacon from heaven).

 **Tourist Information**

## Tourist Offices

Once you leave Sevilla, there are no other *turismos* in Andalucía. See the description of Sevilla for contact information.

## Transport

You can avoid the industrial route out of Sevilla by catching one of the frequent buses to Italica. After Guillena, it's difficult to travel along the camino by bus or even taxi, and Almadén de la Plata is completely cut off from public transport. El Real de la Jara has buses to and from Sevilla and points north.

## Money

There are banks with cash machines in Sevilla, Camas, Santiponce, Guillena, Castilblanco de los Arroyos and El Real de la Jara.

## Accommodation

*Albergues* aren't staffed and their quality varies from extremely basic mattresses on the floor to luxurious dormitory accommodation. The ability to speak a bit of Spanish will be invaluable when searching for the *albergue* and the key to get in.

## Shopping

**El Jueves**, the famous Thursday bric-a-brac market in La Feria in Sevilla, has been going strong since the thirteenth century when it was described by Cervantes. The nearby district of **La Macarena** holds flea markets each Thursday and Sunday. Every town along the camino has at least one well-stocked shop for supplies. Most bakeries and cafés do not open until at least 8.30am, so early starts mean skipping the dawn caffeine hit.

## Events & Festivals

Sevilla's **Semana Santa** is one of the most famous festivals in Spain, deriving from the penitence rituals of medieval *cofradías* (brotherhoods). From Palm Sunday to Easter Sunday, half a dozen or so *cofradías* leave local churches for the cathedral at half-hour intervals, led by *nazarenos* (penitents) cloaked in macabre peaked hoods and followed by floats carrying religious images. The processions are massive and can take the whole day, and even the *cofradías* closest to the cathedral walk for at least four hours.

A couple of weeks after the religious processions of *Semana Santa*, Sevilla lets its hair down for the April **Feria**, the largest *fiesta* in Andalucía. The best parties are private ones in *casitas* (local

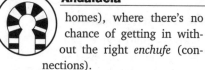

homes), where there's no chance of getting in without the right *enchufe* (connections).

Each Thursday in June, Corpus Christi processions wend their way along Sevilla's streets, which are strewn and scented with herbs. Sevilla's **bienal de flamenco** showcases the world's best flamenco performers in September and October of even-numbered years.

# Rest Days & Detours

It may seem a bit lazy to have a rest day before walking even a kilometre, but **Sevilla** is a gem of a city that deserves at least a few days to explore. If you want to get off to a fast start, take a day to visit the ruins of **Italica** and bypass it on your first day of walking.

# Sevilla

**⊕ ✗ 🛏 € ❶ 🛒** (1007km)

Sevilla is a city of contrasts. It's bejewelled with splendid Moorish architecture yet renowned for its Christian festivals, and it's a pious Catholic city so famous for its exuberance and passion that three famous operas are set here: *Don Giovanni*, *Carmen* and *The Barber of Seville*.

Founded as Hispalis by the Romans on the site of an Iberian settlement, Sevilla was an important town in the late Roman Empire. Intellectual life flourished under the Visigoths who arrived a few centuries later, particularly under bishops Leovigild and his more famous brother Isidro, who argued in *Seven Books Against the Pagans* that Rome's downfall wasn't caused by Christianity. Sevilla became the most powerful state in Moorish Al-Andalus in 1031, and was made capital of the Almohad lands in the late twelfth century, before being captured by

the Christians in 1248. At the beginning of the sixteenth century, Sevilla prospered when it was given an official monopoly on Spanish trade with the Americas, but by 1700 the Río Guadilquivir had silted up and trade had moved south to Cadiz. Sevilla was captured quickly during the Spanish Civil War, seized by General Queipo de Llano who made notorious wartime propaganda broadcasts from the city. Expo '92 attracted 16 million visitors to the city, triggering a tourist boom that's still evident in the city's crowded *tapas* bars every evening. Still, huge tracts of Expo land lie vacant, waiting for promised development that never came.

Sevilla's massive, squat, Gothic **cathedral** is a building of superlatives rather than a superlative building. In 1401, after 150 years of using the Almohad mosque as a place of Christian worship, local churchmen dreamed up "a building on so magnificent a scale that posterity will think we were mad." Measured by volume, it's the biggest church in the world, surpassing St. Peter's in Rome and St.

Paul's in London, and the interior is dominated by the world's largest *retablo* (altarpiece). Most of the mosque was demolished to make way for the church, but the Christian architects retained El Patio de los Naranjos, an orange-treed patio that still contains the font used to perform ablutions, and La Giralda, the mosque's magnificent 94m-high minaret. **La Giralda**, one of the finest examples of Almohad architecture, was used not only as a place to call the faithful to prayer but also as an observatory. The tower was once topped by four copper spheres that could be seen from a day's horse ride away and acted as a beacon for travellers. You glide rather than climb to the top of the tower, ascending via a series of ramps wide enough for two horses. The view over the city is breathtaking, and it's possible to see the route of the Vía de la Plata heading north over the Sierra Morena.

Inside the cathedral, the vault contains the coffins of Fernando III and Pedro the Cruel. Above ground, Columbus' tomb is held aloft by the four great Christian Kingdoms, although it's not clear whether the explorer's remains are here or in the Dominican Republic, where they were originally interred. Historians are hoping that DNA testing of the bones will settle the dispute over his final resting place. The exhibits in the Sacristia Mayor include the Alfonsine Tables, a reliquary of tooth and bone that was Alfonso X's security blanket, and the keys to the city given to Fernando III by the city's Jewish and Muslim communities when he captured Sevilla.

The **Alcázar** is undoubtedly the best example of Mudéjar art in Spain, with gorgeous patios, star-shaped ceilings and beautiful gardens. The Abbadid court here decorated the palace with gruesome flower pots made from the skulls of their enemies; they also found room for a harem of 800 women. The Almohads converted the palace into a citadel and it became part of Sevilla's extensive fortifications. The Alcázar was extensively remodelled in Mudéjar style by Pedro the Cruel, who much preferred Sevilla's Moorish romanticism to the coldness of Old Castilla. Pedro was a controversial king also known as *El Justiciero* (the Just), although probably not by his half-brother Fadrique or by Abu Said of Granada, both of whom were murdered here on his orders. Among Pedro's hauls from murdering Abu Said was a huge ruby that he eventually presented to Edward of England; the Black Prince Ruby now gleams from the front of the English coronation crown. Although subsequent rulers built some spectacularly out-of-place additions, it's worth checking out Carlos V's palace for its sumptuous Flemish tapestries.

The **Torre del Oro**, a twelve-sided tower named for the reflective *azulejos* that once covered its exterior, was built by the Almohads in 1220 when it formed part of the city walls. It now stands alone by the river providing shade for river-tour touts. Popular legend tells that the **Casa de Pilatos** was modelled on Pontius Pilate's home in Jerusalem. It's studded with Crusaders' crosses and contains Roman statues from Italica, including a bust of Antinous, Hadrian's male lover. Sevilla's oddly shaped bullring, **La Maestranza**, was squeezed into its current location by the surrounding buildings that sprung up during its construction between 1760 and 1880. If you're not in town for a bullfight, you can still visit the Museo Taurino and hear La Maestranza's magnificent acoustics.

The **Hospital de la Caridad** was funded by Miguel de Mañara, a notorious seducer and murderer. On receiving a disturbing vision of his own death and funeral, de Mañara repented his wicked ways and became a pious monk devoted to helping the sick. His early life was said to be the model for Don Juan, and his tomb in the hospital bears the epitaph he requested, "Here lie the ashes of the worst man the world has ever known." The hospital chapel contains a series of lovely paintings by Murillo and some macabre images commissioned by the death-obsessed de Mañara, including one of a bishop decomposing in his coffin.

In the north of the city, the **Iglesia de San Salvador** was built on the site of an Umayyad mosque, founded in 829. The minaret forms part of the church's bell tower, and the upper half of an arcade is preserved in the church façade, which was built with reused Roman Corinthian capitals and may have formed part of the mosque courtyard.

*Carmen* fans should visit the **Fábrica de Tabacos**, the eighteenth-century tobacco factory where Carmen rolled her own alongside thousands of women. According to English traveller and author Richard Ford, the workers were subject to "an ingeniously minute search on leaving their work, for they sometimes carry off the filthy weed in a manner Her Most Catholic Majesty would never dream of."

Sevilla also has a few other **museums** worth visiting. The Museo de Bellas Artes is housed in the Convento de Merced, northwest of the cathedral, and contains an impressive collection of Spanish art, including works by Goya, Murillo and Zubarán. Christopher Columbus may have been the most famous guest of the Cartuja de Santa María de las Cuevas, but Napoleon's troops

made more of a mark, using the beautiful ceiling for target practice. The restored monastery is now the serene setting for the Centro Andaluz de Arte Contemporaneo, an imaginative space for the best in modern Andalucían art. South of the city, visit Parque María Luisa for its beautiful palms and orange trees, and for the Museo Arqueológico, which has finds from Italica.

**Turismos** can be found on Avenida de la Constitución 21 (☎ 954 221 404) and Calle Arjona 28 (☎ 954 221 714). You can get a *sello* from the cathedral entrance nearest the treasury.

### Accommodation

**$ Hostal Romero**, Calle Gravina 21 (☎ 954 211 353)

**$$ Hostal Bienvenido**, Calle Archeros 14 (☎ 954 413 655)

**$$$ Hostal Londres**, San Pedro Mártir 1 (☎ 954 212 896)

**$$$$ Hotel Doña María**, Don Remondo 19 (☎ 954 224 990)

Begin your adventure along the Vía de la Plata at the west face of the cathedral on Avenida de la Constitución, where you'll be seen off by the statue of Santiago Peregrino, surrounded by his fellow apostles in an impressive stone doorway. Immediately cross the road and turn right, following the first of thousands of yellow arrows, then take the second left into Calle Garcia de Vinuesa at a scallop shell *azulejo*. Turn right almost straight away onto Calle Jimios and immediately fork left, then keep straight on along Calle Zaragoza. There are yellow arrows at regular intervals, usually painted low down.

Many of the older houses along the way out of Sevilla have a *zaguán* (entrance porch) with a *cancela* (iron gate) and windows grilled with iron. The men who wooed their sweethearts through these barriers were said to *comer hierro* (eat iron). Turn left when you reach the junction with Reyes Católicos, a much bigger road than the narrower streets so far; yellow arrows are obscured here. Cross over Avenida Cristobal Colón and walk over Puente de Isabel II into Triana.

Once home to the city's *gitano* (gypsy) community, Triana is famous for *flamenco* and for the ceramic factories where *azulejos* are still painted by hand. The working class *barrio* also has a more sinister history; the Inquisition's first *auto-da-fé* was held here in 1481, and it was the scene of a brutal Nationalist massacre during the Spanish Civil War in 1936. In July, the Feria de la Velá celebrates Santa Ana, Triana's patron saint.

Take the first right after the bridge along Calle San Jorge, passing a statue of Juan Belmonte, probably Spain's most famous bullfighter, and the *azulejo*-covered Mercado Triana. Turn right along Calle Callao, pass Callejon de la Inquisición, and immediately curve left onto Calle Castilla. Save breakfast until you get to Triana, where bars open at 7am and serve *tostadas*, a local delicacy of toast smeared with lard. Cross the busy Calle Ronda de Triana, then veer right soon afterwards to climb a flight of steps and cross another busy road. Immediately turn left to cross Avenida Carlos III.

The route splits here, both options passing through industrial areas. You can turn left to walk along the riverbank — not as nice an option as it sounds — but we turn right to head towards the town

of Camas. After 100m, veer left to cross an old Expo car park and turn left to cross Canal Corta de la Cartuja. Even though the camino follows a smelly, barren wasteland of a dirt road, this is a good area to spot hoopoes dusting themselves down, hollowing out divots in the dirt as they do so. Keep straight on through a tunnel under the E803 and things soon get more civilized as you enter the outskirts of Camas on a wide boulevard. After about 500m, turn first right, following signs for *centro ciudad*. Go straight on at a roundabout, passing the eighteenth-century Iglesia de Santa María de Gracia.

**Camas** (⊞⏚✕🍴€, 1002km) is slowly becoming a suburb of Sevilla and sprawls with rundown industrial buildings. Its name comes from a mistranslation of the Muslim Abu-Alkama. On a nearby hill is a shrine to Santa Brígida, originally built by Irish monks who sailed here up the Río Guadalquivir. You can stay just on the other side of town at the **Hostal El Madero** ($, ☎ 954 391 299).

Head straight through Camas and, when the town finally ends, keep straight on over a large roundabout, following the signs to Santiponce. Plod along on the sidewalk alongside the main road through an industrial zone, passing the Hostal El Madero after 1km; the sidewalk ends 500m later, but there's a wide hard shoulder. In another 500m, keep straight on at a roundabout as the sidewalk reappears. You'll soon enter the town of Santiponce, which sits on the ruins of the oldest section of the ancient city of Italica. Follow the main road as it curves to the right, passing on the right-hand

**Map 1** (key page 214)

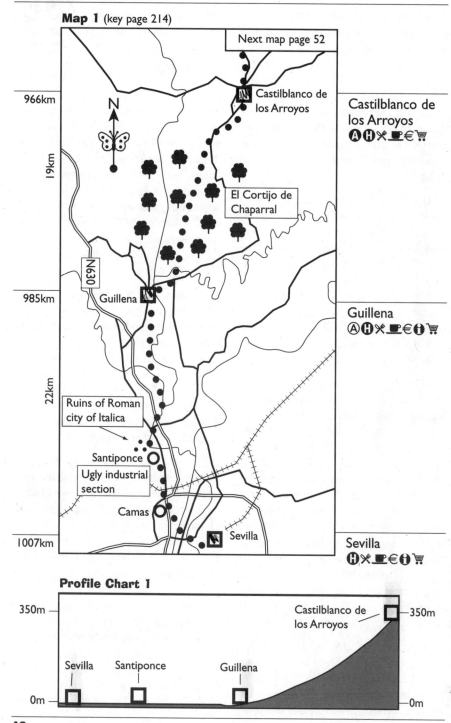

Next map page 52

966km

N

Castilblanco de
los Arroyos

Castilblanco de
los Arroyos
Ⓐ⊕✕▦€🛒

19km

El Cortijo de
Chaparral

N630

985km

Guillena

Guillena
Ⓐ⊕✕▦€🛈🛒

22km

Ruins of Roman
city of Italica

Santiponce

Ugly industrial
section

Camas

1007km

Sevilla

Sevilla
⊕✕▦€🛈🛒

**Profile Chart 1**

350m — 

Castilblanco de
los Arroyos
— 350m

Sevilla    Santiponce    Guillena

0m — 
— 0m

side of the road the entrance to the Monasterio de San Isidro del Campo, which has been visible for some time. The monastery was built by Cistercians monks on the orders of Guzmán el Bueno. You can still visit the church and part of the cloisters, open every morning except Mondays.

In **Santiponce** (⓿✖☎€⓿☕, 997km), you can stay at the **Hotel Anfiteatro Romano** ($$$, ☎ 955 996 704) or the **Casa Rural Señora Carmen** ($$, ☎ 955 996 637). Near the end of town, turn right to visit the Roman theatre and the small *turismo*, then right again 30m later. Otherwise, continue on the camino and reach Italica in 500m.

Founded in 205BC by Scipio Africanus as a home for veterans of the war against Carthage, **Italica** was one of the earliest Roman cities in Hispania. The town really took off in the second century under Emperor Hadrian, who along with Emperor Trajan was born here. Many of the town's monuments were built under Hadrian's patronage, including temples centred around the cult of Trajan, his predecessor. The Moors weren't that interested in Italica and moved their town to Hispalis (now Sevilla), possibly because the Río Guadalquivir changed course around the time of their arrival. Whatever the reason, their decision preserved many of Italica's monuments. Italica's amphitheatre is worth the price of admission alone. The fourth-largest amphitheatre in the Roman world, its impressive scale makes it easy to imagine the titanic gladiatorial battles that kept tens of thousands of roaring spectators enthralled. Much of the seating is lost and the stone reused for other buildings, but many of the vaulted galleries under the seats are still intact, as are the underground passages beneath the floor of the arena, through which animals and other participants were moved.

Although most of the town's artefacts are in the Museo Arqueológico in Sevilla, you'll see *in situ* mosaics throughout Italica. Some of the best are at The House of the Exedra, where the latrine floor is decorated with monochromatic images of pygmies riding ostriches; The House of the Peacocks, aptly named for its fine mosaic of the colourful birds, and The House of Hylas, which has splendid geometric mosaics. Los Baños de la Reina Mora (Baths of the Moorish Queen) contains a 21m-long swimming pool; nineteenth-century excavations show it to be the largest bath complex in Roman Spain. The site is open daily except Mondays, and is free to EU citizens.

Leaving Italica, pass the Restaurant Ventorillo Romano in 1km and keep straight on, following signs for Algaba and Córdoba and crossing the very busy N630. There's a lot of road building going on here, so the road patterns may change in the near future. After 300m, veer left down a track and keep straight on through a clump of eucalyptus, then 100m later, turn left to avoid a bridge. Almost immediately, you have two options, both waymarked. Either keep straight on, the best choice in bad weather or if cycling, or turn right on a less busy route with a tricky section across an irrigation ditch. It's common to see horse-drawn carts along the track and hares in the fields next to the camino. After 1km, pass a fig tree and a farm off to the left, and keep straight on at a crossroads of tracks. The two routes join 300m from here. About 750m later, keep straight on a dirt track as the main road curves right towards a stream. Cotton fields line the camino on both sides, then after 400m these give way to an electric fence that keeps in the fierce-looking local cattle. Veer left as the fence ends, still walking on a dirt track which, in an effort to stop vehicles getting bogged down, is now littered with broken *azulejos* (tiles).

Carry on through fields of cotton and sunflowers, then in just under 1km, turn right at a junction with a larger track. Shortly afterwards, the dirt track becomes concrete to protect it from washouts during seasonal flooding, then crosses a stream and heads towards a concrete tower, passing a farm on the left and climbing slightly. From the top of the rise, you can see the whitewashed village of Guillena ahead.

About 4km from the top, after walking through fields of olives and corn, the dirt track curves to the left; turn right here, following yellow arrows. Pass huge cactus bushes 500m later, and keep straight on to follow a path downhill to a stream, which you cross via stepping stones. Turn left at the far bank and enter Guillena in about 1km, passing a cemetery on the right. Cross a small square 300m later and walk up Calle Real, reaching the shady Plaza de España 200m later.

# Guillena
Ⓐ🄷✕💼€🛒 (985km)

An ancient Roman town — a milestone found here is in the archaeological museum in Sevilla — Guillena was fortified during the Muslim era. Later, the town's reconquest by Fernando III was crucial in his efforts to take Sevilla for the Christians. Today, it's a pretty town of whitewashed houses with broad mustard-yellow trims; the iron grilles on the lower-storey windows are reminiscent of Sevilla. The *ayuntamiento* is next door to the fifteenth-century Mudéjar Iglesia de la Virgen de la Granada. The remains of a castle have been converted into the town bullring, and if you're here during the town's annual September *fiesta*, you'll be able to catch a *corrida* (fight).

Guillena's spartan **albergue** (no mattresses, cold showers, donation) is in the *polideportivo* (sports complex). Pick up the keys from the *policía local*; to get there turn left at Plaza de España, right at the main road, then turn right past Bar Lolo and bear left. To reach the *albergue*, head past the *mercado municipal* and turn left at the bottom of the hill on the outskirts of town. There's sporadic water supply in the changing rooms, which double as sleeping area; pilgrims may prefer to sleep outside under the stars in good weather. The **Bar Hostal Francés** (**$**, ☎ 955 785 177) is a better option if rooms are available.

Follow the wide road out of Guillena. Pass a modern sports complex then turn right, cross the Rió Rivera de Huelva 300m later via a causeway, then follow a stony dirt road to the right at the other bank. Walk through an industrial wasteland, which soon changes to farmland with huge prickly cacti lining the road. After almost 3km, reach a main road, cross over a roundabout and walk past a group of industrial buildings. This is the tiny community of **Venta** (💼), its bar hidden amongst modern warehouses.

Turn right 100m later, passing bamboo on the left, then turn left on to a dirt road through orange and olive trees. Pass a sign soon afterwards for the Vía Pecuaria Cañada Real de las Islas, a medieval cattle drove road that's being partly revived.

Climb gradually through undulating terrain, being sure to stick to the main path as this area is popular with hunters. After 2km, pass a fortified building away to the right and enjoy excellent views of Guillena and Sevilla. After about 4km on this track, pass a sign showing that you're now in the Parque Natural de la Sierra Norte de Sevilla. About 500m later, after a downhill section, keep straight on as the track curves to the left, then pass through a makeshift gate and over a cattle grid into El Cortijo de Chaparral, a local *latifundia* (large estate).

Follow a narrow dirt path past a map of the region 50m later, and look out for yellow arrows painted on low stones and tree trunks as you proceed through a holm oak forest. In a couple of kilometres the terrain becomes rockier and drier as the landscape changes to heathland. Look out for crested larks which, along with hoopoes, are common in these hills. Just 1km later you're back in farmland and large olive plantations, although the track is still lined with scrub. The route passes through a series of gates; be sure to leave these as you find them.

As the scrub opens up, the track widens and becomes sandy, and you start to hear traffic to your right. Eventually, veer right as the track joins a gravel road, and reach the tarmac A3102 about 1km later. There's a modern *miliario* (milestone) here, erected by the local Friends of the Camino; you'll see more of these distinctive stones throughout Andalucía.

Climb steadily uphill, keeping a look out for a track on the right-hand side of the road. This indistinct track disappears from time to time, but becomes more permanent after about 2km, then veers away from the road 1km later and joins a wider dirt track. In another 300m, keep straight on as the track curves to the left to join a paved road, and head towards the large building on the hill up a narrow track blocked to traffic by boulders. Pass through a forlorn-looking botanical garden and keep straight on as you reach a small group of factories.

Turn left at a narrow tarmac road, then turn right 30m later to walk on a path alongside the main road, passing the Hotel Castillo Blanco on the right. Some 150m later at a pyramid-shaped sculpture based on a Cervantes tale, there are two options. Either keep straight on for the *albergue*, 300m downhill behind the petrol station, or turn left down Avenida de España and follow the camino onwards towards Santiago.

# Castilblanco de los Arroyos
Ⓐ❶✕▣€🛒 (966km)

A beautiful hillside town, Castilblanco's cobbled streets are lined with elegant whitewashed terraced houses trimmed with colour and decorated with iron-grilled windows. There are fantastic views over the surrounding countryside, particularly from the *albergue*. Cervantes set his novella *Las Dos Doncellas* here, a tale of betrayal, cross-dressing and ultimate redemption, ending in the best possible way with a pilgrimage to Santiago (although things do almost come undone at the very end). The Mudéjar Iglesia

## Map 2 (key page 214)

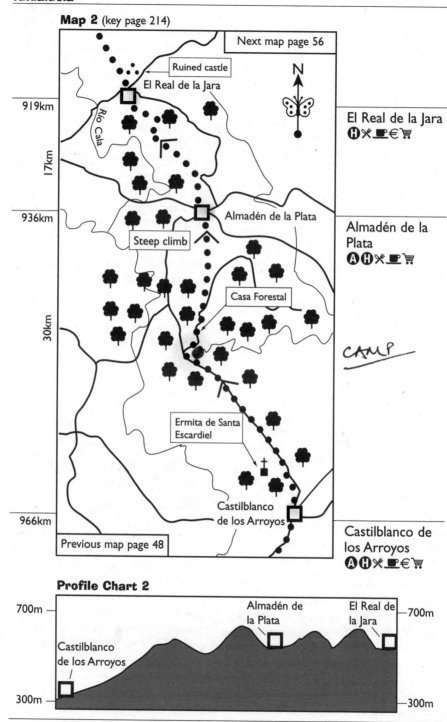

Next map page 56

Ruined castle

El Real de la Jara

919km

Río Cala

17km

El Real de la Jara
ⓗ✕💻€🛒

936km

Almadén de la Plata

Steep climb

Almadén de la Plata
Ⓐⓗ✕💻🛒

Casa Forestal

30km

CAMP

Ermita de Santa Escardiel

Castilblanco de los Arroyos

966km

Previous map page 48

Castilblanco de los Arroyos
Ⓐⓗ✕💻€🛒

### Profile Chart 2

700m

Almadén de la Plata

El Real de la Jara

700m

Castilblanco de los Arroyos

300m

300m

del Divino Salvador dates from the sixteenth and seventeenth centuries, but has been unsympathetically restored.

Castilblanco's **albergue** (8 single beds, hot showers, donation) is in a lovely purpose-built building; ask for the key at the petrol station. Alternatively, you can stay at the **Hotel Castillo Blanco** ($$, ☎ 955 734 523).

___

Before leaving Castilblanco, make sure that you're carrying plenty of water as there's nowhere to fill up for 16km. To leave town, you can either head downhill from the *albergue* on the main road (unmarked) and turn left 300m later at the turning for the Ermita de Santa de Escardiel, or follow the more pleasant route through town, described here.

Return uphill to the roundabout with the Cervantes monument, and take the tree-lined Avenida de España. Turn left on to Calle Juan Ramon Jimenez, then one block later turn right past the Iglesia del Divino Salvador on Plaza de la Iglesia. Keep straight on down Calle Miguel Hernandez past a statue dedicated to local pensioners, and houses that retain iron rings in the outside walls so that you can hitch your horse. Keep to the Avenida de España as it curves left, veer left at a small roundabout, then reach a large stone horse trough and meet up with the main road. Turn left here and join the alternative route from the *albergue*.

Cross a concrete bridge on the edge of town and follow the main SE185 as it climbs up and over rolling hills. Although you're on a paved road, there's usually a shoulder to walk on. The first cork oaks of the Vía de la Plata appear and there are fine views, as hoopoes, jays and cirl buntings flutter in the fields. In 4km, pass a sign for the Ermita de Santa de Escardiel. In another 7km, head steeply uphill, before the road flattens out as you pass a microwave tower on the left. Another 4km later, pass a road sign for the Parque Natural de la Sierra Norte. Soon afterwards, turn right off the main road through a gate into the Parque Forestal de El Berrocal, where a small gatehouse offers some miniscule shade. Unfortunately, if the gate is locked, you'll have to keep following the main road all the way to Almadén de la Plata; cyclists will find this an easier route.

Once in the park, there are cork oak trees as far as the eye can see; be sure to keep a close look out as deer are also a common sight. Follow the narrow, rough paved road past a watchtower on the left, then head downhill to the Casa Forestal, where you can fill up with water at a tap. Walk through another gate and continue downhill as the road winds its way slowly through cork oaks and passes an artificial lake off to the right. After several kilometres the mature oak forest peters out and younger trees appear, protected from nibbling deer by fences.

Even the meagre shade provided by this effort at reforestation soon disappears and the camino leads into a large natural bowl that can be a furnace in hot weather. Ignore a dirt track that leads off to the right and pass a small green metal cross on the left of the road, then walk through a narrow pass next to a river.

Keep straight on 1km later at a junction with a sign for Los Berrocales, then in 150m, when you're almost next to some ruined buildings, turn left on to a dirt track, passing a modern *miliario* on the right and some houses on the left.

Climb slowly through an area of replanted pine, then pass through a gate to head uphill through a landscape of scrub with the occasional lonely oak tree. Ahead you can see the ridge that you must climb to get to Almadén de la Plata. The scrub is interrupted by fire barriers, bizarre-looking straight lines that scar the landscape. They may not been easy on the eye, but they're necessary to prevent fires such as those that destroyed vast tracts of southern Spain in summer 2003. Pass through another gate and keep straight on, ignoring the more established tracks that branch left and right.

The camino is now a wonderful single track through grassland and oak. Steel yourself before tackling the last steep uphill of the day; there's a definite sting in the tail of this climb. About a third of the way up, the track splits at a bend; keep right to follow a steeper, less well-travelled trail, then in about 300m rejoin the main track just below the summit.

On the top of Cerro del Calvario there are two viewpoints with maps showing local features, and you can see Almadén de la Plata below. The climb down is steep with sections of loose gravel and passes through more cork trees. Halfway down, pause at the shrine perched on a jutting rock for fine views of the valley below. Go through another gate on the way into town and walk over chunks of the marble that once made the town wealthy.

At a T-junction, turn right, then take the first left into town. Keep straight on until the main road, then turn right past

a large marble horse trough, and turn left to walk past the church and the *ayuntamiento* (town hall).

# Almadén de la Plata
Ⓐ Ⓗ ✗ ⬛ 🛒 (936km)

Nestled in the Sierra Morena, Almadén de la Plata has an isolated feel.: on the whole it's been downhill for Almadén since its Roman heyday, when marble was quarried here. Although the town was eventually reconquered by the Knights of the Order of Santiago, the artistic influence of the Moors is still evident. The sixteenth-century Iglesia de Nuestra Señora de Gracia is lovely, and the early twentieth-century *ayuntamiento* has a distinctive square Torre del Reloj from which there are great views. Before you leave town, you need to call ahead to the Finca Arroyo Mateo (☎ 954 735 049) to ask that the gate to the *finca* be left open for you on your route the next day.

The excellent **albergue** (30 beds, hot showers, donation) is on the top edge of town. There are some very good restaurants, where you can sample the town's delicious sausages. You can also stay at the **Hostal Casa Concha** ($), behind the bar of the same name.

Walk uphill out of town past the Plaza de Toros and 200m later turn left at a junction going downhill, heading through fields of holm oak and large cacti alongside the camino. Curve around a hill, then keep straight on over a junction, through a gate and into a large field with holm oaks, passing a small water hole on the right. The fields here are jammed full of free-roaming pigs and horses that feign indifference to pilgrims. Walk by a posh new *finca* with a very out-of-place manicured lawn. Veer right just afterwards over a small concrete bridge, then in 100m keep your eyes peeled as the camino turns left to follow a single track that heads up and over a hill.

Eventually, cross a river bed (usually dry) and turn left on to a dirt road. Pass a *miliario* on the left. Keep on this road for a couple of kilometres, passing a small farm and ignoring a left turn just afterwards. Just 500m after the farm there is a well with good water. Keep going until you reach the gate for the Finca Arroyo Mateo, which will be unlocked if you have called ahead; remember to close the gate behind you. The camino heads downhill as it snakes towards some farm buildings. Take a sharp right-hand turn 200m after the gate, then walk behind the farm buildings and head steeply downhill. The path can be loose, so watch your footing here. The *finca* is a hunting reserve, well-stocked with deer and game birds. It's common to see Egyptian and griffon vultures circling overhead and you may also spot the rare black vulture.

At the bottom of the hill, cross a river bed, then climb a small rise and cross another arm of the Arroyo Mateo, the stream gives its name to the *finca*. Follow the track as it curves uphill in a long, slow climb, and stunning views open up. Just before cresting the hill, pass a small building on the right, then once at the top, follow the undulating ridge until you reach a gate under some power pylons. Go through the gate and keep following the ridge, but be careful, as this stretch is not well marked. If you have binoculars you can get a close look at the

castle above Santa Olalla del Cala straight ahead. El Real de la Jara is hidden around the hill on the right.

The track becomes more established as you pass through a series of gates; be sure to leave these as you find them, as there are many sheep and the occasional sheep dog. The route curves around to the valley bottom where you walk though open fields and holm oaks. Pass some modern ruins on the left and head straight on, ignoring a junction off to the left. Soon afterwards, pass a 3km milestone, and follow this road all the way to El Real de la Jara. At the 1km milestone, there's a plaque dedicated to Jose Luis Salvador Salvador, a key figure in the modern revival of the Vía de la Plata.

You don't see El Real until you're almost on top of it and there are suddenly great views of the castle. Enter the town on Calle Pablo Picasso, turn right at a T-junction, then left along Calle Real and follow this all the way through town.

There's a comfortable, lived-in feel to **El Real de la Jara** (❶✕ ▣€☗, 919km), where it seems as if everyone's family has lived here for generations, and innocuous doors hide magical courtyards and gardens. The village owes its name to the Camino Real, the main route between Andalucía and Extremadura before the modern N630 was built. The Mudéjar Iglesia de San Bartolomé has a *retablo* with a painting attributed to Zurbarán. There are wonderful views of the town from the *castillo* that dominates the skyline, and you can walk along the restored castle walls. Beds are available at the **Pensión Salvadora** (**$**) at Calle Real 70, and you can get a *sello* from the Guardia Civil across the road. There's

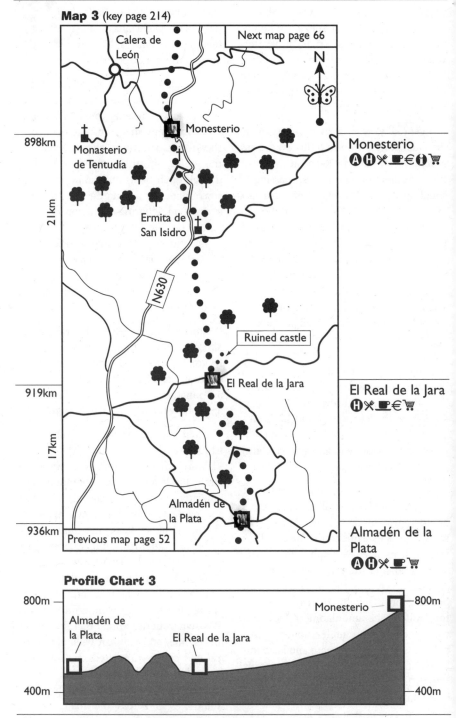

**Map 3** (key page 214)

Calera de León

Next map page 66

N

898km

Monesterio

Monesterio

Ⓐ🅗✂🍴🛒€ⓘ🛒

Monasterio de Tentudía

21km

Ermita de San Isidro

N630

Ruined castle

919km

El Real de la Jara

El Real de la Jara

🅗✂🍴€🛒

17km

Almadén de la Plata

936km

Previous map page 52

Almadén de la Plata

Ⓐ🅗✂🍴🛒

**Profile Chart 3**

800m — Monesterio — 800m

Almadén de la Plata

El Real de la Jara

400m — — 400m

excellent food at Meson La Cochera, opposite the church.

As you leave town on Calle Real, the paved road becomes a walled dirt lane through farmland, then after a short climb and descent you'll get views of another magnificent ruined *castillo* on the right. Pass a modern *miliario* on the left and cross a concrete causeway over a stream that marks the modern boundary between the provinces of Sevilla and Badajoz. Pass the wonderfully dilapidated *castillo* soon afterwards.

The route continues through mostly flat farmland with holm oak and cork oak that provide welcome shade. Sheep, cows and goats are your only companions as the route is little used by motorized traffic. Soon, three peaks come into view ahead: Monesterio is just over the middle peak, still more than 15km away. After a few kilometres the land becomes more barren, shade begins to disappear and you get increasingly lovely if slightly disheartening views of the highest point of the Sierra Morena ahead.

Some 10km after leaving El Real, ford a stream that can be packed with frogs, then in 1km, ford another stream, a good spot to see herons. Pass a summer-only campsite on the left, then 300m later pass a small whitewashed domed chapel at the campsite's edge. Cross a tarmac road and keep straight on along a dirt track. In about 300m, the track veers close to the N630, which you will shadow all the way to Monesterio. Keep to this track 100m later as you enter eucalyptus trees that offer welcome shade on a hot day. In another 200m, pass the Ermita de San Isidro on the left. The *ermita* was built to mark one of the many resting places of those who transported the body of San Isidro from Sevilla to León. There's an a important *romería* (religious procession) to this spot on May 15.

The track begins to narrow and moves a little further away from the main road. Keep climbing uphill and after 1km keep straight on at a crossroads as the track narrows to a path. About 2km from the *ermita*, the camino leaves the dirt path and follows an old tarmac road, then crosses the busy N630 just afterwards.

Walk alongside the N630 on a narrow path next to the road, although it may be easier to walk along the road itself in wet, muddy weather. After 2km, cross a tarmac road that leads to a campsite in the Río de Cala valley, then immediately veer left down another old tarmac road. You'll rejoin the road in a few hundred metres, but the camino soon veers left once more to follow a dirt track just to the left of the road. The track widens after about 1km and passes a chicken farm on the left in a further 1km. It's uphill for a while here, a long, steady though not overly steep slog. Those who are flagging may be spurred on by the sight of vultures circling overhead looking for an easy meal.

At the top of the climb you'll reach the Cruz de Puerto, where there's a picnic area. There are also views of Monesterio up ahead. Walk along the N630 into Monesterio, passing fruit and sausage factories, and a sign for the Vía de la Plata in Extremadura. On the left, just as the town begins, you'll see the Cruz Roja, which houses Monesterio's *albergue*.

## Regional Map (key page 214)

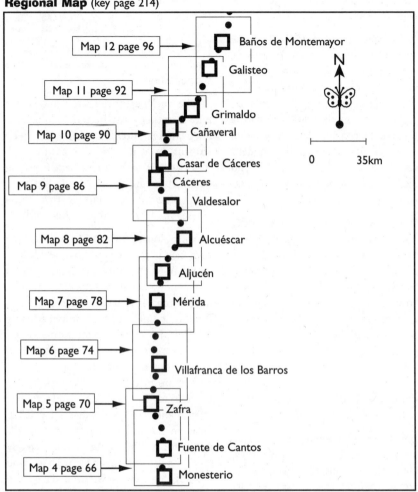

| | Map 12 page 96 | → | Baños de Montemayor |
| | Map 11 page 92 | → | Galisteo |
| | Map 10 page 90 | → | Grimaldo / Cañaveral |
| | Map 9 page 86 | → | Casar de Cáceres / Cáceres / Valdesalor |
| | Map 8 page 82 | → | Alcuéscar |
| | Map 7 page 78 | → | Aljucén / Mérida |
| | Map 6 page 74 | → | |
| | Map 5 page 70 | → | Villafranca de los Barros / Zafra |
| | Map 4 page 66 | → | Fuente de Cantos / Monesterio |

N

0      35km

## What's the Weather Like?

| | Jan | April | July | Oct |
|---|---|---|---|---|
| **Sun** | 5hrs | 9hrs | 13hrs | 7hrs |
| **Rainfall** | 6cm | 4cm | 0.2cm | 5cm |
| **Maximum Temp** | 17°C | 28°C | 41°C | 30°C |
| **Minimum Temp** | -2°C | 5°C | 13°C | 9°C |

Average hours of sun, total average rainfall in cm and average temperature in degrees celsius

# Extremadura

## Monesterio to Baños de Montemayor

A vast, flat and sparsely populated stretch with long gaps in between villages, Extremadura can be a challenging section. But the route is enlivened by constant reminders of the region's Roman past and by its rich agricultural present; come in autumn and you'll walk alongside vines heavy with fruit and fields of grazing *cerdos ibéricos*, Extremadura's famous pigs. A few cities will tempt you to rest for a while; Zafra has an elegant, understated old centre and a lively September *feria*, Mérida is the best place to visit Roman Spain, while Cáceres' conquistador-built *solares* (manor houses) sit crammed inside Roman-Moorish walls.

 **Walking**

### Geography

Cut off by the Sierra Morena to the south, the Sistema Central to the north and to the east by the Montes de Toledo, Extremadura is a vast lowland; even though your immediate surroundings can be barren and flat, you're never too far from a view of the hills that encircle the region. At first the landscape seems little different from northern Andalucía, with rolling hills, holm oaks and grazing pigs. As you head north, you'll pass through the Tierra de Barros, a rich agricultural region just south of Mérida famous for its olives and wine. You'll cross some of the Iberian peninsula's most important rivers along the way; Mérida lies on the Río Guadiana, which flows into the sea at the southwestern border with Portugal, whereas the Tajo, which you'll cross at the vast Alcántara reservoir, bisects Portugal as it heads towards Lisbon. At its northern extremes, Extremadura suddenly becomes lush and green as you climb towards the flat tablelands of the *meseta*, with oak, beech and chestnut announcing your arrival at Baños de Montemayor, the final town of the region.

### Trails

The camino traces the Roman road from Mérida to Astorga for much of the route through Extremadura. You'll cross Roman bridges, see exposed sections of Roman paving and pass *miliarios* (milestones) at many points along the way. In keeping with Roman tradition, modern, concrete *miliarios* are being placed at many junctions along the route in time for the 2004 Holy Year. Otherwise, waymarking is inconsistent; yellow arrows are prevalent and clear in some places, but the route can be confusing in others, particularly in northern Cáceres and through major towns. The Vía de la Plata also follows the Cañada Real, a broad drove road that dates from medieval times. In winter, the *transhumancia* saw thousands of sheep, goats and cows herded from northern Spain to graze on the plains of Extremadura. Although the Cañada Real is seldom used now, there's been some effort to revive it, including a much fanfared journey from Madrid that has taken place each year since 2001. You'll often see white painted arrows marking the drove road in a northern and southerly direction; watch out, as these don't always follow the same route as the camino.

The biggest problem for pilgrims in Extremadura is the long distances between towns and villages. It's 38km from Carcaboso to Aldeanueva del Camino, for example, and not only does this make for an exhausting day, it makes carrying enough water, particularly in summer, a real challenge.

## When to Go

In spring, the landscape is green and the wildflowers are spectacular. The land can be soggy at this time, and the tracks become sticky with Extremadura's red mud after even a little rain. This is also the time of year when the region's network of tiny, criss-crossed streams are at their fullest, and fording them can be tricky. Summer can be sweltering, and temperatures can soar above 40ºC; not only is it uncomfortable for walking, but it can be difficult to sleep at night too. It's usually still hot in September, and warm in October, so autumn is a lovely time to visit; you'll get a first-hand look at olive and grape harvests along the route. The trails are usually dusty so you'll rarely be slowed down by squelchy stretches. Winters can be cold and rain can dampen your enthusiasm, but finding somewhere warm to sleep may be more of a concern, since very few of the *albergues* and other places to stay have heating.

# Flora & Fauna

Southern Extremadura is planted with vines and olives, interspersed with holm oak and cork oak woodlands and arid, barren stretches. Livestock line the route too, and the south is particularly famous for its **cerdos ibéricos** (pigs). Further north, you'll see more sheep and cattle, often accompanied by helpful cattle egrets that pluck insects from the animals' coats. Elsewhere, much of the land is set aside for hunting, and your Sunday morning stroll will be punctuated with the sound of gunfire. If the hunters don't get to them first, you may see foxes, wild boar and wolves. Other mammals, not considered fair game, include the wild cat, Egyptian mongoose and otter.

Above you, flocks of migrating **birds** fly to sunnier or cooler lands in spring and autumn. The region is also an excellent place to see birds of prey such as the short-toed, booted, imperial, Bonelli's and golden eagles, and red and black kites. Rarer birds that nest in the region include black storks and black-shouldered kites.

In or around pools of water, look for the European pond terrapin, a small dark amphibian often with yellowish spots and streaks. The Iberian midwife toad, a small, stocky-legged amphibian that's almost entirely confined to Extremadura, also lives near water. The *lacerta hispanica* (Spanish lizard) is common throughout the region, and you may also see the spiny-footed lizard, a striped lizard which lives only in Spain and Portugal: young lizards have distinctive black stripes and a vivid red tail.

 # People & Culture

There are times along the camino when you'll wonder if anyone actually lives in Extremadura as hours go by before you'll bump into another soul. It's true that the region is sparsely populated, and it's not really been crowded at any time in its history. Still, the **Romans** sited the capital of their province of Lusitania here in 25BC, and Mérida is the best place to see their cultural and architectural marvels. Extremadura's empty landscape made it unattractive to some visitors; once the Romans were driven out, the Visigoths simply barrelled straight through, finding little to detain them.

The **Moors** stayed a little longer, leaving behind monuments in Mérida and Cáceres, and improving on Roman irrigation and agricultural techniques. But the flat landscape made keeping hold of Extremadura difficult, and the region became known as the *tierras despobladas* (deserted lands), acting as a kind of buffer zone between Moorish Andalucía and Christian Castilla in the Middle Ages, and changing hands frequently during the *reconquista*. Many of the towns along the Vía de la Plata were fortified during

this time, leaving behind impressive Almohad and Christian walls. Once the Christians finally took control in the thirteenth century, they divvied up the land between the powerful orders of knights that helped win the war. Sadly, not only were the knights hopeless farmers, leading to a drop in production, the granting of land to the rich and powerful left many locals without a means to earn a living. With nothing to lose, many of them followed local boys Hernán Cortes, conqueror of Mexico, and Francisco Pizarro, conqueror of Peru, to the Americas, and returning **conquistadores** built sumptuous *solares* (manor houses), most notably in Cáceres.

**Farming** is still the main way of making ends meet in Extremadura; there's very little industry in the region and, since the 1950s, there's been a relentless trickle of emigration as *extremeños* who find it hard to make a living from grapes or olives head to the cities to make some money. The population of the region is now lower than it was in 1940, and Mérida has only 10,000 more inhabitants than it did in Roman times. Even though things are better now than during the *años de hambre* (years of hunger) of the late 1940s when rural Spaniards were reduced to eating boiled grass and weeds, standards of living in rural Extremadura are still far below those of much of the rest of Spain.

 # Food & Drink

Extremadura is best known for its **cerdo ibérico**, a particular breed of pig that yields very fine sausages and *jamón serrano* (cured ham similar to *prosciutto*), and inspires enough pork dishes to stack the menu of every restaurant you'll stop at along the way. Monesterio proudly names itself the sausage and ham capital of Extremadura, and celebrates El Día de Jamón each September, lauding the town's most famous food with a festival that now spills over into a week-long affair. Try *almondigas* (pork meatballs), usually served as a *tapa*, or *caldereta extremeña* (a thick stew).

Extremadura's more sophisticated cuisine mostly came from the region's monasteries. French soldiers during the Peninsular War were said to be so impressed by the local food that they brought a cookbook back home introducing, amongst other things, *foie gras* to the French diet. Lovers of offal should head for Fuente de Cantos, where *chanfaina*, the local lamb offal stew, is so popular that a festival on the last Sunday in April is named after it. Fuente de Cantos is also the place for sweet-toothed pilgrims, with excellent *pastelarías* (pastry shops) and *confiterías* (sweet shops).

Extremadura's rivers provide very good *trucha* (trout) and *tenca* (tench); in August, the villages around Cáceres celebrate El Día de la Tenca with fishing contests and special meals. The region's hunters bag *javalí* (wild boar), *conejo* (rabbit), *cordonices* (quail) and *faisán* (pheasant) for the dining table. Extremadura has adopted many dishes from nearby Portugal, particularly her smaller neighbour's trademark *bacalao* (salted cod); try one of the many varieties on offer in Mérida's excellent restaurants. While in Mérida you should also sample *caracoles* (snails), a local delicacy served in spicy sauce and eaten with a toothpick.

Every inch of the Tierra de Barros, just south of Mérida, is given over to vines and olives. The area produces excellent **olive oil** and drinkable **wine**, including an aromatic, intensely coloured red from Salvatierra de Barros, a small village southwest of Mérida. Casar de Cáceres is known all over Spain for **Torta de Casar**, its trademark take on sheep's cheese. A round cheese with a hard rind, the centre is so creamy that it's almost liquid and best eaten with a wooden spoon. The cheese was so coveted in medieval times that it was used instead of money to pay the taxes that financed the *reconquista* in Extremadura. Still scarce, and still made by hand, the sheep's milk is gently warmed, curdled with wild thistle, then left to cure.

# Tourist Information

## Tourist Offices

There's very little information on the Vía de la Plata, aside from the two interpretation centres at either end of Extremadura, in Monesterio in the south and in Baños de Montemayor in the north. *Turismos* are often closed out of peak season but can provide helpful information, particularly on the routes out of major towns. Contact information for individual *turismos* is listed under relevant towns.

## Transport

Mérida and Cáceres are well served by rail, with about five trains a day from

Madrid; RENFE also serves Zafra. Thanks to the N630, it's easy to get a bus to and from Monesterio, Fuente de Cantos, Los Santos de Maimona, Villafranca de los Barros and Almendralejo. Bus services are trickier in northern Extremadura, and you'll need to rely on more sporadic local services.

## Money

Extremadura is well equipped with banks and you'll rarely go more than a day without finding a bank machine. Do your in-person banking in the morning, as very few places re-open after the *siesta*.

## Accommodation

Expect an extreme range of accommodation options, from space on the floor of a town hall or even a swimming pool to excellent *albergues* and hotels. Access to many of the *albergues*, particularly the basic roof-and-floor variety, is dependent on finding the person with the keys. If you're having problems, head for the *ayuntamiento* during business hours or the local bar at other times.

## Shopping

If you're in need of a *bordón* (walking staff), hold out until Aldeanueva del Camino, where local artisans make fabulous examples. You'll find good quality leather goods throughout the region, particularly riding boots, saddles and other horseriding paraphernalia, and Extremadura is also a good place to buy ceramics, pottery and embroidery. If you neglect to stock up on sausages and *jamón serrano* in Monesterio, the sausage and ham capital of Extremadura, there will be plenty of opportunities to get pork products along the Vía de la Plata.

The Tierra de Barros around Almendralejo is the best place to buy wine, olives and olive oil.

## Events & Festivals

In the first week of September, head to Monesterio for the town's annual **Día del Jamón**. As well as tastings, you can take courses in how to cure ham and meet local producers; the festival is so popular that it now stretches over a week. A few days later, the Romería de la Virgen de la Tentudía is held each September 8 at the monastery that gives the town its name. Food festivals are popular elsewhere too; Fuente de Cantos celebrates the region's offal stew during La Chanfaina at the end of April. **Galisteo** has a stack of peculiar traditions but is most famous for the bizarre La Vaquilla, where cows are left to run amok inside the walls of the old town.

Culture buffs are well served in Extremadura: Cáceres' annual **WOMAD** (World of Music, Arts & Dance) festival attracts more than 50,000 world music fans each May, Mérida's Festival de Teatro Clásico takes over the Roman theatre in July and August, and Cáceres fast forwards a few centuries at the summer Festival de Teatro Medieval. Both Cáceres and Mérida are also worth visiting during Semana Santa.

# Rest Days & Detours

Close to Monesterio, the **Monasterio de Nuestra Señora de Tentudía** has a special place in Spain's religious history. Tentudía comes from "hold the day," when the Virgin Mary is said to have held off the sunset during a crucial battle between Christians and Moors so that the Christians, who were on top in the fight, could finish off their foes. The monastery that was built in honour of the miracle is a mix of architectural styles and ironically incorporates the courtyard of the mosque that once stood here. The stunning Capilla Funeraria de San Agustín has a domed roof, whitewashed walls and high arches, and the Gothic-Mudéjar *retablo mayor* is made entirely of *azulejos* in reddish hues to represent the blood spilt in the battle and the long-delayed sunset. To reach the complex, follow the signs off the camino just after Monesterio to Calera de León, then follow the marked path to the monastery. Alternatively, make the day to Monesterio a short one and catch a taxi from the town to the site.

From Alcuéscar, detour to the ruined Moorish fortress of **Montánchez**, built with Roman stones and fragments of Visigothic carving from an early church and containing a twin-chambered Arab cistern. The castle changed hands many times during the *reconquista* and was finally conquered in 1230 by the Order of Santiago, who refortified the building.

Take some time off walking once you get to Carcaboso, just north of Galisteo,

and hop on a bus 11km east to the lovely town of **Plasencia**. Founded in 1178 and surrounded by double walls and 68 semicircular towers that rise above the Río Jerte, Plasencia's lively Tuesday market, held in the Plaza Mayor since the twelfth century, attracts hundreds of visitors each week. Monuments include the town's back-to-back cathedrals, the Catedral Nueva and Catedral Vieja, and the Museo Etnográfico Textil Provincial. There are also some excellent restaurants here, particularly La Alacena de Chus.

Along the camino, three towns stand out as potential rest day candidates. Foremost among them is **Mérida**, a living museum of Extremadura's Roman past with enough sites to occupy fervent archaeologists and plenty of fabulous restaurants to appease non-historians. **Zafra**'s compact centre makes for easy wandering as most of the sites are next to the town's twin arcaded squares, the Plaza Grande and Plaza Chica. Although it can be fun to visit at the end of September, when the Feria de Zafra, a massive agricultural fair, takes over an ugly site just outside town, it's impossible to find accommodation at this time of year. Further north, stop off in **Cáceres** to visit its *casco antiguo*, a walled old town of lovely *solares* (manor houses) built by returning *conquistadores* in the fifteenth and sixteenth centuries.

# Monesterio

ⒶⒽ✗⚐€❶☕ (898km)

The largest town along the Vía de la Plata since Sevilla, Monesterio seems at first to be little more than a glorified truck stop, with restaurants and cafés strung along the N630. Off the main road, there are some interesting narrow streets, among which you'll find the rather forlorn-looking Iglesia de San Pedro Apostól. The late *mudéjar* church was built from brick and salvaged Roman columns in the town's fifteenth and sixteenth century heyday, when links with the powerful Order of Santiago brought money and prestige. Nowadays, Monesterio's wealth comes almost exclusively from pigs. The town proudly claims to be the ham and sausage capital of Spain: the **Día del Jamón** de Monesterio in the first week of September includes videos, courses and plenty of tastings. Despite these attractions, most visitors head to the town's namesake Monesterio de Nuestra Señora de Tentudía some 15km away (see page 63).

The helpful **turismo** (☎ 924 516 737) is on Calle Extremadura, and the nearby Centro de Interpretación General de la Vía de la Plata on Plaza del Pueblo 8 gives a taste of the Vía de la Plata in Extremadura with a short video, photographs and explanations in Spanish.

## Accommodation

The **albergue** (6 beds, extra mattresses, hot showers, donation) is in the Cruz Roja on the N630 at the start of town; get the key from Hotel Moya next door.

**$ Hotel Leo**, Calle Extremadura 2 (☎ 924 516 428)

**$ Hostal Extremadura**, Calle Extremadura 103 (☎ 924 516 502)

**$ Hostal Puerta del Sol**, Calle

Extremadura 67 (☎ 924 517 001)

**$$ Hotel Moya**, Calle Extremadura 278 (☎ 924 516 136)

---

Walk up Calle Extremadura and follow it until the end of town. A couple of hundred metres later, turn left at the end of a football stadium down a dirt road. This soon becomes a flat, walled lane, a pleasant route past lots of holm oaks and the occasional fig grove, although the stream on the left is a little fetid when the water is low. In 500m, you can detour left across this stream to visit Calera de León, 8km away along a marked route. The town itself was one of the strategic and religious centres of the Knights of Santiago, and the monastery they built is worth a visit for the magnificent Gothic-Renaissance two-storeyed cloister. Another 7km further on, again on a marked route, is the area's religious and architectural highlight, the Monasterio de Tentudía.

Some 200m after the turning for the detour, turn left to cross the stream via a concrete bridge. The track soon begins to climb past fields of holm oaks and grazing pigs, then curves left a little under 1km later and flattens out. Along this stretch of the route, you'll see white Vía de la Plata markings and rustic wooden signs; although these mostly follow the camino, it's safest to ignore them and follow the yellow arrows instead. On the hill to the left you can see the Monasterio de Tentudía.

Pass a brick building just as the camino flattens out, then keep straight on 100m later, ignoring a track to the

**Map 4** (key page 214)

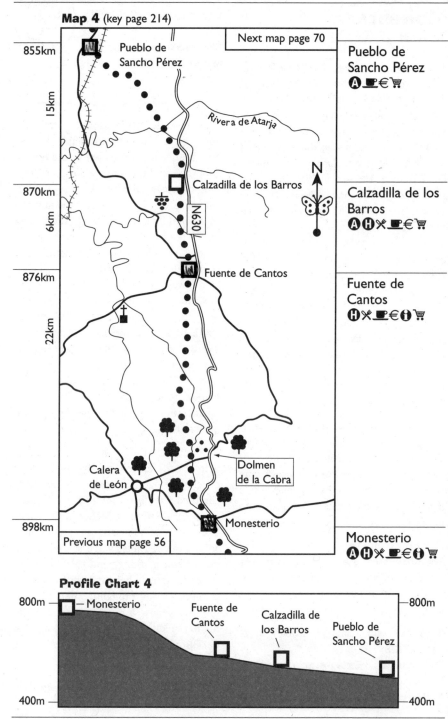

Next map page 70

855km

15km

Pueblo de
Sancho Pérez

Rivera de Atarja

870km

6km

Calzadilla de los Barros

N630

N

876km

22km

Fuente de Cantos

Calera
de León

Dolmen
de la Cabra

898km

Monesterio

Previous map page 56

Pueblo de
Sancho Pérez
Ⓐ ☕ € 🛒

Calzadilla de los
Barros
Ⓐ Ⓗ ✕ ☕ € 🛒

Fuente de
Cantos
Ⓗ ✕ ☕ € ⓘ 🛒

Monesterio
Ⓐ Ⓗ ✕ ☕ € ⓘ 🛒

**Profile Chart 4**

800m — ☐ Monesterio

Fuente de
Cantos

Calzadilla de
los Barros

Pueblo de
Sancho Pérez

800m

400m

400m

left. A little more than 500m later, pass a whitewashed farm building on the left; up ahead there are good views of the rolling plains of Extremadura and although they look pretty flat from here, you'll soon realize that there are plenty of ups and downs.

Just under 1km later, cross a minor road to walk over a cattle grid and between a pair of concrete posts. In another 200m, the track forks, and there's a gate on the left. The clump of vegetation to your right, about 10m off the camino, hides the Dolmen de la Cabra. More than 5000 years old, this megalithic passage grave was built, like others in Spain and Portugal, to face the rising sun. The complex is some 22m in diameter, and although only a small section has escaped the encroaching weeds, there are some huge, impressive stones intact.

Back on the camino, take the left-hand fork; soon, there are excellent views of the whitewashed town of Calera de León away to the left, particularly its huge monastery. To your right, there are rolling hills, one of which is topped by a ruined *castillo*. About 2km from the dolmen, the route forks; take the right-hand fork, continuing straight ahead. The landscape becomes open and less intensively farmed here, and there's lots of broom and holm oak.

A little more than 500m later fork left, passing through a gate. There's a lot of grazing in this area, so make sure that any closed gates are firmly shut behind you. This stretch of the camino is very well-marked with yellow arrows and prettified with rustic wooden Vía de la Plata signs. The track soon narrows and the landscape becomes still more sparse, with open grassland dry and bleached blonde in summer and autumn; there's little to distract you aside from the occasional bird of prey. Just 500m later a yellow arrow directs you to shadow the fence to your right; it's just as easy to stick to the main track, which veers first away from and then back towards the fence in less than 200m.

Pass through a gate, some 2km after the last one, and soon a great view of rolling plains and Fuente de Cantos emerges. In another 500m keep straight on at a crossroads with another dirt track, heading downhill towards a river. Look out for cattle egrets here, helpfully picking bugs from the backs of the area's many grazing sheep.

About 1km later, pass a walled-in olive grove; listen and watch out for songbirds here and along the Arroyo del Taconal, which you'll reach in a few hundred metres. Cross the river via stepping stones (you may get your feet wet after rain) and climb steeply, veering to the left in less than 100m. In another 1km, you'll pass a farm away to your right that raises ostriches. In dry weather, the track's soft, sandy soil is bliss for tired feet, although after rain it can get squelchy.

Just past the farm, take the right-hand track as the route forks. About 500m later there's a wooden cross, a carved wooden map of the Vía de la Plata and, intriguingly, a videocassette case. Open it, and you'll find a book and pen in which pilgrims can record their details and messages of encouragement to each other. Keep straight on here, climbing steadily as you have been since crossing the stream; the reward is fantastic views of the Sierra Morena behind you.

The camino from here to Fuente de Cantos undulates, and sometimes you'll get clear views of the town whereas at others it disappears from sight. Watch out for red kites and other birds of prey searching for rodents in the fields. In 3km, pass modern farm buildings on the right, then cross the Arroyo del Taconal again a little more than 500m later, and cross it once again in another 200m, veering right and heading towards the N630.

Just before the track reaches the road 1km later, take a left-hand fork. In another 1km, at a tarmac road on the outskirts of Fuente de Cantos, veer left then cross the road after 20m and walk up Calle San Julián. A few hundred metres later, turn right at Calle de Quintos, which curves left in 50m. Turn right 50m later and arrive at the Iglesia de la Virgen de la Granada, which dominates the Plaza de la Constitución.

# Fuente de Cantos
**ⓗ✗🛏️€ⓘ🍴** (876km)

Fuente de Cantos is a pretty, whitewashed town whose pedestrianized streets, multitude of shops and intriguing architectural features make for a pleasant evening *paseo*. Most of Fuente de Cantos' hotels line the N630 at the top of town, from which there are excellent views of the surrounding plains. Like Monesterio, Fuente de Cantos became wealthy on the backs of the local pigs, and you'll be able to sample every conceivable cut of pork in the town's restaurants, where food is a cut above the standard *menú del día*.

Fuente de Cantos' most famous son is the painter Francisco de **Zurbarán**, a contemporary of Velázquez whose depictions of saints and still lifes are characterized by vividly contrasting light and colour. You'll need to visit the Iglesia de Nuestra Señora de Candelaria in Zafra or the Prado Museum in Madrid to see his best work, but Fuente de Cantos maintains the Casa Museo de Zurbarán and an interesting display in the *albergue turístico*.

Fuente de Cantos' small **turismo** is on Calle Olmo.

## Accommodation
Fuente de Cantos has no municipal *albergue*, but the **Albergue Turístico** on Calle Los Frailes (☎ 924 580 035), in the gorgeously converted Convento de los Frailes de Zurbarán is a great place to stay. More like a *parador* with bunk beds than any *albergue* you've seen so far, the €15 per person price includes a sit-down or packed breakfast. To get there, follow the street to the left of the Iglesia de la Virgen de la Granada, turn left into Plaza del Mercado, then left down Calle Arias Montano, which becomes Calle Frailes.

**$ Hostal Casa Vicenta**, Calle Real 33 (☎ 924 500 852)
**$$$ Hotel Rural La Fábrica**, Calle Real 117 (☎ 924 500 042)

From the Iglesia de la Virgen de la Granada, head along Calle Pizarro, then turn right on to Calle Olmo, passing the turismo on the left-hand side of the road. Keep straight on, ignoring the sign for the Casa Zurbarán, cross over Plaza Olmo and follow Calle San Juan. Keep straight on out of town, following part of the Calzada Romana, although it no longer looks much like a Roman road;

perhaps the remains are buried underground. You'll start to see the first grape vines of the camino so far, a sure sign that the soil and landscape have changed after days of dusty grassland. To your right, away from the camino, is a large metal bull, and the sculpture looks particularly impressive in the early morning light.

After rolling along the Roman road for almost 7km you'll find yourself at the outskirts of **Calzadilla de los Barros** (🅐🅗✗💻€🍴, 870km), where an *azulejo* sign highlights the village's tourist attractions. Foremost among these is the fortified fifteenth-century Iglesia Parroquial del Salvador, a stocky brick building topped with storks nests; the church has been declared a national monument, and it's well worth a look at its fabulous Gothic-Renaissance *retablo*. Follow Calle Fuente de Cantos into the village, turn right on to Calle Manuela Martes and reach the Plaza de España. You can stay at the village **albergue** (beds, hot showers, kitchen, donation), well signposted but almost 2km from the centre of the village, or alternatively at the **Pensión Rodriguez** ($, ☎ 924 584 701) on the N630.

Leave the Plaza de España via Calle Encornacion, then make a sharp right turn on to Calle Zafra, leaving the village on a dirt track. Cross a stream 500m out of the village and soon afterwards begin walking through fields. In just over 1km, the camino nears a bend in the N630 and veers left to follow a disused tarmac road parallel to the highway; anise plants help to mask the smell of exhaust fumes. Fork left at a dirt lane 500m later, walking through quiet fields next to the Rivera de Atarja. Cross a small tributary of the river

via stepping stones, then climb uphill past a *finca*. This is an isolated stretch of the camino, and you'll walk over rolling hills and past olives and vines for more than 10km, ignoring turnings for the Ruta de los Ancestros and Camino de las Cañadas.

You'll eventually reach civilization and views of Puebla de Sancho Pérez at some train tracks. Cross over these and follow the dirt road towards the village. **Pueblo de Sancho Pérez** (🅐💻€🍴, 855km), which you'll come to in 2km, has a basic municipal **albergue**, a few bars and a couple of shops. Cross a paved road and keep straight on along Calle Sancho Pérez to the large, pedestrianized Plaza de España, where you'll find the Iglesia de Santa Lucía. Turn right in front of the church, then first left down the Paseo de Extremadura, following it for a few hundred metres until you reach the main road.

Yellow arrows are difficult to see here; look for a dirt track next to a stream on the other side of the road. Follow this track as it meanders past buildings and then crosses a modern concrete bridge over some train tracks. On meeting the train tracks again in a couple of kilometres, turn left to follow the tracks through the train yard. The route here is confusing, and you're unlikely to see a yellow arrow until you reach the other side of Zafra; the trick is to pass between the lovely but derelict old station on the left and the new freight station on the right to emerge on Avenida de la Estación, which will take you all the way into the centre of Zafra.

At the end of Avenida de la Estación, turn left at a small park, then turn right

**Map 5** (key page 214)

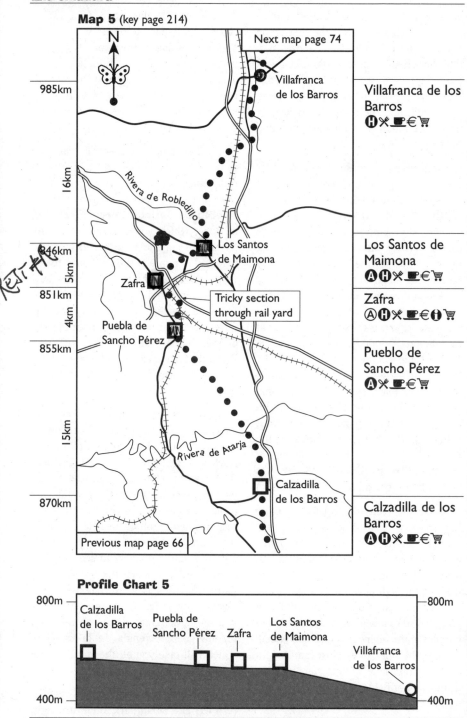

985km

16km

Rivera de Robledillo

Next map page 74

Villafranca
de los Barros

Villafranca de los
Barros
🅗✕🍺€🛒

846km

5km

Zafra

Los Santos
de Maimona

Los Santos de
Maimona
🅐🅗✕🍺€🛒

851km

4km

Tricky section
through rail yard

Zafra
🅐🅗✕🍺€🛈🛒

855km

Puebla de
Sancho Pérez

Pueblo de
Sancho Pérez
🅐✕🍺€🛒

15km

Rivera de Atarja

870km

Calzadilla
de los Barros

Calzadilla de los
Barros
🅐🅗✕🍺€🛒

Previous map page 66

**Profile Chart 5**

800m

Calzadilla
de los Barros

Puebla de
Sancho Pérez

Zafra

Los Santos
de Maimona

Villafranca
de los Barros

800m

400m

400m

along Glorieta Comarcal into the Plaza de España, a large square with a fountain. On the opposite side of the plaza, walk up the pedestrianized Calle de Sevilla, a culture shock of shoe shops and clothing stores that leads to the Plaza Grande.

# Zafra
Ⓐ🅗✕💻€🛈🍴 (851km)

An elegant walled town of narrow cobbled streets that open on to stunning squares, Zafra has a Moorish feel, so much so that Spaniards call it little Sevilla. Spend a few hours lounging in the graceful arcades of the **Plaza Grande** and the **Plaza Chica**, originally a fifteenth-century marketplace, to avoid the summer afternoon sun; both are lined with cafés should you feel the need for refreshment.

Stay in the Plaza Grande to visit the Gothic-Renaissance **Iglesia de la Candelaria**, whose *retablo* is graced by Francisco de Zurbarán's nine magnificent painted panels. If you're motivated enough to venture further, start with the nearby Alcázar de los Duques de Feria, built in the fifteenth century over a Muslim fortress. Gutted by Napoleon's troops in 1822 and boasting a lovely marble patio by Juan de Herrera, the castle is now a *parador*.

Despite a laid-back, timeless atmosphere, Zafra has some trendy bars and stores, and you'll have no problems eating well at the city's excellent restaurants. Wash your food down with the region's excellent wines; the turismo can arrange tours of nearby *bodegas* (wineries) if you want to investigate them further.

Zafra's **turismo** (☎ 924 551 036) is on the Plaza España.

## Accommodation
Zafra's on-again, off-again **albergue** is rumoured to be in the grounds of the Feria de Zafra, the town's agricultural fair. It's currently closed for renovations, and permanently closed for the duration of the fair each autumn; ask for keys at the *policía local* (☎ 924 554 513).

**$ Hostal Arias**, Carretera Badajoz-Granada, km72 (☎ 924 554 855)

**$$ Hotel las Palmeras**, Plaza Grande 14 (☎ 924 552 208)

**$$$ Hotel Plaza Grande**, Calle Pasteleros 2 (☎ 924 563 163)

**$$$$ Parador de Zafra**, Plaza Corazón de María 7 (☎ 924 554 540)

From the Plaza Grande, take Calle Tetuán, then turn to walk alongside the Colegiata de la Candelaria along Calle Conde de la Corte. Cross over the Avenida da Fuente del Maestre and keep straight on up Calle Ancha and Calle San Francisco. Reach a roundabout and keep straight on, heading for the Torre de San Francisco, the only remains of a convent founded by the Duques de Feria in the fifteenth century. Yellow arrows out of Zafra are difficult to find; if you get lost in town, ask for directions to the Torre de San Francisco. Once past the tower, begin the slow climb up the Sierra de los Santos past small farms and posh houses, turning around for good views of Zafra. Once you've reached the top, in a couple of kilometres, you'll be treated to the welcome sight of Los Santos de Maimona below. Zigzag down to town, keeping straight on until you reach the main square in about 2km.

In **Los Santos de Maimona's** (🅐🅗✕💻€🍴, 846km) main square,

**71**

you'll find the Gothic Iglesia de Nuestra Señora de los Ángeles, with a beautiful Plateresque Puerta del Perdón. Pilgrims who are unable to continue the camino can pass through this door and receive the same time off purgatory as those lucky enough to continue to Santiago de Compostela.

Los Santos' origins are Roman, and the town is famous as the site where the disc of Theodosius was discovered. Now in the Museo Arqueológico in Madrid, this huge, delicately engraved silver dish was issued to celebrate the tenth anniversary of an emperor who briefly brought peace to the Roman Empire in the late fourth century. Later, Los Santos de Maimona was an important centre of the Knights of Santiago, who were largely responsible for repopulating the town after the *reconquista*; their former headquarters is now the *ayuntamiento*.

Head here if you want to stay in Los Santos' **albergue** (30 beds, hot showers, kitchen, donation); it's 2km out of town, and you'll need to get a key from the police, who can also drive you there or give directions. The *albergue* is up a very steep hill from which there are great views, particularly at sunset. Buy some food before you leave, as there's a fully equipped kitchen, and bring some earplugs, as the hill is a favourite hangout of the town's bored teenagers, who are very keen on fast cars and loud music. Alternatively, the **Pensión Sanse 2** (**$**, ☎ 924 544 210) has cheap rooms.

To leave town, take the street to the left of the Iglesia de Nuestra Señora de los Ángeles. Follow Calle Blanco Madrid, turn right at a T-junction then turn first left to reach a busy road. Cross this road, keeping straight on past a bar. Next to a small square, turn left along Calle Maestrazgo, then take the first right on to a wide boulevard. Turn first left then first right, then cross an old bridge over the Rivera de Robledillo, following a line of young trees planted for some welcome shade. In 100m, turn right up a paved lane, then in another 100m at a bend in the road, turn left on to a small single track, keeping left when it joins a larger dirt track soon afterwards. Pass a few farms, olive groves and grape vines, and keep heading in the direction of some power lines. Turn right on meeting a larger dirt road, then 500m later keep left at a fork as you reach the crest of a hill.

From here, there are lovely views of the surrounding countryside, as well as two wells; check them before drinking the water, as they're not always well maintained. Follow the dirt road past fields of vines for about 4km, before the camino leads you along a dirt track between two fences, leaving the vines behind and climbing slowly uphill. As you reach the top of the hill, Villafranca de los Barros comes into view.

Go downhill through a large olive grove, passing between a small water tower on the left and a ruined building on your right; look carefully for yellow arrows as the route is not well marked. Soon, the track becomes clearer, and you see a motorway up ahead. Some 300m before reaching the motorway, turn right at a crossroads with another dirt track, walking over a level crossing 300m later. Turn left in another 200m to walk alongside the N630, then in 200m turn right along a dirt road. Note that this junction is occasionally fenced off; you may need to detour around an olive tree nursery.

Once you're safely on the right road, keep straight ahead for about 1km, then turn left opposite a large warehouse and follow the road across a stream. Climb uphill past some new houses before re-entering vineyard country and heading downhill into Villafranca de los Barros. Follow Calle Zurbarán into town, cross a bridge, pass the covered market and cross a main road. Turn left soon afterwards down the pedestrianized Calle Larga and reach the Plaza de España in 100m.

# Villafranca de los Barros

Ⓗ✕💼€🛒 (830km)

Villafranca de los Barros is a small town with all facilities and an excellent market. Of Roman origin, there's little to detain the pilgrim aside from the sixteenth-century Iglesia de Santa María, which has a good Gothic façade and a Santiago Peregrino carved in the altar. If you do decide to stay, **Hotel Diana ($$, ☎ 924 525 408)** is close to the centre of town on the *carretera*, has a good restaurant and a café popular with local matrons and teenagers. Pilgrims can get a *sello* from the *ayuntamiento* at the top of the Plaza de España. At the beginning of May, religious processions centred around holy crosses and crucifixes pass through Villafranca's streets.

From the Plaza de España, walk up Calle Santa Joaquina de Vedruna. At another square in 200m, turn left then immediately right up Calle Calvario. In another 200m, reach the Plaza de la Coronada,

where there's a Spanish Civil War monument; walk across the square, then turn left along Calle San Ignacio. Pass a Jesuit college on your right and 200m later, as the main road curves left, keep straight on along a tarmac road, suddenly finding yourself outside Villafranca and in open countryside. Keep straight on 100m later along a tarmac road, ignoring a dirt road to the right. The large white building away to your left is a winery; the surrounding area is renowned for its wine and there's a potent smell of crushed grapes at harvest time. Cross another tarmac road 100m later and keep straight on along a dirt track, passing an olive and vine nursery on the right.

The terrain is flat and without shade, and there are vines here as far as the eye can see. Most of the grapes are picked by hand into a large bucket made from recycled rubber tyres, then balanced on top of a worker's head and dumped into an open-topped wooden truck. The trucks, piled high with grapes and pulled by puffing tractors, are a common site in autumn as they putter towards the wineries of nearby Almendralejo and Torremegía. There are few yellow arrows on this stretch, but the route is straight and it's difficult to go wrong. About 3km after crossing the tarmac road, keep straight on, ignoring the track to your left. You'll see quite a few greyhounds in this area, bred to hunt hares and rabbits. In another 2km, fork left down a narrower dirt track. Occasionally, you'll see vines staked out *espalier*-style, which makes grapes easier to pick by machine.

In 4km, turn left at a broad dirt track, looking carefully for yellow arrows as

**Map 6** (key page 214)

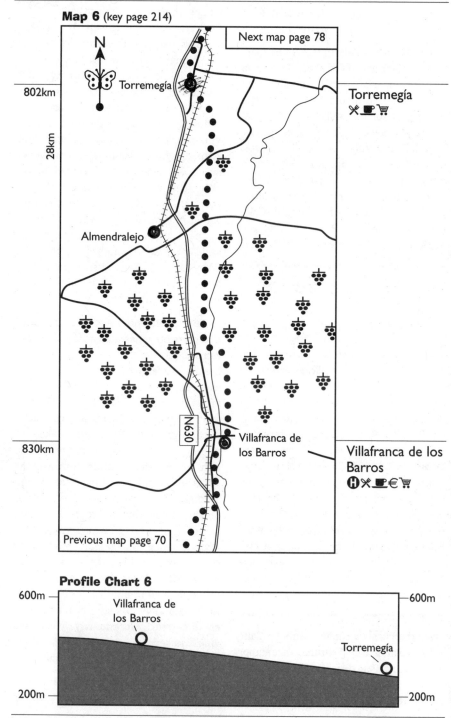

N

Torremegía

Next map page 78

Torremegía

802km

28km

Almendralejo

N630

Villafranca de
los Barros

830km

Villafranca de los
Barros

Previous map page 70

**Profile Chart 6**

600m

Villafranca de
los Barros

Torremegía

600m

200m

200m

there are very few places to put them in an area devoid of trees and fences. Keep straight on 1km later as a road joins from the left and keep straight on 200m later, ignoring the track to the right. The olive trees here are the first plants other than vines that you've seen for quite a few kilometres and they provide a habitat for songbirds and shade for a break.

In another 300m, cross a concrete bridge over a rather polluted stream. You're still walking on a very straight road, of Roman origin, with little to distract you apart from a group of houses away to your right about 3km after the bridge. Ignore a track to the left soon after passing these houses, and climb slightly, reaching a paved road in a little more than 1km. Keep straight on here to continue along the camino, or turn left to go to Almendralejo, 3km away.

Should you decide to detour to **Almendralejo** (❶▪️✗✖️€❶), and it's another 28km to the next accommodation in Mérida if you don't, you'll find a sizeable town famous for its wine production. While you're here, as well as visiting one of the town's *bodegas*, take a look at the sixteenth-century Iglesia de la Purificación, which boasts a Gothic-Plateresque façade, a lovely tower and a seventeenth-century *retablo*. The church eaves are home to a colony of kestrels, which breed in the area. Also worth a visit is the Palacio del Marqués de Monsalud, now the *ayuntamiento* but for a few years in the nineteenth century was home to Almendralejo's most famous son, the revolutionary poet Espronceda. You can stay at **Hostal La Perla** ($$, Plaza de la Iglesia, 12, ☎ 924 661 020), **Hotel España** ($$, Avenida San Antonio 69, ☎ 924 670 120) or

**Hotel Vetonia** ($$$, 2km NE of town on the N630, ☎ 924 671 151), and eat very well at one of the town's restaurants, where *judiones* (beans with pigs' knuckles or partridge) are a speciality. The **turismo** (☎ 924 670 507) on Calle Mérida 2 can suggest other accommodation options. To return to the camino, follow the road to Alange, which cuts just over 1km off the route.

If you don't detour to Almendralejo, keep straight on, and you'll soon see the town away to your left. In about 800m pass a water treatment station to your right, then in another 800m cross a tarmac road (this is the road that returns from Almendralejo). Even though your immediate landscape is flat, there are mountains to the right and the pass straight ahead is the Puerta de Sevilla, which you'll walk through to enter Mérida.

In 3km, keep straight on at a crossroads with another dirt road. There are more olive trees here; these are usually harvested two workers to a tree, the pair standing on ladders and handpicking the olives into a basket worn slung in front of each worker. In another 2km, pass a grand house on the right, then cross a bridge over a stream in another 1km. Keep straight on 50m after the bridge as the main road curves right, then pass a small water reservoir 500m later.

The crops diversify as you approach Torremegía, which you've been able to see for some time now, and you'll walk past hay and sunflowers. In another 500m, and just after the camino reaches a railway, turn left to go under a railway tunnel. If it's waterlogged, you can keep straight on here and turn left to cross the railway via a road bridge about 500m further on (yellow arrows lead both ways). Otherwise, walk through farmland and keep straight on to enter Torremegía on Calle Calzada Romana.

**Torremegía** (✗⚏☕, 802km) is an odd, nondescript town. Its modern houses are soulless and single-storey and there's a peculiar air of neglect around its unusually wide, rubbish-strewn streets. You'll have to turn left off the camino to visit its basic café-restaurants.

Keep straight on along Calle Calzada Romana, which changes to a dirt road at the end of town, where a clump of eucalyptus trees provides some shade. Fork left on to a dirt track after a few hundred metres, heading towards a water tower. Keep straight on 100m later, ignoring a track to the right, then pass the municipal cemetery to the left as the track curves to the right to shadow the N630. There are actually two roads here: the N630 to your immediate left and the newer A66 another 100m or so further away.

About 1km after leaving Torremegía pass a garden centre on your right, then 300m later cross a stream via stepping stones sometimes hidden by reeds and scented with mint. In another 400m, pass a bizarre road sign storage depot, then cross a side road to Alange and keep straight on; this stretch of the camino is well marked all the way to Mérida.

In about 300m the camino becomes paved as it follows the old road to Mérida, and a group of eucalyptus trees provide some shade. Cross a railway line 400m later and keep straight on along the old road. Unfortunately, this road joins the N630 about 500m later, and you'll walk alongside the N630 for about 2km, until you see a yellow arrow directing you right to the old road once more. Just before the old road curves back to rejoin the N630 in another 200m, turn right down a grassy path through eucalyptus trees. From here, a shady spot for a rest, there are good views of Mérida, some 8km ahead.

In 200m, turn left as the grassy track joins a dirt road. In another 2km, turn left to join a wider dirt track, then keep straight on as the track curves left 500m later, following another dirt track. In another 500m, turn left to join a broad dirt track, then take the right-hand fork 500m later. Keep straight on in another 100m at a crossroads with a dirt track, and walk through vines again. About 300m later, keep straight on along a left-hand fork, heading downhill through holm oaks and olive trees. At the bottom of the hill, pass a farm on your left, then turn right 500m later to walk along a stony road.

The route slowly becomes less stony and more industrial as Mérida comes into focus; one of the first buildings you'll be able to pick out is the city's blood-red Plaza de Toros. After another 2km, cross over a tarmac road and walk to the Río Guadiana just 50m away. Turn left to walk alongside the river along a *camino peatonal*, a recreational route for cyclists, joggers and walkers. Pass under a road bridge, getting great views of the Puente Romana up ahead and the stylish, modern Puente Lusitania behind it. You can also clearly see the town walls on the other side of the river, and the middle of the Río Guadiana is dotted with reed-choked islands, home to hundreds of egrets. In a little more than 500m, you'll reach the bridge.

There can be few grander entrances to a city than via Mérida's 60-arch pedestrianized Puente Romana, one of the finest examples of Roman engineering in Spain and one of the largest bridges ever built by the Romans. Probably dating from the time of Trajan, the bridge has been restored at various periods and was in use for traffic until the Puente Lusitania was built in the 1990s. Enter Mérida and pass the Puerta del Puente on the right, heading up the Calle del Puente to the Plaza de España.

# Mérida

Ⓗ✕⮘€❶🛒 (786km)

Mérida was founded in 25BC as a colony for retired Roman soldiers, and in its heyday was the economic and cultural capital of the province of Lusitania, controlling the roads to Olisipo (Lisbon), Asturica (Astorga), and Toletum (Toledo) and home to 40,000 people. Now a UNESCO World Heritage site, you'll bump into the city's Roman past wherever you turn, from restored monuments to dozens of *ad hoc* excavations; when a building is demolished, archaeologists get to assess the site's historical significance before developers can move in.

The best place to start an exploration of Mérida's Roman past is the city's superb **Museo Romano** (free on Saturday afternoons and Sundays; closed Mondays). A glorious red-brick building designed to show the excellent collection from various angles and levels, it centres around an airy, arched main hall, built to the same height of the city's Acueducto de los Milagros. Display highlights include vast, colourful mosaics,

intact statues, and the remains of an *in situ* Roman road and villa.

The most impressive of Mérida's many monuments is undoubtedly the 6000-seat **Teatro Romano**, built at the end of the of the first century BC. Plays were performed from the magnificent but substantially restored two-storey colonnaded stage, rich with marble columns, statues and capitals, for spectators who sat on the remarkably well-preserved semi-circular rows of stone benches. If you've timed your visit for high summer, check out the Festival de Teatro Clásico, held in July and August. Next door, the **Anfiteatro Romano** was built within a few years of the *teatro* and staged rather more gruesome entertainments. Fights between gladiators were commonplace, as were battles to the death between unfortunate slaves and captives; often, exotic animals were thrown in for added interest. You can walk around the amphitheatre floor, wander amongst the seating and explore the network of passages and rooms beneath.

Visit the Casa del Anfiteatro and the Casa del Mitreo for some incredible **mosaics**, particularly the fabulous cosmological depiction of celestial, terrestrial and aquatic gods in the Casa del Mitreo. Other Roman sites worth looking at include the Circo Romano (hippodrome), the Temple of Diana and the Forum Pórtico. Save the Arco de Trajano (Trajan's Arch) and the soaring Acueducto de los Milagros for later; you'll pass by both on your walk out of Mérida.

But it's not just Mérida's Roman past that make it a great place to while away a day or two. The city was one of the earliest Christian communities in Spain and flourished under the Visigoths. The thirteenth-century Romanesque **Iglesia de Santa**

**Map 7** (key page 214)

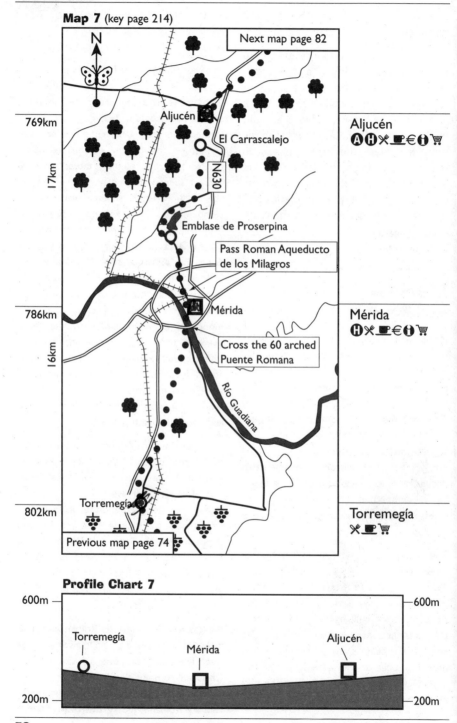

N

Next map page 82

Aljucén

769km

El Carrascalejo

N630

17km

Emblase de Proserpina

Pass Roman Aqueducto
de los Milagros

786km

Mérida

16km

Cross the 60 arched
Puente Romana

Río Guadiana

Torremegía

802km

Previous map page 74

Aljucén

**Ⓐ🅗✕💻€ⓘ🛒**

Mérida

**🅗✕💻€ⓘ🛒**

Torremegía

**✕💻🛒**

**Profile Chart 7**

600m ——

Torremegía

Mérida

Aljucén

200m ——

—600m

—200m

Eulalia was built over a fourth-century shrine to a child saint said to have been roasted alive by the Romans. Recent, imaginative excavations have preserved the Romanesque church and turned the basement into a Visigothic museum that includes Santa Eulalia's shrine and a fifth-century basilica. If you'd like to know more about Mérida's Visigothic past, visit the Museo de Arte Visigodo, just off the Plaza de España.

The Moors made their mark in Mérida too, best seen at the **Alcabaza**, one of Spain's oldest Moorish buildings. The striking cistern is well preserved and of a style rarely seen outside North Africa, and you can also access the top of the town walls alongside the Río Guadiana. The site has been almost continuously occupied since Roman times and was once home to the Order of Santiago.

Once you tire of old monuments, indulge in a meal out or a *tapas* crawl through Mérida's winding streets. The city's restaurants are wonderful and even the smallest bar will serve creative and unusual dishes; try the region's famous *caracoles* (snails) or one of the fabulous dishes adapted from nearby Portugal, particularly *bacalao* (salted cod). Alternatively, collect picnic ingredients at Mérida's excellent *mercado municipal*.

Mérida has two **turismos**; the most helpful is next to the *teatro* on Paseo José Álvarez Buruaga (☎ 924 315 353) and the other is on Calle Santa Eulalia (☎ 924 381 368).

## Accommodation

Mérida has no pilgrim *albergue*, but pilgrims can stay free of charge in the city's comfortable youth hostel 5km out of town in the industrial area; ask for directions at the *ayuntamiento* in the Plaza de España, where you can also get a *sello*.

$ **Hostal Residencial Senero**, Calle Holguín 10 (☎ 924 317 207) is helpful, friendly and provides *credenciales* in summer.

$$ **Hotel Lusitania**, Calle Oviedo 12 (☎ 924 316 112)

$$$$ **Hotel Nova Roma**, Calle Suárez Somonte 42 (☎ 924 311 261)

$$$$ **Hotel Melía Mérida**, Plaza de España 19 (☎ 924 383 800), a highly recommended luxury hotel with substantial off-season discounts

---

Leave the Plaza de España via Calle Santa Julia, just to the right of the Hotel Melía Mérida; there are no yellow arrows on the way out of Mérida. Walk past the Museo de Arte Visigodo as the street curves right, then turn first left into Calle Trajano. Pass under the Arco de Trajano (Trajan's Arch), a spectacular 15m-high arch of large granite blocks that would have been clad in marble in Roman times. Although the arch itself has nothing to do with the Emperor Trajan, you're now on the Kardo Maximus, one of Mérida's principal Roman streets, thought to have provided access to a temple devoted to Trajan's imperial cult.

Turn right into Calle Almendralejo then left pass the *correo* (post office) into Plaza de la Constitución. Keep straight on along Travesía de Almendralejo, then cross Calle Almendralejo and turn left then first right into Calle Calvario. In 500m or so, you'll reach the Río Albarregas. Cross a road and walk under the railway via an underpass and turn left then right to cross the river via a Roman bridge that dates from the first century BC.

From here, there are stunning views of the immense **Acueducto de los Milagros**, 50m away. This magnificent, towering aqueduct stretches for almost 1km from the city outskirts into the centre of Mérida, and provided the last link in a chain of channels that carried water from the Proserpina reservoir 5km away. A staggering feat of engineering that wasn't completed until the third century, the aqueduct's remarkably well-preserved brick and granite arches stretch to 25m high.

At the other side of the bridge, continue straight on along Calle Vía de la Plata. Yellow arrows, which have been missing since you first entered Mérida, reappear here, then almost immediately split. The right-hand fork (marked CR), follows the more authentic route out of town, tracing the way of the Calzada Romana but now shadowing the busy N630.

It's much more pleasant to take the left-hand route (marked EP), which heads towards the Embalse de Proserpina, and is described here. Keep straight on at a roundabout immediately afterwards and walk along the side of the road, being careful as there's no shoulder for most of the way. In 1km, keep straight on at another roundabout, then cross the motorway via a bridge 500m later. The road becomes much quieter now, and you've swapped the light industry of Mérida's outskirts for a more familiar landscape of fields. Pass a bar 500m later and begin to climb slightly before passing a cross on your left in another 500m. Nearly 1km further on, keep straight on at a roundabout just before you reach a campsite: there's a restaurant here, and some more around the reservoir, which you'll soon reach.

The **Embalse de Proserpina** (✗⬛) was the biggest reservoir in the Mediterranean Roman world and supplied most of Mérida's water. Its extensively restored granite dam wall is 21m deep and stretches to almost 500m in length; you can also see preserved staircase towers. In summer it's a pretty spot, popular with weekenders from Mérida, who own or rent holiday homes on the water. Food stalls line one side of the reservoir, whereas quieter reaches are home to flocks of egrets.

Keep on the road as it curves around the reservoir, then in a couple of hundred metres, next to a food stall, veer right to walk along a *camino peatonal* next to the water. In a little under 1km, return to the road as it begins to veer away from the reservoir. You're walking through undulating pasture dotted with holm oaks; look out for rabbits here.

About 2km later, and about 200m after passing a white house to your left, veer left off the road down a dirt track. There is initially a maze of junctions, but all are well marked with yellow arrows. Take the left-hand fork 100m later, then curve right in 50m and fork left 100m later. The landscape here is hillier than it's been for some time and there are holm oaks everywhere. It's a great place to see songbirds like the great tit, and the area is also home to the massive, striking great horned owl.

Cross a cattle grid 1km later and pass some farm buildings in another 1km, then cross another cattle grid 300m further on, as **El Carrascalejo** comes into view. Go through a gate 500m later, marked with a yellow arrow and the cross of Santiago, and enter the tiny village, where there are no facilities. The lovely stone Iglesia de Nuestra Señora de la Consolación is a sixteenth-century church with a Renaissance façade and porch. Turn right to walk past the church, then turn left at the end of the church, passing a stone carving of the town's coat of arms depicting holm oaks and the cross of Santiago.

Walk downhill out of El Carrascalejo. Pass a house on the right, then 50m later keep straight on at a *cruceiro* along a broad dirt road. There are vines alongside the camino, the first you've seen since Mérida. Fork right about 1km after the *cruceiro*, but be careful here: in late 2003 motorway construction was altering the route of the camino, so be sure to watch out for yellow arrows. Just over 500m later, there's a cross at the top of a rise put here by the Albergue de Aljucén de San Andrés in 2001.

In another 1km, enter **Aljucén** (🅰️🅗📟🍴, 769km) and fork right. It's a friendly little one-street village, with camino imagery in the Iglesia de San Andrés, and it's a lovely place to spend a couple of hours or the night. Get the key for the **albergue** from the first house on the left in the village. Turn left, and continue uphill to the *albergue*, or turn left again after the village bar to continue along the camino. You can also stay at a **casa rural** on the main street, which also does meals.

Walk downhill out of Aljucén, passing the *casa rural*, then turn right at the end of this road to head out of town. You'll reach the N630 in 1km or so: turn left here to walk along the road. Cross the Río Aljucén, then turn right just before a couple of petrol stations (one has a bar)

along a dirt road. The junction is marked with a massive yellow arrow and a cross of Santiago.

You're now entering the **Parque Natural de Cornalvo**, a landscape of holm oaks, pasture and scrubland. In spring, it's a gorgeous carpet of wildflowers, and in autumn, you'll walk through broom, tall white orchids with ghost-grey stems and autumn crocuses. The park is home to amphibians rarely seen outside the area, such as the European pond terrapin and the Iberian midwife toad, a small, stocky, nocturnal amphibian. After rain, look for the striking fire salamander, black with vivid yellow blotches; sadly, you're more likely to see dead ones along the route, crushed by farm vehicles. A great place to see birds, the park is home to two pairs of nesting black storks and three pairs of black-shouldered kites, there's also a notable colony of black kites.

In a little less than 2km, fork right at a modern cross of Santiago. Cross a cattle grid 300m later, then take the right-hand fork in another 100m. The big boulders that dot the landscape make arable farming too difficult; dry stone walls enclose livestock and mark out hunting zones. Pass through a gate 2km after the last junction, then keep straight on at a crossroads with another dirt track about 500m further on. After 300m, turn left at a track between two boulders along a grassy path through trees that parallels the main track, then turn left 100m later along another dirt track.

The landscape changes to scrub here and is dominated by cistus bushes, although you'll still see lots of holm oaks. In 500m, pass through a gate; you'll start

**Map 8** (key page 214)

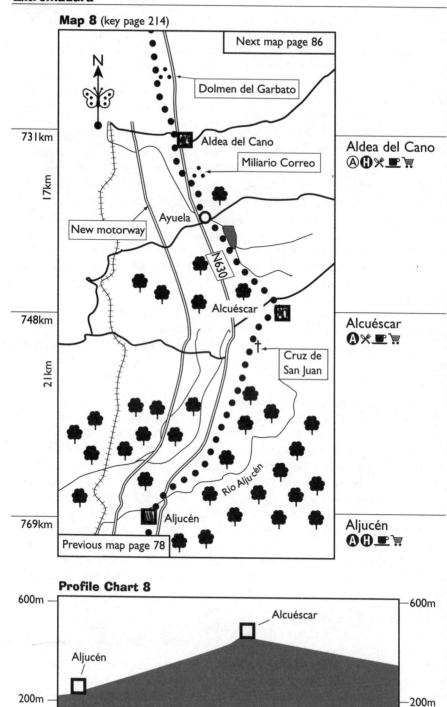

N

Next map page 86

Dolmen del Garbato

731km

Aldea del Cano

Aldea del Cano
Ⓐ🅗✕💻🛒

17km

Miliario Correo

New motorway

Ayuela

N630

Alcuéscar

748km

Alcuéscar
Ⓐ✕💻🛒

21km

Cruz de
San Juan

Río Aljucén

769km

Aljucén

Aljucén
Ⓐ🅗💻🛒

Previous map page 78

**Profile Chart 8**

600m ────────────────────────── 600m

Alcuéscar

Aljucén

200m ────────────────────────── 200m

to see cork oaks in this area. Just 1km later, fork right then pass through another gate in 200m. At the next junction in a little under 1km, take the right-hand of three tracks. Cross a stream, pass through another gate in 500m or so, then after another 1km enter an open field via yet another gate. Keep walking through this massive field, almost 2km across, along a track lined with lavender, then pass through a gate on the other side.

In just over 1km, you'll reach the Cruz de San Juan, a stone cross. Also known as the Cruz del Niño Muerto, the cross marks the spot where a young shepherd boy on his way to a midsummer *fiesta* was devoured by a wolf. At the top of a hill 2km later, turn right to walk downhill, following the signs to Alcuéscar. The farmland changes here, and you'll pass vines, olives and livestock; to your left the flat landscape stretches for as far as you can see. In just after 1km, turn right on to another dirt track, turn right again 30m later then fork right in another 100m; the track soon becomes cobbled as you walk uphill.

Pass a cattle trough and in about 1km reach a paved road and the start of the small village of **Alcuéscar** (❶✕▣▣🛒, 748km). Turn left and walk downhill along Calle Fuente de la Orden, then turn left at a T-junction and keep straight on for about 200m. Cross the main road; the **albergue** (8 beds, extra mattresses, hot showers, donation) is in the Casa de la Misericordia de la Congregación de Esclavos de María y los Pobres, where monks generously provide pilgrim accommodation in a wing of a monastery that cares for disabled men. Pilgrims sleep on narrow beds in tiny cells and can also eat a delicious dinner; be sure to leave a donation so that this practice can continue. From Alcuéscar, you can detour to the recently restored Visigothic Basilica de Santa Lucia, on a small hill some 3km away along a well-signed path from the Plaza de España.

To leave Alcuéscar, keep straight on the narrow road. In 500m, veer right at a fork in the road along a dirt track that leads you through fields, then 200m later at another fork under a power line, turn left. Keep to the main track as it zigzags north through olive groves and fields, a peaceful scene although you can hear snatches of the N630 in the distance.

After 1km or so you can see houses off to the left and the landscape is drier, with scattered oak trees. Keep straight on at a junction, walking along a dirt track, a wire fence on either side separating you from fields of holm oak; in the early morning it's often possible to see foxes here. In 1km, veer right to join a larger track that leads towards **Las Casas de Don António**, looking out for the Embalse de Ayuela on your right.

Join a paved road, then turn off it to walk down a dirt track towards the village. Pass a modern water channel, then cross a lovely medieval bridge (originally Roman) across a tributary of the Río Ayuela. Turn left on the other side of the river and follow the paved road that skirts **Ayuela** (▣) and leads to the N630. It's worth detouring into the pretty village to wander about its old streets and to visit the fifteenth-century Iglesia de Nuestra Señora de la Asunción.

At the end of the village, the tiny Ermita de la Virgen del Pilar contains a statue of Santiago Matamoros. Turn right at the road, passing a café, and follow a dirt track that parallels the N630. After about 1km and just past the gates to the Casa de Santiago de Bencaliz, you'll pass an upright *miliario* (Roman milestone), known as the *miliario correo*, as the notch chiselled into it was used to drop off post for the Casa de Santiago de Bencaliz. You're walking directly atop a Roman road, which excavations have shown is about 50cm below the current level of the track.

In another kilometre, pass a Roman bridge, looking a bit sorry for itself and somewhat overshadowed by the larger motorway bridge nearby. Soon afterwards, cross the N630 and follow the track on the other side of the road. After 1km, pass a second *miliario*, leaning slightly just to the left of the track. Keep heading straight on and shortly afterwards join a larger dirt track, still heading in the same direction.

Pass a sports field on the right, then reach the road to **Aldea del Cano** (Ⓐ🄷✕💺🍴, 731km). Turn right here to detour to the village, where pilgrims can sleep on the floor of the village school; ask for keys at the Bar-Restaurante Las Vegas on the N630. You can also stay at the **Casa Rural Vía de la Plata** ($$) on the main square. The Gothic Iglesia de San Martín has an early sixteenth-century *retablo mayor*.

Otherwise, keep straight on, entering a scrub land of broom and holm oak in 1km. Fork right, looking to your right for views of an old farm and a castle on the hill. Cross a small stream and veer right uphill. The Dolmen del Garbato is on a ridge just to the right of the camino; sadly for the curious, the megalithic monument is fenced off. To the west, there are good views of the Sierra de San Pedro. Keep straight on, heading for the Cáceres air club. Cross straight over the runway here, looking out for landing aircraft, then pick up the track on the other side of the airport. An old well on the left is a good place to see European pond terrapins.

Head uphill, and soon get your first views of Valdesalor; look to your right as you pass red and white aerials to see a large fortified mansion. There is no shade on the long approach to the village, and the trail is lined with broom as you descend to the Río Salor. To your right are two upright *miliarios* that at first glance look like fence posts, although those with binoculars can make out the inscription.

Just before the village cross the eleven-arch Roman bridge over the Río Salor, then head into the village on a dirt track that parallels the N630. **Valdesalor** (Ⓐ✕💺🍴, 719km) is a small, modern village dominated by the main road alongside it. Pilgrims can stay on the floor of the Casa de la Cultura in the main square; there are mattresses but no bathroom, although if the *ayuntamiento* is open, you can use its shower and toilet. You can get meals at the Hogar del Pensionista, which also has a toilet and the keys for the Casa de la Cultura. The bar-restaurant near the petrol station on the other side of the village opens at 8am for breakfast.

Leave Valdesalor via the track alongside the N630. Shortly after the bar-restaurant, cross on to the right-hand side of the road, with views of a factory pumping out pollution to the right and a dilapidated country manor to the left.

Keep on the right-hand side of the road as you cross a side road, then walk under the N630 via a foot tunnel. Once back in daylight, turn right and take the lower of two tracks that cuts out a corner of the N630 and leads up to the top of the Sierra de las Camellas via a stony track. With luck, the wind will be blowing the fumes from the nearby factory away from you.

Just after the top of the hill known as the Puerto de las Camellas, cross carefully back over the N630 and follow the dirt track on the other side. From here, Cáceres is laid out before you, its urban sprawl taking up the whole of the northern horizon and its old town perched strategically on the hill to the left.

Halfway down the hill into Cáceres, a stretch with no shade at all, fork right just before a small white *finca* to walk along a dirt track between wire fences. Ignore a left-hand turn and head towards the warehouses you see before you, veer left at a stone wall then keep right at a fork soon afterwards. Walk past the warehouses until you reach a main road.

Cross the road at some traffic lights and take the smaller road on the left, heading towards the fortified old town. This section is not well marked, but just keep straight on for about 1km, passing a large hospital. Shortly after passing the San Francisco clinic, turn right at a fork in the road, passing the Museo de Cultura.

Climb the steep cobbled road that leads past the Convento de Santa Clara, through the Puerta de Mérida and into the old town. Keep heading uphill along the narrow, incongruously named Calle Ancha (wide street), passing the helpful *turismo*, and then zigzag through the narrow streets to the Plaza de Santa María.

# Cáceres
Ⓗ✕⬛€ⓘ🛒 (707km)

Cáceres became suddenly wealthy as gold from the conquest of the Americas poured into town, and the returning *conquistadores* seemed to be in competition to create the grandest *solares* (manor houses) imaginable; the result is a compact walled **casco viejo** (old town) built almost entirely in the fifteenth and sixteenth centuries. The history of the walls themselves stretches back still further, to Roman times; both the walls and the Puerta del Cristo may be original, although the city's continuous occupation has stymied any archaeological excavation. The walls, and many of the towers that top them, were fortified by the Almohads towards the end of the twelfth century, and were strategically important in the struggle between the Christian Kingdom of León and the Muslims for control of Extremadura. Interrupting the Christian-Muslim ding-dong was a maverick Portuguese adventurer, Geraldo the Fearless, who seized Cáceres and created what amounted to an independent fiefdom until he was deposed by Fernando II in 1169. The military Order of Santiago was founded here in 1170 to defend the city from Muslim attack, but Almohad forces retook Cáceres just four years later.

Many of Cáceres' **solares** are open to the public for free, and wandering in and out of grand houses emblazoned with the stone-carved shields of the families that built them is a lovely way to spend a few hours. Some of the *solares* are particularly special. The

### Map 9 (key page 214)

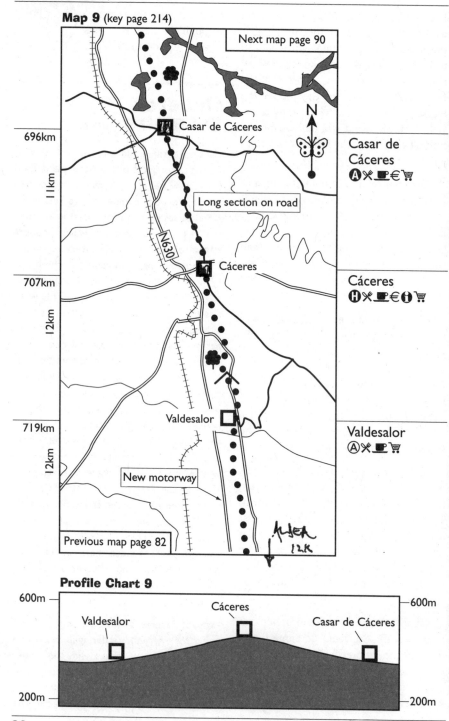

Next map page 90

N

696km

11km

Casar de Cáceres

Casar de
Cáceres
Ⓐ✕🖴€🛒

Long section on road

N630

707km

12km

Cáceres

Cáceres
Ⓗ✕🖴€ⓘ🛒

Valdesalor

719km

12km

Valdesalor
Ⓐ✕🖴🛒

New motorway

Previous map page 82

### Profile Chart 9

600m

Cáceres

600m

Valdesalor

Casar de Cáceres

200m

200m

Casa de Toledo-Montezuma has a distinctive domed tower, but it's best known as the place where *conquistador* Juan Cano de Saavedra, a follower of Cortés, brought back a daughter of the Aztec Emperor as his bride. The late fifteenth century was a time of damaging infighting amongst Cáceres' nobles, and an edict from Isabel la Católica ordered the *solares'* fortified towers destroyed. The Casa de las Cigüeñas (House of the Storks) was the only building allowed to preserve its original tower, as its owner was a close supporter of Isabel. The Casa de las Cigüeñas isn't the only building where storks nest, and you'll see the birds all over the city, including on the spires of the fifteenth-century Iglesia de Santa María, Cáceres' Gothic cathedral, where you can slip a coin into a slot to light up the lovely sixteenth-century carved cedar *retablo*.

More recent history has touched Cáceres too; the Casa de los Golfines de Abajo, a *solar* with a gorgeous façade, served briefly as Franco's headquarters in 1936 and it was here that Franco had himself proclaimed Generalísimo and Chief of State. If you want to know more about Cáceres' past, check out the Museo de Cáceres; its most impressive exhibit is the twelfth-century *aljibe* (cistern) which is all that remains of the Muslim fortress inside the walls.

Cáceres' past attracts a steady stream of tourists, but the city isn't simply a museum piece: the town boasts some fine restaurants and Cáceres' sizeable student population drives a vibrant nightlife. There are also some fabulous spring and summer festivals, from the Fiesta de San Jorge at the end of April to the Feria de Cáceres in May and June, a riot of fireworks and bullfights. The town's WOMAD festival attracts top world music acts and as many as 70,000 people gather here on the second weekend in May.

## Extremadura

Cáceres' **turismo** (☎ 927 247 172) is on the camino itself, on Calle Ancha 7.

## Accommodation

**$ Albergue Turístico Las Veletas**, Calle General Margallo 36 (☎ 927 211 210) has 4- and 6-bed dorms

**$ Pensión Carretero**, Plaza Mayor 23 (☎ 927 247 882)

**$$ Hostal Alfonso IX**, Calle Moret 20 (☎ 927 246 400)

**$$$ Hotel Iberia**, Calle Pintores 2 (☎ 927 247 634)

**$$$$ Parador de Cáceres**, Calle Ancha 6 (☎ 927 215 800)

Leave the old town via the Arco de la Estrella, built by Manuel Churriguera in the eighteenth century, and enter the Plaza Mayor, a big square made to seem even more vast after the cramped cobbled streets of the *casco viejo*. Leave the square via Calle Gabriel y Galán, then turn left into Calle Zapatería, which changes its name twice before finally settling on Calle General Margallo. At the roundabout next to the Plaza de Toros, turn left down Calle Escampleros, which leads downhill out of town.

The next 6km are some of the most unpleasant of the camino so far, as you walk along the shoulder of the busy C520 with no shelter from the elements. Be careful of traffic, particularly on blind corners and hills, then just as you begin to lose hope that this horrible stretch will never end, cross a small bridge and turn left, taking a dirt track away from the road.

This track rolls up and down towards the newly built motorway, which may well reduce the traffic on the C520 for a

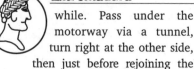

while. Pass under the motorway via a tunnel, turn right at the other side, then just before rejoining the main road, turn left down a dirt track. You can see the flat Río Almonte basin before you, then, in a few kilometres, you'll eventually see Casar de Cáceres.

Once at the edge of town, head for the bandstand in the town park. Pick up a lovely shady promenade here, which you follow for about 1km, then cross a road and keep straight on along the Calle Larga Alta until you reach the tiny Plaza de España.

# Casar de Cáceres
Ⓐ✗ 💼€🛒 (696km)

Casar de Cáceres is a small, very friendly town; you'll find it impossible to get lost as concerned locals are forever checking that you know the way to the excellent **albergue** (24 beds, hot showers, kitchen, donation) in the Plaza de España. Get the key from Café Majuca on Calle Larga Alta, and a *sello* from the *ayuntamiento*, just opposite the *albergue*. The Iglesia de la Asunción has a lovely *retablo* and a baroque wooden painted Santiago to the left of the altar. There are a couple of good restaurants and supermarkets on the main street, but the thing to eat in Casar de Cáceres is **Torta de Casar**, the town's famous sheep cheese; pale yellow, smelly and so runny that you'll need to eat it with a spoon.

Leave Casar de Cáceres on the main street, now called Calle Larga Baja, and keep straight on as the town ends less than 500m later at the Ermita de Santiago, which contains a modern stat-

ue of Santiago Matamoros. The road becomes a dirt track here, then 1km later passes the Pozo Canario, a massive well with no accessible water. In 300m, pass a round hut with a conical roof, which houses an interpretation centre for the Vias Pecuarias (sheep drove roads). Keep right here, climbing gradually uphill. You're surrounded by pasture, and there are few sights apart from vast skies and endless, village-less views. There's also very little shade, and wise pilgrims will greedily gobble up the pitiful shelter provided by the odd cork oak alongside the camino. About 1km after the interpretation centre keep straight on, ignoring the dirt track to your left. You'll soon get a glimpse of the Embalse del Espino, a small reservoir to your left. On the right you can see the Río Almonte, and the mountains ahead form part of a chain that stretches from the Serra da Estrela in central Portugal to the Sierra de Gredos just west of Madrid. The track is bordered on either side by intricate dry stone walls, hemming in the area's many cows.

After a few kilometres the land becomes more barren, dotted with boulders, broom and holm oaks. Keep straight on past the gate to the Finca la Higuera, some 5km after the last junction; there's a collection of three *miliarios* in 300m. About 150m later, ignore a gate to the right, then keep straight on 30m later through another gate and fork right 20m later. In another 400m or so, fork left, then pass through a gate 300m later; make sure that you leave this gate and the others in the area exactly as you find them, as there are lots of cattle and sheep. From here, there are fabulous views of the surrounding plains. In 200m, there's another group of *miliarios* to the left of the camino. Just over 500m later, go through a gate, passing farm buildings to your right, then fork right at a junction 150m later. Watch for yellow arrows here, and keep straight on through a gate in another 150m. A boulder to the right is worn away, possibly from the gentle but persistent rubbing of centuries of sheep.

In another 2km, pass between a pair of gateposts, then keep straight on 100m later as a track joins from the left. Pass a farmhouse on the left 100m later and get your first view of the Embalse de Alcántara ahead. You can also glimpse Cañaveral in the distance and the N630 away to the left. Keep straight on about 1km after the farmhouse, passing ruined stone houses with massive thick walls. Cross a cattle grid 200m later, then turn immediately right to walk down a narrow dirt path. Soon, you're very close to the N630, but instead of joining it, the camino parallels the road, clambering up and down small river valleys. Look out for birds of prey here, particularly the Bonelli's eagle.

After almost 2km of this undulating path, the camino meets the N630, where you turn right to walk along the road. The N630 is a busy road, miserable to walk along, although the construction of the nearby A66 may ease some of the traffic. You'll have to follow the road in order to cross the Río Almonte and the Río Tajo, and although there are yellow arrows to the left of the road, these direct you to steep paths overgrown with thistles and other prickly plants. Just 300m after joining the road, cross the Río Almonte, getting lovely views of the reservoir from the bridge.

In 1km, pass the junction to Hinojal

on your right and the Estacion de Río Tajo, the train station, below you on your left. In 1km, cross the bridge over the Río Tajo, which eventually empties into the sea at Lisbon, some 300km away. In another 1km, pass the entrance to the Club Nautico Tajomar, then 100m later, opposite the entrance to the now-closed Café Miraltajo, turn right off the road on to a stony track. If you're not sick of the N630 yet, keep straight on to detour to the ruined Puente Alconétar, a second-century Roman bridge alongside the reservoir, and the nearby Torre Floripes.

Otherwise, walk steeply uphill, with ever improving views of the reservoir. A little under 2km from the road, curve left then cross first one cattle grid, then another 400m later. On the ridge to your left, near the village of Portezuelo, is a ruined castle. The landscape here is scrubland with occasional grazing and very little shade, and although the views can be spectacularly sparse, there's very little to distract you aside from another cattle grid 2km later. There are many animal pens and corrals here, and even the broom that provided feeble shade up to now disappears. Pass through a gate 200m after the cattle grid, then walk over another cattle grid 300m later, taking care, as this one's a bit wobbly.

In 2km, as the main track curves right, veer left down a narrower track. Nearly 300m later, veer right at a fork, following a circuitous route towards Cañaveral over rolling hills and avoiding steep valleys. The terrain becomes more barren here, and there's less evidence of livestock, although as you approach Cañaveral the landscape changes again,

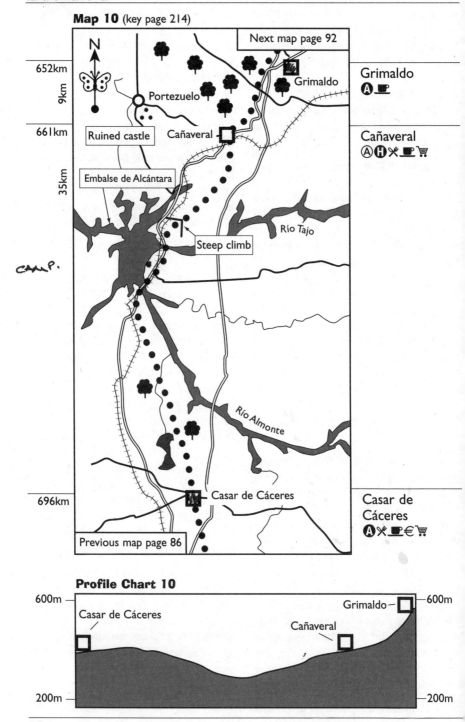

**Map 10** (key page 214)

N

652km

9km

Portezuelo

Grimaldo

Next map page 92

Grimaldo
Ⓐ☕

661km

Ruined castle

Cañaveral

35km

Embalse de Alcántara

Cañaveral
ⒶⒽ✕☕🛒

CAMP.

Río Tajo

Steep climb

Río Almonte

696km

Casar de Cáceres

Casar de
Cáceres
Ⓐ✕☕€🛒

Previous map page 86

**Profile Chart 10**

600m

Casar de Cáceres

Cañaveral

Grimaldo

600m

200m

200m

and becomes reminiscent of rural Wales or Scotland, albeit after a prolonged drought.

Cross a cattle grid 500m after the last junction, then in another 500m or so, arrive at a fork in the route. The left-hand route, marked Caña, takes you down to Cañaveral on a steep path; the right-hand route, marked CR, bypasses the village and is not described here. Head steeply downhill on a steep path worn from the rock, a well-marked route that soon reaches a dirt track. Turn left here, then pass through a gate 100m later and arrive in 200m at the four-teenth-century Puente de San Benito. Pass a sign for the Ruta de los Molinos and reach the N630 in 250m. Turn right here, passing the sign for Cañaveral and crossing a railway bridge.

In 300m, turn left up Calle de Monrobel, passing a fountain in 20m and arriving at the beautiful Iglesia de Santa Catalina in the centre of **Cañaveral** (ⒶⒽ✕🍴🛒🍺, 661km) 200m later. Set in a lovely arcaded square, the serene fourteenth-century church is a model of Romanesque grace and restraint. Cañaveral is also known for its *chimineas antiguas* (old chimneys), and many of the town's houses are fronted by massive, thick wooden doors and iron grilles. Opposite the church is the *ayuntamiento*, where you can get a *sello*. Here, in theory, you can also get the key to Cañaveral's outdoor **swimming pool** (located at the entrance to town), where pilgrims can stay the night on the floor of the changing rooms, although the townspeople are keen to encourage you to move on to the *albergue* in Grimaldo, another 9km away. Less hassle, and more comfortable, is the **Hostal Málaga** ($, ☎

927 300 067) in town on the N630.

To leave Cañaveral, turn right at the main square, then turn left on returning to the N630 about 400m later. After 1km or so, pass a turning on the right to the railway station, then turn left off the road 300m later and veer right almost immediately down a dirt track in front of the Ermita de San Cristóbal. The fountain just off the path to the right is dry, but it's worth taking a swig of your water as there's a sharp climb to come.

Keep on the track as it curves left 100m later, then in a little under 1km turn left at a junction, heading uphill. In another 100m, follow the track as it heads right, ignoring the left-hand track to a quarry, keep left 50m later to continue uphill, then veer left 30m later, climbing very steeply through scrub. After a couple of hundred metres the camino flattens out as it enters a pine forest. Keep straight on 1km or so after entering the forest, ignoring the track to the right. In 100m, turn right to walk down a narrow tarmac road, heading downhill through cork oaks. Turn right at a T-junction just under 1km later, then turn left just before you reach the N630 at a now-closed hotel.

Take the dirt track in front of the hotel, which soon narrows to a path winding through cork oaks. Watch for yellow arrows and strips of yellow plastic tied to trees as the path mostly follows the line of a barbed wire fence. This is a lovely walk, with lots of chances to see songbirds like the long-tailed tit. Cross a stream after about 2km, then walk through a gate a little under 1km later on a dirt path, following a stone wall to your right. Much of this area was burned in

**Map 11** (key page 214)

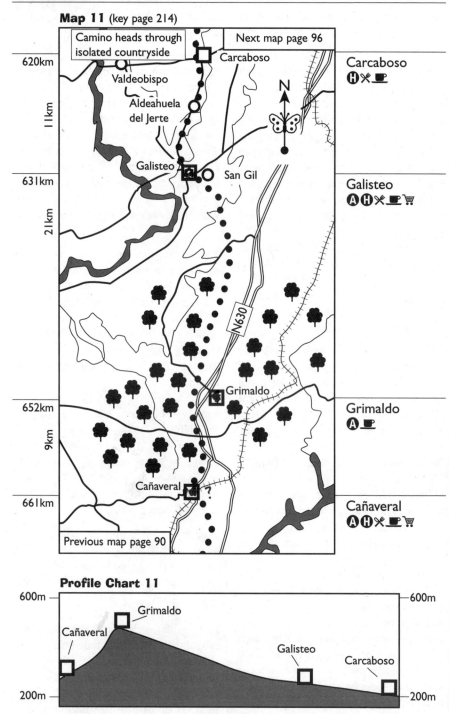

Camino heads through isolated countryside

Next map page 96

620km

Carcaboso

Valdeobispo

Aldeahuela del Jerte

11km

N

Galisteo

San Gil

631km

21km

N630

Grimaldo

652km

9km

Cañaveral

661km

?

Previous map page 90

Carcaboso
Ⓗ ✕ ☕

Galisteo
Ⓐ Ⓗ ✕ ☕ 🛒

Grimaldo
Ⓐ ☕

Cañaveral
Ⓐ Ⓗ ✕ ☕ 🛒

**Profile Chart 11**

600m — — 600m

Grimaldo

Cañaveral

Galisteo

Carcaboso

200m — — 200m

the summer of 2003, part of a series of forest fires that devastated tracts of Spain and Portugal.

Very soon afterwards, you'll pass a sign to Grimaldo. To detour to this village, some 600m off the camino, turn right here up a dirt path, heading under the new motorway and passing a few houses, and arrive in **Grimaldo** (**A**__) at the N630. Pick up the keys to Grimaldo's new **albergue** (10 beds, hot showers, donation) at the Bar Grimaldo next door.

Back on the camino, cross a road 1km after the Grimaldo turning and keep straight on along a dirt track that narrows to a path, walking through fields and holm oaks. Cross a track a little under 1km later (you may have to duck under a fence here) and keep straight on as the path becomes indistinct shortly afterwards. In another 1km pass through a gate, and the track becomes clearer and broader.

Keep straight on 100m later, ignoring a gate to the left and following a stony path sandwiched between two fences. This is a lovely stretch of the camino; you're walking along the Calzada Romana, there's some shade from holm oaks, and birds of prey fly above you. Pass through a gate just under 2km later, walking over rolling hills. In just under 1km and shortly after a long, flat stretch, walk downhill, then watch carefully near the bottom of the hill for a turning to the right down a narrower grassy path; it's well marked once you see it, but easy to miss, particularly if you're zooming past on a bicycle.

Pass through a gate 300m later. The track widens on the other side of the gate, then passes through another gate in just under 1km. In about 500m, come to two adjacent gates and go through the right-hand one. You're at the top of a rise now, with good views ahead of a silhouetted bull on a hill in the distance. Come to another two gates 200m later and turn left, then turn right immediately afterwards to keep heading in the same direction on the other side of a dry stone wall.

Up ahead, Galisteo is just visible, although still a long way off. There's no track here, just a meandering route through pasture; the route stays close to the wall and yellow arrows are much in evidence, painted on holm oaks. In 1km, turn right to go through a gate. This time, turn left to keep walking in the same direction, now with the stone wall on your left. Pass through a gate 500m later then, in a little under 1km, you'll suddenly see the Embalse de Riolobos; curve left to follow the line of a fence here and walk downhill towards the N630. As the path flattens out, pass through a gate and turn left on to a broad dirt track. Cross a stream 50m later and turn left on to another dirt track, then turn left in another 50m and right in 20m to take a steep path up to the road.

Turn right to walk along the N630. After about 1km, turn left down a broad dirt road that leads to Finca Valparaiso, crossing a cattle grid. In 500m, fork right as you get good views of Galisteo ahead, then cross another cattle grid 50m later. There's very little shade on this stretch as the oaks have disappeared, replaced by low-growing broom. In another 500m, keep to the track as it curves right, ignoring a fork to the left. Climb slightly with

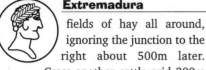

fields of hay all around, ignoring the junction to the right about 500m later. Cross another cattle grid 300m later then almost immediately cross a small bridge over a canal and turn right to walk alongside the water. This part of the country is much greener than anything along the Vía de la Plata so far, irrigated by an extensive network of canals like this one. When the terrain undulates, water is carried on gorgeous, stone-arched aqueducts.

After about 1km, turn sharp left to walk away from the canal and to the left of some farm buildings. You're getting closer to Galisteo, and the efficient irrigation means that locals can grow corn and vegetables. Pass through a gate 300m later to walk along a stone track; it can get boggy here from overflowing water channels. Walk through two more gates, 100m apart, and find yourself on a broad gravel track. Pass a picnic area under a shady weeping willow 50m later, then head downhill towards the Arroyo de las Monjas and cross it via a concrete bridge 500m later.

Walk uphill out of the small valley, coming to a junction in the camino 200m later. Keep straight on for San Gil (signposted SG), or turn left for Galisteo (signposted Glto), which is the route described here. In 50m, turn right and go up a final stiff climb, passing near one of the lovely stone aqueducts, and getting great views of Galisteo from the top. In 300m, cross a tarmac road and keep straight on along a gravel road. Cross another tarmac road 100m later, then turn left at the Bar-Restaurante Los Emigrantes. Turn right in 150m to walk into Galisteo's old walled town, or keep straight on this road to continue the camino.

# Galisteo

Ⓐ Ⓗ ✕ ◼ ☕ ☷ (631km)

Galisteo is a lovely, compact town founded by the Almohads in the ninth and tenth centuries and entirely encircled by the 11m-high **walls** they built to keep out attackers. The ramparts have been extensively restored, and you can climb steep stone steps at various places to reach them; the view, particularly at sunset, is breathtaking. The Torre del Homenaje, known locally as Picota, is a distinctive conical tower with an octagonal base that was erected during fourteenth-century renovations of the Moorish Alcazar. The Iglesia de Santa María is a mish-mash of architectural styles, with a Mudéjar apse, sixteenth-century Gothic nave and an eighteenth-century Baroque *retablo*; the belltower is separate from the rest of the church.

Galisteo is a place of bizarre **traditions**. La Calva, a game with murky origins, involves throwing a cylindrical stone weighing some 3kg at a wooden post about 15m away, and La Alborá is a wedding tradition in which the groom, bride and best man are serenaded by Galisteo's townsfolk on the eve of the big day. On Nochebuena (Christmas Eve), locals stage a slapstick Nativity play with shepherds dressed in regional costumes and toting shotguns. Yet even these eccentricities are overshadowed by **La Vaquilla**, Galisteo's unique cow-running festival, established by the first Duques de Galisteo in 1436. Although it begins with fairly tame dancing and music, the climax comes when the four gates into Galisteo's walled centre are closed, young cows are let loose in the middle of town, and the town's women run around ahead of them. Even the town walls don't always provide refuge from the understandably annoyed beasts; on one occasion, a rogue cow actually managed to climb up to the ramparts, a staggering achievement given the narrowness and steepness of the steps.

## Accommodation

Galisteo's **albergue municipal** (4 beds, hot showers, donation) is about 600m past the far side of town along the camino. It's not in the best condition and only has four beds, but there's plenty of room to sleep on the floor. Pedro Serrano, keeper of the keys, lives at Plaza de España 5 in the middle of the walled old town. A nicer option is to stay in the **private albergue** (4 beds, extra mattresses, hot showers, kitchen, €6) run by Mesón Rusticiana, an excellent restaurant that serves delicious local cuisine, some 400m before the *albergue municipal*.

**$ Bar Los Emigrantes** (☎ 927 452 142) offers a few rooms and breakfast, and serves a hearty, home-cooked *menú del día*.

---

Follow the road out of Galisteo, passing the Mesón Rusticiana and the *albergue municipal*. At the bottom of the hill, cross Galisteo's beautiful fourteenth-century medieval bridge, decorated with a coat of arms. Climb slightly and turn right at a junction, then keep straight on at the next junction soon afterwards. Follow this road for 5km and pass through the village of **Aldeahuela del Jerte** (🛒🍷). Canals cut through the landscape, making the countryside much more green than the rest of Extremadura.

A few kilometres later, as the road nears Carcaboso, pass a large brick factory on the left, and soon afterwards reach the edge of the village. The camino goes straight across a road and continues on a narrow street through **Carcaboso**

(🅷🍽️✗). If you're after some sustenance, turn left at the road to detour to the very welcoming **Bar Ruta de la Plata ($)**, which serves the biggest *café con leche* on the camino and offers cheap beds. From Carcaboso, you can detour to visit Plasencia (see page 64).

At the far side of Carcaboso, turn right on to a dirt track near three large stone crosses. The route curves through fields until you're faced with a decision 500m later. It's easiest to follow the bicycle sign and keep straight on to the Canal del Jerte (see below), but adventurous walkers can turn right here to head in a disturbingly southeastern direction. Keep calm, as the route soon crosses a stream and curves back towards an abandoned ruin. Turn left just before the ruin, then pass through a gate 300m later into a large cattle field.

Follow the track as it curves around to a large barn on top of a hill, from where there are panoramic views of the countryside. Keep straight on at another gate and enter a forest of holm oak, looking out for yellow arrows painted on the trees. After about 1km, the track heads downhill. Here, confusing yellow arrows point left along a narrow overgrown track and over a narrow water channel, but it's easier to continue for another 200m to the edge of a field and pass through a gate on the other side.

In another 200m, turn left at a paved road parallel to the Canal del Jerte, where the bicycle route emerges. Turn right 100m later to walk through a gate and climb a long hill on a dirt track through holm oaks. After about 1km of climbing uphill, pass an interesting stone

**Map 12** (key page 214)

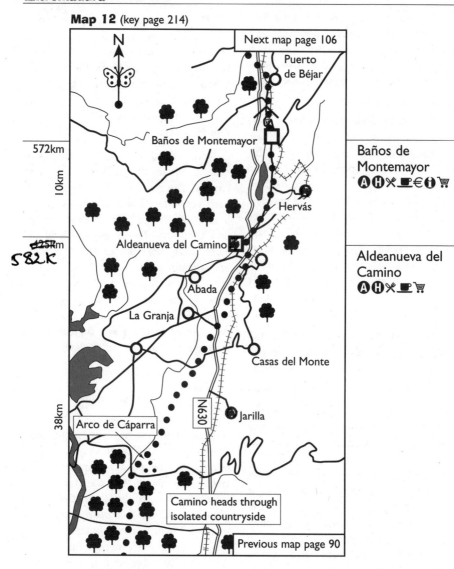

Next map page 106

N

Puerto
de Béjar

572km

Baños de Montemayor

Baños de
Montemayor
🅐🅗✕🍽️€ℹ️🛒

10km

Hervás

125km
582K

Aldeanueva del Camino

Aldeanueva del
Camino
🅐🅗✕🍽️🛒

Abada

La Granja

Casas del Monte

38km

N630

Jarilla

Arco de Cáparra

Camino heads through
isolated countryside

Previous map page 90

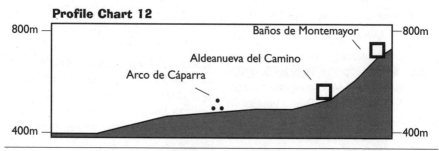

**Profile Chart 12**

| | |
|---|---|
| 800m | 800m |

Baños de Montemayor

Aldeanueva del Camino

Arco de Cáparra

| | |
|---|---|
| 400m | 400m |

corral on the left, then go through a gate 200m later. Look out here, as in another 200m the camino breaks away from the dirt track to the right to follow a narrow path through holm oaks. This is the start of one of the most beautiful, and most remote, stretches of the whole camino. The route shadows a stone wall on the right as it curves around trees and large boulders, and lots of shade protects the pilgrim from the elements.

In a little more than 1km, the camino approaches a stone wall. Turn right through a gate then go immediately left to keep heading north. The route once jumped a series of walls here and occasional yellow arrows on the other side of the wall can be confusing, but the new gate makes any leaping unnecessary. Fans of Roman Spain may want to hop back over the wall soon afterwards, however, to look at a couple of *miliarios* that are now tantalizingly out of reach.

The route keeps winding through holm oaks for about 4km before cork oaks begin to appear, a sign that you are nearing the end of this stretch. Pass through a makeshift gate in a stone wall and go around a brick corral. A little while later, pass through another gate, and climb up to a water hole, looking out for European pond terrapins that scurry into the water when disturbed. Cross two large fields, hop over a gap in a stone wall and cross over the narrow paved road to Oliva de Plasencia. You may be able to get water at the house on the left here.

You're now walking on a broad dirt track between two stone walls 50m apart. This is a fantastic stretch of Roman road that heads almost dead straight to the Arco de Cáparra. It has also been used for centuries as the Cañada Real, a drove road to move sheep and cattle from summer pastures in northern Spain down to Extremadura. There's been some revival of interest in the Cañada Real in recent years, with a fair bit of waymarking (look for white painted arrows) along the way. The Roman road, just to the right of the route, is slightly raised and clearly visible, and this section also has some inviting shade and great views of the Sierra de Gredos. After about 5km, pass a *finca* on the left then 1km later pass another, called Casablanca, on the right, with Roman stones in the garden. Pass an abandoned building with a sundial on it, and soon see the Arco de Cáparra straight ahead. The camino passes directly beneath the arch in an in-your-face reminder of the route's Roman origins.

The Roman town of Caprera was on the Roman Camino de la Plata from Hispalis (Sevilla) to Salamanca and the silver mines of Asturias. It's a fascinating place to visit, not least because it's in the middle of nowhere, having been abandoned. The site is dominated by the magnificently preserved four-sided arch that gives the **Arco de Cáparra** its name. Probably built in the second century by a local citizen, the whole of the squat, unusual arch, including the vaulting, has been preserved. The arch likely formed the entrance to the forum and recently there's been extensive excavation of the surrounding site, including the forum itself, Roman baths and the well-preserved main street. Helpful information plaques and an interpretation centre explain the various monuments and the site's history.

To continue along the camino, cross straight over a narrow paved road 200m later (turn right here for the interpretation centre), walk briefly on an old tarmac road then pick up a walled dirt track almost straight away. The landscape is more arid now with much less shade, but it's clear that you'll soon be leaving the Extremadura basin behind as the Sierra de la Candelaria come into view ahead and to the left. Keep going for 2km until you reach a gate, then pass through it into an open field, cross two streams and reach a tarmac road.

You're now faced with a long stretch of tarmac that can be murder on tired feet, but although there are sections where it is possible to find a path through the scrub to the right of the road it's often quicker to stay on the tarmac. Just to make your walk a little more miserable, there's also no shade on this stretch. In 2km, come to a junction. Turn right here to stay at the **Hostal Asturias ($,** ☎ 927 477 057) on the N630 in Jarilla, some 3km off the camino. In another 4km, there's an S-bend in the road. Soon afterwards, keep straight on at a junction until the tarmac ends in another 2km.

The next section is very confusing and poorly marked with yellow arrows, and is not suitable for cycling pilgrims, who should follow the N630 to Aldeanueva instead. As the tarmac ends, turn left to cross a river bed, then turn immediately right to go under the N630 bridge. Once under the bridge, hop over the wall on your left and walk diagonally across the large field on its other side. There are yellow markers on concrete pylons in the field. Once you reach a wall on the other side of the field, look for two gates very close together leading to a small field on your right. Go through the gates, or clamber over them if they are padlocked.

The camino becomes more obvious from now on, and you'll be less stymied by obstacles. Follow a dirt track to the left as it leads uphill through a beautiful cork oak forest. As you climb, pass a couple of ruined buildings on the right, looking out for the unusual stone trough in front of the second one. On meeting another wall soon afterwards, hop over it and turn left to walk along a lovely, shady walled lane. Follow the lane over rolling hills, pass a reservoir on the left, and keep straight on, ignoring turnings to the right and left.

On your right, you'll pass a tiny shelter set up for shepherds using the Cañada Real. Head down into a small valley and up the other side to walk alongside the motorway. Keep straight along this lane until you meet a motorway overpass. Climb up to the overpass, then turn left to walk along it into Aldeanueva del Camino, taking the first road on the right into the village.

# Aldeanueva del Camino
Ⓐ Ⓗ ✕ ▬ 🛒 (425km)

Aldeanueva del Camino is a gorgeous village and a lovely place to stay. The village houses boast cluttered balconies laden with flowers and there's a beautiful medieval humpback bridge over the Río Ambroz.

In the river, you'll often see chestnut branches soaking in the water; the damp wood will later be worked into the region's famous baskets and staffs. If you choose to walk without a *bordón* (walking staff), you'll be regarded as a curiosity, and villagers may try to persuade you to buy one of the beautiful local examples. The Iglesia de Nuestra Señora de Olmo, one of two parish churches in the village, has an elegant, star-vaulted dome.

The tiny **albergue** (4 beds, hot showers, donation) is in a yellow building on the left just before you reach the main square; get the keys from Bar La Union just across the bridge from the square. The **Hostal Montesol** ($, ☎ 927 484 335) on the N630 at the other side of town, has rooms and does meals, or you can stay at the **Hostal Roma** ($$, ☎ 927 484 038), another 500m away.

---

Leave the village via the lovely main street, cross the medieval bridge and arrive at the N630 about 1km after the *albergue*. Turn right here, passing the Hostal Montesol, then reach a roundabout in 500m. Take the right-hand exit signposted Hervás, then at a second roundabout almost immediately afterwards turn left, still following signs to Hervás.

It's a 4km detour from here to the lovely village of **Hervás**, known for one of the best preserved *juderías* (Jewish quarters) in Spain, a maze of narrow medieval streets and irregular squares. The first Jews arrived in these hills at the beginning of the fifteenth century and were among the foremost merchants by the time the Inquisition decimated its population at the end of the fifteenth century. Among the buildings worth exploring are the *ayuntamiento*, the

Palacio de los Dávilas and the Iglesia de San Juan, which has a baroque *retablo*. There's a helpful *turismo*, and you can stay at the **Hotel Sinagoga** ($, ☎ 927 481 191). You don't need to retrace your steps to return to the camino; follow the signs to Baños de Montemayor and you'll join the N630 about 5km further on.

If you decide not to visit Hervás, keep on the road, which you'll follow more or less all the way to Baños de Montemayor. After 5km, pass the Hervasfiel campground on the left, where there's a restaurant, and the second road to Hervás on the right. At the top of a rise in another 1km, follow a yellow arrow that leads you off the road for a short 500m stretch. Up ahead, you can see the impressive hills that hide the Puerto de Béjar pass and soon, as you round a corner, you'll see Baños de Montemayor ahead. Shortly after a large sign with a snowflake on it (warning of the region's sporadic winter road conditions), turn left off the main road down a dirt track, which again offers a short section of relief from the tarmac. There's been a fair amount of cash injected into the region around Baños to preserve and highlight the area's Roman roads, and the example you're now walking on is a particularly good one. In a few hundred metres, you'll rejoin the main road next to the Ermita del Humilladero. Soon afterwards, turn right to walk into the centre of Baños, heading uphill along Calle Mayor past the Iglesia de Santa Catalina and towards the *ayuntamiento*.

## Regional Map (key page 214)

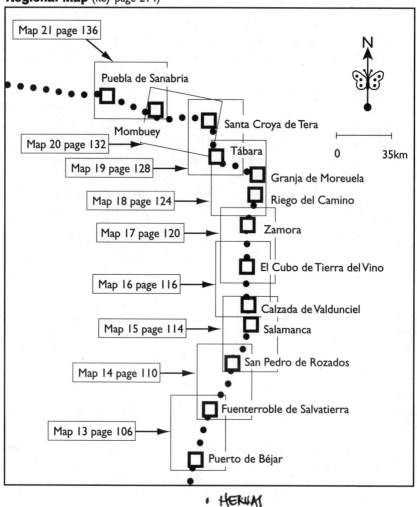

Map 21 page 136

Puebla de Sanabria

N

Santa Croya de Tera

Mombuey

Map 20 page 132

Tábara

0        35km

Map 19 page 128

Granja de Moreuela

Map 18 page 124

Riego del Camino

Map 17 page 120

Zamora

El Cubo de Tierra del Vino

Map 16 page 116

Calzada de Valdunciel

Map 15 page 114

Salamanca

San Pedro de Rozados

Map 14 page 110

Fuenterroble de Salvatierra

Map 13 page 106

Puerto de Béjar

· HERNAS

## What's the Weather Like?

|            | Jan   | April | July  | Oct   |
|------------|-------|-------|-------|-------|
| **Sun**    | 4hrs  | 8hrs  | 12hrs | 6hrs  |
| **Rainfall** | 6cm | 5cm   | 2cm   | 2cm   |
| **Maximum Temp** | 7°C | 15°C | 35°C | 18°C |
| **Minimum Temp** | -1°C | 3°C | 11°C | 6°C |

Average hours of sun, total average rainfall in cm and average temperature in degrees celsius

# Meseta

## Baños de Montemayor to Puebla de Sanabria

The Vía de la Plata climbs up towards Puerta de Béjar and the red soils of the *meseta*, a vast, high tableland that covers much of central Spain. The landscape is mostly flat, and although some pilgrims find the monotony tiring, others find it inspiring. The plains can be hauntingly beautiful, and it's not all desolate wilderness: Salamanca is a boisterous university town, and mellower Zamora boasts fabulous restaurants and smooth Toro wine, which is rarely found outside Spain.

 **Walking**

## Geography

The vast expanse and huge skies of the *meseta* are striking and strange, swinging from depressingly monotonous to exhilaratingly infinite in the space of a kilometre. The hills at the start and end of the *meseta* will provide some distraction, but mostly your senses will be overloaded by an endless flatness.

Roman engineers solved the problem of where to cross the southern Sistema Central Massif by choosing the narrow gap between the Sierra de Gredos and the Sierra de Francia to link their ever-expanding empire. The only problem with their solution is that the Vía de la Plata crosses the Sierra de Béjar instead, rolling hills more in character with Galicia than the flat plains that surround them. The higher mountains snag passing clouds and squeeze out what little water they contain. As a result, the area receives a slightly higher rainfall than the surrounding plains, and moisture-loving ferns and poplars give the landscape a refreshing green tinge.

The flat tabletop of the high *meseta* is slowly being eroded by the three great rivers of the region: the Río Tormes, Río Duero and Río Esla. Multiple dams dot their length, and their waters support large scale irrigation, making this area perfect for farming crops and grazing cattle. The need for electricity is also transforming the foothills of the Sierra de la Culebra in the north, where modern wind turbines crown the ridges, providing green power for the surrounding population.

## Trails

The route is well-marked through most of the *meseta*, although there are few yellow arrows in the centre of Salamanca and Zamora, and after Granja de

Moreruela the quality of the waymarking deteriorates considerably.

Throughout the region, heavy rains can churn the dirt tracks into killer mud that sticks to everything and makes walking a real chore. At Granja de Moreruela, the Vía de la Plata splits. One branch heads north, joining the *camino francés* in Astorga after passing through the towns of Benavente, Vilabrázaro, Alija del Infantado and La Bañeza. We describe the less-travelled way northwest to Ourense, a peaceful, rural route through gorgeous countryside and tiny villages.

## When to go

Summers are hot, winters are cold and though the brief spring and autumn seasons are more bearable, the wind can still be bone-chilling. Start early in summer and you'll miss the worst of the heat and catch a wonderful dawn chorus. Wrap up in winter to enjoy crisp, cloudless days that make for wonderful walking.

The wheat fields and scrubland of the *meseta* initially seem lifeless and deserted, but if you stop for a while and leave the camino treadmill, you'll hear and see a stunning array of birds.

One of the most distinctive is the **great bustard**, a stocky, Canada goose–sized bird that loves the *meseta*'s wide open spaces. In spring, the males rustle their tails in a dramatic courtship display; their size and fluffy white feathers make a group of males indistinguishable from a flock of sheep at a distance. Intensive cultivation and tree planting are eroding the bustard's habitat, and a hunting ban may paradoxically reduce numbers further, as landowners now have no incentive to conserve territory for the former game bird.

Up above, the skies are a bonanza of aerial hunters. You can see kestrels, peregrine falcons, Egyptian vultures, hen harriers and Bonelli's eagles. It takes more patience to look for birds that live low to the ground in fields or scrubland, and at first you're more likely to hear the melodic songs of the *meseta*'s many **larks** — there are short-toed, Dupont's, crested and calandra larks here — than to see the well-camouflaged birds. Much easier to spot is the bold, coral-coloured crest of the **hoopoe**, which has distinctive black and white bars on its tail and wings, and flies in such an ungainly, undulating style that it seems to fall from the sky with each wing beat.

The lack of rain on the *meseta* means that flowers either burst quickly into life in the rains of spring and autumn, or conserve moisture and heat in tubers and bulbs. Orchids, cornflowers, vetch and corn poppies are a riot of colour among the seemingly endless, straw-coloured fields, whereas moisture-loving plants crowd rivers, streams and ponds.

Castilla y León can justly claim to be the cradle of Spanish culture. One of the first regions to be won back by the Christians after the Muslim invasion, Spain is so entwined with **Castilla** that the Spanish even call their language *Castellano* (Castilian).

*Meseta* architecture is at its finest in Salamanca, a lively city of yellow sandstone buildings centred around the magnificent Churrigueresque Plaza Mayor. Zamora's heyday came earlier, and its city walls enclose a lovely compact centre crammed with Romanesque treasures. More modest folk have been equally creative. In many *meseta* villages, notably Montamarta, houses are made from adobe, a logical choice in a bone-dry climate, where it's cheap to build and repaired by simply patching the walls with more straw and mud. Hobbit-like underground **bodegas** (cellars) are a common sight on the outskirts of villages and towns, providing cool storage for wine and other produce. The round- or horseshoe-shaped buildings that sit plum in the middle of fields are **palomares** (dovecotes). Pigeon droppings are a valuable source of nitrogen-rich fertilizer, and these game birds also make their way to the dinner table.

Bullfighting *aficionados* flock to the area around Salamanca, not for any grand spectacles but for its reputation as a breeding ground for the country's best **toros bravos** (bulls). Although you'll see a fair few cows along the camino, you're unlikely to meet the male of the species, as they're far too precious to be allowed to stalk unsuspecting pilgrims.

# Food & Drink

Castilla y León is known for its **pork**, particularly the suckling pig, traditionally roasted in a baker's oven with pine branches, broom, rosemary and thyme. Pork is also a main ingredient of the region's heavy stews, padded out with pulses and rice-blood sausage.

Keep vampires away with Castilla's famous **sopa de ajo** or *sopa de castellana*, a soup made by frying bread in paprika and lots of garlic, pouring on stock and cracking an egg on top. A staple food in hard times, *sopa de ajo* is now appearing in the finest restaurants.

**Ribeira del Duero** wines are now firmly established on the international scene, and the Duero basin in the south of Castilla y León now attracts almost as much attention as its more famous Riojan cousin. These deep burgundy wines have more acidity than Rioja wines due to the extreme temperature fluctuations in the region.

Further along the Río Duero, some 40km east of Zamora, the tiny **Toro** region is the up-and-coming wine-growing part of Spain. Although only demarcated as an official wine region since 1987, the area's primary grape variety, Tinta de Toro, has been grown here since medieval times, when most of the land was given to the cathedral authorities of Santiago de Compostela. The region's sandy soils mean that there's little need for irrigation, and they also prevented the vines from being destroyed by the *phylloxera* disease that ravaged many southern European vineyards in the nineteenth century. Contact the *turismo* in Zamora to arrange a visit to local winemakers.

Zamora has some excellent restaurants, and one of the town's delights is a visit to the many pastry shops on Calle

Alfonso IX for a slice of *empanada*, a vast, shallow pie usually made with meat.

Culinary adventurers should try *cresta*, deep-fried rooster comb, a local delicacy that you'll see in *tapas* bars.

# 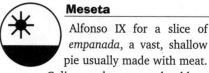 Tourist Information

## Tourist offices

You'll find tourist offices in Baños de Montemayor, Salamanca and Zamora. Contact information for the *turismos* is under individual towns.

## Transport

Salamanca and Zamora are both well-connected bus and train transport hubs, and the southern section of the meseta is easy to get to from all over Spain. Further north, it's difficult to get from Granja de Moreruela to Mombuey by public transport.

## Money

There are cash machines and banks in Baños de Montemayor, Salamanca, Aldeaseca de Armuña, Zamora, Tábara, Santa Croya de Tera, Rionegro del Puente and Mombuey.

## Accommodation

*Albergues* vary in quality, space and facilities, from the basic comforts of the bare bones *albergue* in San Pedro de Rozados to Santa Croya de Tera's new and stylish private *albergue*. Each has an individual character because they're usually run by local people rather than provincial authorities. The distances between accommodation are often far, making for

long stages, and there are no *albergues* in Salamanca or Zamora.

## Shopping

Salamanca and Zamora are modern cities with everything a pilgrim could need. In between, supplies and opening hours can be limited.

## Events & Festivals

Those lucky enough to pass through Salamanca and Zamora during Semana Santa will be greeted by massive celebrations that do their best to rival the more famous Easter celebrations of Sevilla. *Salamantines* celebrate the Día de San Juan de Sahagún on June 24, but the city really lets it hair down for the two-week *Feria* that starts on September 7.

Like all good towns that make a living from tourism, Baños de Montemayor's calendar is packed with festivals. The most popular is the Fiesta de los Mayores y los Emigrantes during the month of August, which also sees the festivals of San Ramón Nonato and Santa Rosa de Lima.

#  Rest Days & Detours

The logical places to take a break are Salamanca and Zamora, pleasant cities to wander around, visit spectacular monuments or simply rest sore feet.

If you're really suffering, the thermal baths of **Baños de Montemayor** will ease all but the most troublesome aches and pains, and the quality of hotels and restaurants help to make this an enjoyable spot to spend some time.

Further off the camino, some 20km south of Salamanca, **Alba de Tormes** is famous for its castle and Convento de Carmelitas Descalzas. The remains of Santa Teresa are buried here and you can still see the cell in which she died. It was here, too, after the battle of Salamanca during the Peninsular War, that Wellington's reserve forces ignored orders to secure the bridge, allowing the defeated French forces used to escape.

Head to **Campillo**, 12km northwest of Zamora, to visit the Iglesia de San Pedro de la Nave. This seventh-century Visigothic church was restored in the ninth century with carved capitals and friezes of a style not common until three centuries later.

Further north, turn left off the N630 just before Granja de Moreruela to walk the 4km to the **Monesterio de Moreruela**, the first Cistercian convent in Spain. Dating from the late eleventh century, the monastery was destroyed by Almanzor and reconstructed in the twelfth century.

# Baños de Montemayor

ⒶⒽ✕💺€ⓘ🍽 (572km)

Baños has been drawing tourists since the Romans discovered the healing properties of the local **thermal waters**. With a constant temperature of 43°C and a high mineral content, it's no surprise that the waters remain a popular treatment for muscular and respiratory problems. Strolling through the streets of Baños de Montemayor, you'll often see robed pensioners scurrying from their hotels to the baths and back as they ease their aches and pains. Nestled at the foot of the Sierra de Gredos, the town is also a popular spot with summer tourists looking to escape the heat of Madrid.

Baños boasts some excellent restaurants and hotels, and a string of tacky souvenir shops that sell baskets, *bordones* (walking staffs) and general tourist tat. Pilgrims can visit the **Centro de Interpretación de la Vía de La Plata**, an excellent introduction to the route in Extremadura. Although it's almost a replica of the centre in Monesterio, it's interesting to see the exhibit again after having walked through the region. The **turismo** (☎ 923 428 012) is in the *ayuntamiento* on the main square.

## Accommodation

The Centro de Interpretación de la Vía de La Plata, Calle Castañar 38 (☎ 679 228 208), has some beds for pilgrims, but doesn't open until late evening.

**Campsite Las Cañadas** is at km432 on the N630 out of town

**$ Pensión Don Diego**, Avenida Las Termas 69 (☎ 923 428 125)

**$$ Hostal Martín**, Plaza Hernán Cortes 4 (☎ 923 428 066)

**Map 13** (key page 214)

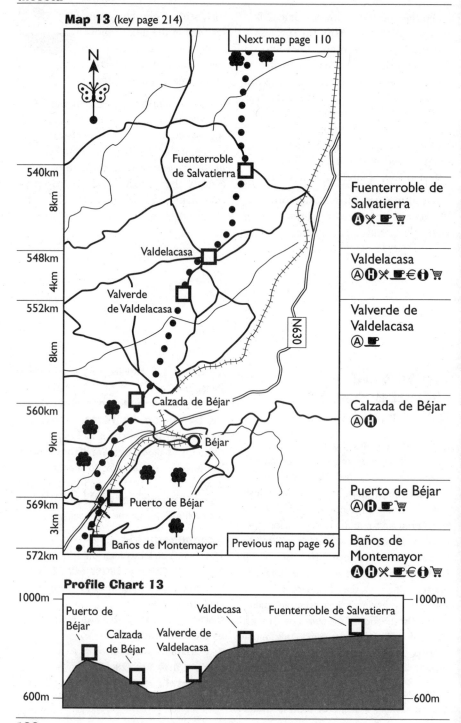

Next map page 110

N

540km

8km

Fuenterroble
de Salvatierra

548km

4km

Valdelacasa

552km

Valverde
de Valdelacasa

8km

N630

560km

Calzada de Béjar

9km

Béjar

569km

Puerto de Béjar

3km

Baños de Montemayor

Previous map page 96

572km

**Fuenterroble de
Salvatierra**
Ⓐ✕☕🛒

**Valdelacasa**
ⒶⒽ✕☕€ⓘ🛒

**Valverde de
Valdelacasa**
Ⓐ☕

**Calzada de Béjar**
ⒶⒽ

**Puerto de Béjar**
ⒶⒽ☕🛒

**Baños de
Montemayor**
ⒶⒽ✕☕€ⓘ🛒

**Profile Chart 13**

1000m

Puerto de
Béjar

Valdecasa

Fuenterroble de Salvatierra

Calzada
de Béjar

Valverde de
Valdelacasa

1000m

600m

600m

**$$ Hostal Galicia**, Avenida Las Termas 139 (☎ 923 428 162)
**$$$ Hotel Balneario**, Avenida Las Termas 54 (☎ 923 428 005)

---

Walk past the *ayuntamiento*, heading uphill to the left on Calle Castillejos soon afterwards. Follow the yellow arrows as they lead steeply up and out of town, passing houses with overhanging balconies that enjoy wide vistas of terraced fields and the flat plains of Extremadura to the south. Turn left at the road to La Garganta, then keep straight on almost immediately at a hairpin bend on the N630 to walk on a well-preserved section of the Calzada Romana (Roman road).

Pass a *cruceiro* on the right 100m later and keep climbing steeply uphill on this ancient cobbled thoroughfare. After 1km, pass a fountain that commemorates the reconstruction of the Cañada Real (livestock drove road). You now leave the province of Cáceres in Extremadura and enter the province of Salamanca and the region of Castilla y León.

Join the N630 soon afterwards and turn right to walk along it. In a little more than 1km, pass a petrol station with a café and a small shop on the left. Turn left off the road 100m later down a dirt track, following a Camino de Santiago sign as you enter the village of **Puerto de Béjar** (Ⓐ❶▣✉🛒, 569km). The parish church hides a magnificent sixteenth-century *retablo* and a carving of the Virgen de la Asunción attributed to Gregorio Fernández. There was once a pilgrims hospice here and you can still stay in the basic **albergue** (mattresses, no shower, donation) in the old school next door to the **Casa Rural Casa**

**Adriano**, where pilgrims can also get a *sello* and a *credencial.*

As you leave Puerto de Béjar, the route changes to tarmac and you pass underneath a motorway bridge. Keep straight ahead 100m later along a dirt road as the tarmac road veers left towards the motorway, then carry on a few hundred metres later to cross the N630 next to a modern *miliario*. Follow a wide lane downhill along a well-preserved section of the Calzada Romana, lined with oak, chestnut, beech and ash trees. Pass a stone farmhouse about 4km later, and turn left to cross the Puente de la Magdalena over the poplar-lined Río Cuerpo de Hombre. Much of the bridge is the original built by Roman engineers almost 2000 years ago.

Curve right 30m later and start to climb gradually, passing a *miliario* on the right almost immediately. You're walking next to a quiet tarmac road on the left, with the Río Cuerpo de Hombre away to your right, up a beautiful valley of fields and trees mercifully unsullied by the motorway. Pass a farmhouse after 1km and a *miliario* after another 1km, then head past the buildings that make up Coloniado San Francisco on the right and join the road near some houses 100m later. In 300m turn off the road again, heading left on a dirt track and climbing steeply. Pass a pig farm 2km later as the track flattens out, and enter Calzada de Béjar soon afterwards.

**Calzada de Béjar** (Ⓐ❶, 560km) is a lovely village of old stone houses with pretty balconies propped up by wooden beams and stone columns. On a hill to the right of the village are the remains of a Roman fort, although access to the site

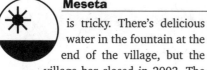

is tricky. There's delicious water in the fountain at the end of the village, but the village bar closed in 2003. The basic **albergue** is in the *ayuntamiento* (mattresses, no shower, donation). You can also stay at **Casa Rural La Gavia** (**$$**, ☎ 923 416 954) on the main street, which serves meals to guests.

Leave town on a paved road and turn left in 500m down a dirt track. Cross a minor road in 1km and pass a row of coppiced ash trees, then keep walking through flat fields along this dirt road for 5km. Pass a Roman *miliario* with good inscriptions, then 300m later turn right on joining a paved road at an abandoned farm. Look out for the curious steel-grey cows in the fields along the camino. Soon after joining the road, turn left to leave it again on a dirt track. In another 2km, fork right and walk over a stone slab bridge.

Pass a *cruceiro* on the right and enter **Valverde de Valdelacasa** (Ⓐ🍷, 552km), a tiny village whose link to the camino is evident. Santiago is Valverde's patron saint, and his cross is in the village's coat of arms. The parish Iglesia de Santiago has a lovely porch that offers shelter from the elements and a curious steeple that seems to be built on the wrong corner of the church. There's a former pilgrims hospital in the house with 1704 over the door. In a pinch, pilgrims can sleep on the floor of the *ayuntamiento*; ask in the old folks' home for the key. The village bar is often closed. Leave Valverde on a tarmac road, then 2km later as a road joins from the left, keep straight on past a sign for Valdelacasa and carry on towards the village.

Perched on top of a windy hill, the curved streets of **Valdelacasa** (Ⓐ🍷, 548km) can be a little confusing to navigate. You'll find the **albergue** (6 beds, hot showers, donation) towards the end of town; ask for the key at the *ayuntamiento*. There's a small but well-stocked shop, and the town boasts three bars that seem to take it in turns to open.

Leave Valdelacasa, cross the main road and keep straight on along a narrow paved road next to small fields bordered by dry stone walls. About 1km later, turn left, following a Vía de la Plata sign down a dirt track and heading gradually uphill. Keep on the track as it curves right 500m later, ignoring a track to the left. In 2km, pass a *miliario* on the right and 100m later keep straight on to take the left-hand fork, heading gradually downhill.

Just over 1km later, pass a house among chestnuts trees on the right, then pass another *miliario* 300m later on the left. Suddenly, there are views across the flat *meseta* and of Fuenterroble de Salvatierra up ahead. About 100m later, yellow arrows direct you right at a crossroads with another dirt track, then immediately left on to a paved road. A better option is to keep straight ahead at the crossroads to follow a dirt track parallel to the road. Almost 1km later, turn right at a Vía de la Plata sign then immediately left to join the paved road. Enter Fuenterroble de Salvatierra in 1km and keep straight on for the *albergue*.

# Fuenterroble de Salvatierra
Ⓐ✕🍷 (540km)

This small village is perched on the edge of the *meseta* and is exposed to the elements, the bleak environment in stark contrast to the warm welcome pilgrims receive at its remarkable *albergue*.

The **Iglesia de Santa María de la Blanca** stood abandoned for years, but has now been heavily restored and boasts a new roof and altar. The defensive tower, older than the rest of the church, once guarded the boundary of the old kingdom of Castilla, and there's a cross of Santiago in the stone window near the altar. Every Easter, huge wooden statues of the apostles are paraded around the countryside by villagers. Outside the church is a preserved section of the Calzada Romana; the middle part has been excavated and signs explain its construction in more detail. There's also a *miliario* with a well-preserved inscription.

Fuenterroble's **albergue** (30 beds, extra mattresses, hot showers, kitchen, donation) is one of the most famous on the Vía de la Plata, smoothly run by the tireless Don Blas Rodríguez, the parish priest who has done much to revive the camino in this region. The ashes of José Luis Salvador Salvador, another driving force behind the Vía de la Plata, are buried in the front wall of the building. The ramshackle, slightly grubby building has things shoved into every available nook and cranny and offers a warm fireplace in cold weather. Pilgrims often join together for communal dinners.

One of the two village bars does meals with advance warning, and there's a tiny shop next door.

With your back to the *albergue*, turn right to follow signs to Liñares and walk along the main road on a gravel shoulder. In 1km, turn right on to a paved road which soon becomes a dirt track, a straight 4km stretch with little shade. The camino eventually enters a holm oak grove. Be careful when the trees end 500m later, as the route is badly marked. The path turns left, then swerves right 100m later on to a dirt track, and left in another 100m down another indistinct track. Pass some beehives on the left 300m later and some farm buildings away to the left in another 300m. Soon afterwards, join a broad track from the left. At a gate 100m later, keep straight on as the main track curves left.

The track goes uphill, passing through some more holm oaks, and you'll soon find yourself following a wide gravel track, still ascending. This a good spot to see eagles, sparrowhawks and vultures soaring on thermal updrafts over the Pico de la Dueña. Keep straight on at a junction with the road to Navarredonda de Salvatierra, about 1km after the gate.

Ignore a track to the left just under 1km later, where there are good views over the *meseta* and a last glimpse of the Sierra de Gredos behind. Turn left on to a dirt track in another 300m, then keep straight on 200m later as a stony track joins from the left. In 500m, turn left just before a cattle grid to walk steeply uphill on a stony path through holm oaks. The camino changes to a narrow dirt path and winds its way through trees as it continues uphill.

Pass a wooden cross in 1km, and another one in 1km. At last, you reach a cross of Santiago near the summit of **Pico de la Dueña**. Perched on a rocky outcrop but annoyingly inaccessible behind a wire fence, this cross marks the highest point (1140m) on the Vía de la Plata between Sevilla and Astorga. As with the Cruz de Hierro on the *camino*

**Map 14** (key page 214)

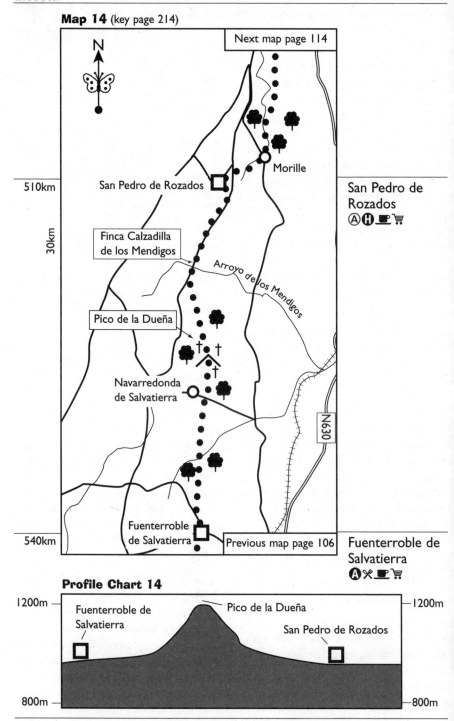

Next map page 114

N

Morille

510km

San Pedro de Rozados

30km

Finca Calzadilla
de los Mendigos

Arroyo de los Mendigos

Pico de la Dueña

Navarredonda
de Salvatierra

N630

Fuenterroble
de Salvatierra

540km

Previous map page 106

San Pedro de
Rozados
Ⓐ🅗☕🛒

Fuenterroble de
Salvatierra
Ⓐ✕☕🛒

**Profile Chart 14**

1200m

Fuenterroble de
Salvatierra

Pico de la Dueña

San Pedro de Rozados

1200m

800m

800m

*francés*, pilgrims traditionally leave a stone at this spot, following a tradition begun by Celts and Romans to ensure safe passage over the mountains. Unlike the Cruz de Hierro, there's no impressive mound of stones and you'll have to make do with lobbing yours over the wire fence.

From the summit, there are good views of the *meseta* as you descend quickly through oak trees. Turn right when you reach a tarmac road at the bottom of the hill, and follow it for 3km, then at a right-hand hairpin bend carry straight on along a dirt path

Regain the road in 1km, cross the Arroyo de los Mendigos, then pass the substantial Finca Calzadilla de los Mendigos. About 300m after the farm, leave the road to walk on a track to the left of the road. As the road curves right 2km after the *finca*, keep following the track, which parallels the road and can get boggy in wet weather. In 3km, turn left on to a minor road signposted San Pedro de Rozados and arrive at the village in 1km.

# San Pedro de Rozados
Ⓐ🅗 💺🛒 (510km)

This tiny village offers a warm welcome to weary pilgrims. Ask for the keys to the *albergue* at Bar El Moreno, where pilgrims can also get dinner and breakfast. Photographs on the bar walls show the local festival of San Blas, when a local pig is ceremonially slaughtered and the meat is used to make sausages and other delicacies. The **albergue** (mattresses, hot shower, donation) is in a rather run down building at the back of the village school, near the Iglesia de San Pedro. More comfortable is the **Pensión Casa Miliario ($)**, also run by Bar El Moreno.

---

Leave San Pedro de Rozados and on the edge of village cross a paved road and walk down a dirt track through open fields. Turn left at a junction in 1km and then just before entering the village of **Morille** bear right at a fork in the road, next to a metal cross bearing the village name. Head straight through Morille, passing the *ayuntamiento* and a medical centre. On the far side of the village, keep going straight past the cemetery and pass a semi-circular metal-roofed barn in 1km. There's not much shade or shelter along this stretch of the camino but the open landscape does offer a good place to see red kites soaring overhead looking for food.

Several kilometres from Morille, at the top of a hill, pass through a gate and enter a holm oak forest. Head downhill keeping to the same path, then pass through another gate next to a fence 1km later. Cross straight over a road and keep straight ahead for 200m, then go through yet another gate and turn left to climb the face of a hill. Once at the top, head downhill into an open landscape, passing a *finca* on the left.

From here, you can see Salamanca in the distance as the camino heads almost directly for the city. It was near here on July 22, 1812, that the tide turned in the Peninsular War. Around the hills near Miranda de Azán, the Duke of Wellington and his 48,000 troops lay in wait for the French army led by General Marmont.

**Meseta**

The battle of Salamanca, which came to be hailed as Wellington's finest, was a complete rout of the French forces. Marmont committed tactical suicide by ordering his troops to march across the face of Wellington's position, exposing the French flanks. Wellington, who up until that moment was known as a cautious commander, ordered an all-out attack and by the end of the day, his forces had decimated Marmont's troops. The French never regained the upper hand in the Peninsular War.

Continue along the dirt track for 5km. Pass the hamlet of Miranda de Azán on the left, then soon afterwards cross a bridge over the Arroyo de Fuente de la Parra. Salamanca disappears from view for a moment, obscured by a small hill which the camino climbs straight over, passing under some power lines. From the top, the panorama of Salamanca is breathtaking.

As you approach the city, new construction will alter the route somewhat; whatever direction the new route takes, it's easiest to head towards the N630, off to the right, particularly in wet weather, when the region's red clay becomes treacherously sticky. Once you're at the N630, turn left and follow the road into Salamanca. Turn left at a large roundabout just before the city centre, then 100m later cross the busy road and follow the Roman bridge across the broad Río Tormes.

The route through Salamanca isn't marked by yellow arrows but directions are straightforward. Turn left at the end of the bridge, just before the Iglesia de Santiago, then turn left uphill next to a large *cruceiro* along Calle Tentenecio.

Turn right at the cathedral on to Calle Rúa Mayor, and enter Salamanca's Plaza Mayor.

# Salamanca
Ⓗ ✕ ▆ € ❶ ☷ (484km)

Extravagant Renaissance and Plateresque architecture and a lively student buzz make Salamanca a wonderful place to relax for a day or two. At night, tourists and native *Salamantines* promenade and *tapeo* around the beautifully illuminated old quarter.

Salamanca's origins stretch back into prehistory. The Iberian settlement here was captured in 217BC by Hannibal who disarmed the men but, in a fit of chivalry, left the women alone. But the women smuggled weapons to their men, who then escaped their captors and fled to the hills. Hannibal was so impressed by this courageous act of deception that he allowed the entire population to resettle unharmed. Once Hannibal left, Salamanca was soon swallowed up into the Roman Empire. The city flourished under the Visigoths, was overrun by the Moors in 715 and was finally captured by the Christians in 1055. It reached its height of influence in the sixteenth century when its architectural style was widely copied, then went into a slow decline until much of the town was destroyed and pillaged by French and British forces during the Peninsular War.

The **Plaza Mayor** is the city's open air masterpiece. Commissioned by Felipe V to thank Salamanca for her support in the War of Spanish Succession, and built in the eighteenth century by Alberto Churriguera, the *plaza* is considered by many to be the most magnificent in all of Spain. The square was once used for bullfights, and the noise a crowd makes on a packed summer evening gives some clue as to the atmosphere of those bloody spectacles. The arcaded shops are decorated with medallions, including busts of famous people; the one of Franco is frequently vandalized.

Salamanca's famous **university** was founded in 1218 by Alfonso X of León, and within 30 years it had been proclaimed by Pope Alexander IV as equal to the institutions at Oxford, Bologna and Paris. By the fifteenth and sixteenth centuries there were 25 colleges and 10,000 students, and its stellar faculty of astronomy helped fund Columbus' trip to the Indies. The Inquisition and its aftermath hit the university hard. Luis de León, a professor, poet and biblical translator, was imprisoned for translating the *Song of Solomon* into Spanish. On his release five years later he began his lecture with, "As we were saying yesterday," and the lectern from which he said the famous words still stands. Religious suppression led to the closure of the faculties of mathematics and medicine and the banning of countless books. By the end of the nineteenth century there were only about 300 students. The Nationalists didn't think much of the university either; one of their popular civil war slogans was "*Mueran los intelectuales*" or "death to intellectuals."

The sixteenth-century university façade rivals the Pórtico de La Gloria in Santiago Cathedral in pictographic detail. The Plateresque sandstone is covered with carved religious and mythical scenes, surrounding the coat of arms of Fernando and Isabel. If you spot the frog in the carving without any hints from the locals, you'll have good luck and be married within a year. The Escuelas Menores building is worth visiting to see *The Salamanca Sky*, a huge astrological fresco, and the neighbouring Sala de las Tortugas has the second-largest collection of tortoises and tortoise-shells in the world. The university library has a display of magnificent globes.

Salamanca rather greedily has two **cathedrals**. The older Catedral Vieja is a mix of Romanesque and Gothic styles, and the dome has Byzantine influences. Heavily damaged in the 1755 earthquake that flattened Lisbon, the building has been completely restored. The curved *retablo* is stunning, with 53 panels painted by Nicolás Florentino, who also created the *Last Judgement* fresco above it. One of the chapels contains the fifteenth-century alabaster tomb of Diego de Anaya, archbishop of Santiago.

The Catedral Nueva was built partly as an external show of Salamanca's power and, more prosaically, to hold up the teetering, adjacent Catedral Vieja. Begun in 1513, the style is mostly late-Gothic, with Renaissance and Baroque additions. The highlights are the Churrigueresque dome built by José Churriguera, and the Renaissance doorways, especially the Puerta del Nacimiento, a dazzling Gothic-Plateresque entrance. More recently, stonemasons have added an astronaut and an ice-cream cone to the Puerta de Ramos. Inside, the choir stalls and *retablo* are by Alberto, another member of the talented Churriguera family. Pilgrims can get a *sello* in the Catedral Nueva.

Towards the centre of town, the **Casa de las Conchas** goes overboard on camino imagery. Studded with scallop shells, the symbol of Santiago, it was built by Rodrigo Maldonado, a Knight of the Order of Santiago. This religious military order was very powerful in Southern Castilla during the *reconquista*, and even today the order includes the heir to the Spanish throne. Built at the beginning of the sixteenth century, the *casa* is now a public library, entered via a

**Map 15** (key page 214)

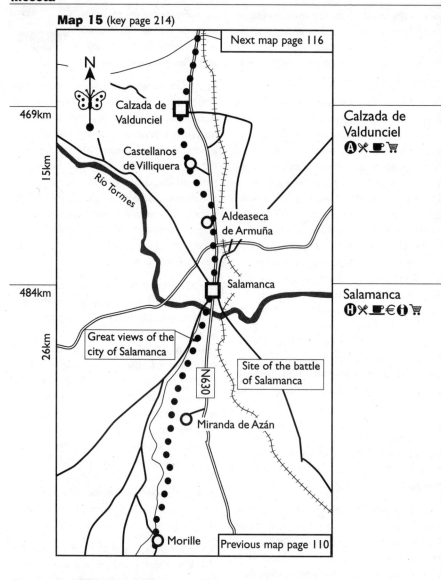

Next map page 116

N

Calzada de
Valdunciel

469km

Castellanos
de Villiquera

15km

Río Tormes

Aldeaseca
de Armuña

Salamanca

484km

Great views of the
city of Salamanca

26km

N630

Site of the battle
of Salamanca

Miranda de Azán

Morille

Previous map page 110

Calzada de
Valdunciel
Ⓐ✕◼︎🛒

Salamanca
Ⓗ✕◼︎€ⓘ🛒

**Profile Chart 15**

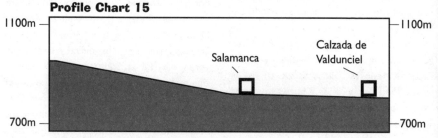

1100m

1100m

Salamanca

Calzada de
Valdunciel

700m

700m

lovely courtyard with wonderful carved capitals and lintels.

The **Museo de Arte Nouveau y Arte Deco** in the Casa Lis is a welcome change for those who are tired of looking at old buildings. The collection is from all over Europe, but the highlight is the colourful art nouveau building itself; enjoying the sun-soaked stained glass windows from the inside is worth the price of admission alone.

The **turismo municipal** (☎ 923 218 342) is on Plaza Mayor 14, and the **turismo regional** (☎ 923 268 571) is next door to the Casa de las Conchas on Calle de la Compañía 2.

### Accommodation

There are two hostels in Salamanca, although neither is specifically for pilgrims. **Albergue Salamanca**, Calle Escuto 13–15 (☎ 923 269 141), is a 10-minute bus ride from the city centre, and the **Albergue Juvenil Lazarillo de Tormes**, Calle Largo (☎ 923 194 249), is in town.

**$ Pensíon Barez**, Calle Meléndez 19 (☎ 923 217 495)

**$$ Hotel Reyes Católicos**, Paseo de la Estación 32 (☎ 923 241 064)

**$$$ Hotel Don Juan**, Calle Quintana 6 (☎ 923 261 818)

**$$$$ Hotel Rector**, Paseo Rector Esperabé 10 (☎ 923 218 482)

---

Walk out of the Plaza Mayor along Calle Zamora and stay on this street until you arrive at a roundabout with a large sculpture of a bull in the middle of it and the modern Plaza de Toro on its far side. Keep left here, following the signs for Zamora, then pass a large supermarket and soon reach the edge of town. The views open out of the flat *meseta* as you stick to the busy N630, passing a junkyard on the right that has large aircraft on display. You'll soon pass the Helmantico football ground, home to Salamanca Football Club, a team that generally wallows in the Spanish second division.

Keep straight on under a bridge for the E80. On the far side of the bridge, turn left off the N630 at the km335 sign, down a dirt track that runs parallel to the N630 and quickly leads to **Aldeaseca de Armuña** (🛒⬛€, 529km).

This lovely small village is slowly becoming a bedroom community for Salamanca, and the number of modern buildings is testament to this. Walk through a modern housing estate along the aptly named Calle Ruta de la Plata, then pass a *frontón* (pelota court) that dates from 1901. Curve left behind the church, then turn right into fields almost straight away, passing under telephone wires. At a junction in 100m turn left, then stay on this main track as it winds downhill heading west.

There's no shade along this section. At a T-junction near the bottom of a hollow turn right and cross a concrete bridge over the Río de la Encina. On the far side of the river, ignore the first junction and then turn right at the second junction just afterwards. This dirt track curves around to climb a small ridge and passes a cemetery on the left heading towards the village of **Castellanos de Villiquera** (⬛, 534km). Pass a squat *cruceiro* that seems to be missing its top section, then carry on past a *frontón* and curve left to the rather splendid church. The sixteenth-century building has a Gothic façade by Rodrigo Gil de

**Map 16** (key page 214)

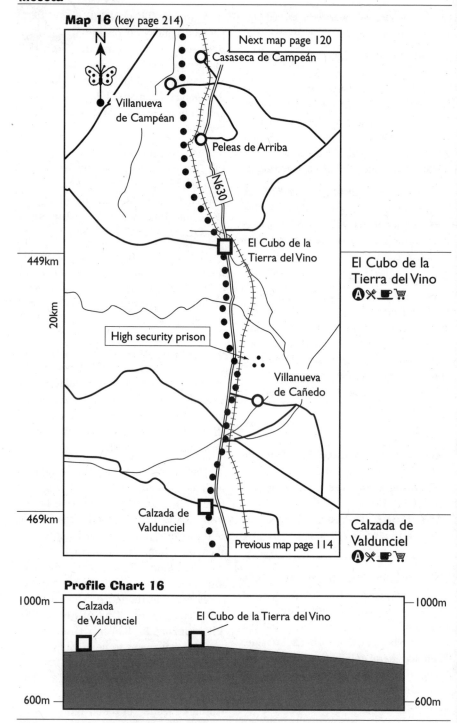

N

Next map page 120

Casaseca de Campeán

Villanueva
de Campéan

Peleas de Arriba

N630

449km

El Cubo de la
Tierra del Vino

20km

High security prison

Villanueva
de Cañedo

Calzada de
Valdunciel

469km

Previous map page 114

El Cubo de la
Tierra del Vino
Ⓐ✕🛏🛒

Calzada de
Valdunciel
Ⓐ✕🛏🛒

**Profile Chart 16**

1000m — Calzada
de Valdunciel

El Cubo de la Tierra del Vino

1000m

600m —

600m

Hontañón, an interesting porch and a sundial dated 1704; the rough walls suggest it was once part of a larger complex. There are two bars in the village, one by the church and the other near the N630.

Keep straight on out of the village. The flat *meseta* makes it easy to see the next village of Calzada de Valdunciel 4km away. Just before you enter it, cross a paved road and pass another *frontón*.

# Calzada de Valdunciel
Ⓐ✕▣☕🛒 (469km)

Calzada de Valdunciel is a rather windswept village, not quite tucked far enough into a hollow in the *meseta*. The twelfth-century Iglesia de Santa Elena has Romanesque and Gothic features but was heavily rebuilt in the sixteenth century. There's an image of Santiago Peregrino in the altar, and carved into the stone of the outside walls is the name of José Antonio Primo de Rivera, a haunting reminder of the civil war.

You can stay at the new **albergue** on Calle Cilla, or at the **Restaurant/Hostal El Pozo** ($, ☎ 923 310 016) on the N630, where there are also a few shops.

Leave the village by taking a bridge across a stream just after the *albergue*, then head uphill on a dirt track. After 500m, turn right and head towards the N630, then turn left along it to begin a long stretch of walking on tarmac.

After 5km, at a turning for Castillo del Buen Amor, you can pick up a dirt track just to the right of the N630. Note that after heavy rain this track can be waterlogged and it may be better to stick to the

road. The track shadows the road for 1km, then just as a large jail looms on the horizon you reach a stretch of disused tarmac road and the camino rejoins the N630. The Vía de la Plata is very badly marked along this stretch. You soon pick up a dirt track on the left-hand side of the road and then traverse a field towards some houses. Faded yellow arrows direct you straight on here, past a pond, through a gate and into some woods. This is a difficult route to follow, and it's simpler to turn right and return to the N630.

Turn left to follow the N630, then take the left-hand turning along the paved road into El Cubo de la Tierra del Vino.

# El Cubo de la Tierra del Vino
Ⓐ✕▣🛒 (449km)

A friendly little village that seems somewhat misnamed, as there's hardly a vine in sight in El Cubo de la Tierra del Vino. You can get meals in Bar Santo Domingo, where José will insist on taking your photo to add to his extensive collection of pilgrim portraits. There's a tiny **albergue** (4 beds, hot showers, €4) in the *ermita* at the far end of the village; you can get the key from house #6 in the main square, opposite the *ayuntamiento*.

Leave El Cubo on the old N630 and cross a bridge over the Arroyo San Cristóbal. Turn left 50m later down a paved road which quickly changes to a dirt track. The camino passes through farmland and initially parallels the railway; it can be muddy and waterlogged after rain. There are still very few vines, but some shade is provided by the holm oaks that line the train tracks.

At a T-junction near a level crossing 5km after leaving El Cubo, turn left to veer away from the railway, then turn right 50m later. The landscape opens up here, and there is very little shade. About 1km later, keep straight on at a crossroads next to some farm buildings, then continue straight on in another 1km, ignoring the track to your left. You can soon see mountains in the distance and the fertile Duero valley ahead, and you'll start to descend slowly through vines and pine. The track curves to the right then, some 500m after the last junction, veers right at a fork to follow a ridge. Lavender lines the route and there are patchwork fields all around.

You'll soon leave the ridge and descend more steeply along a section that can be particularly thick with sticky red mud. About 1km after the last junction, keep straight on at a crossroads with another dirt track, fork right at a group of poplars in another 1km, then fork left 50m later. Watch for birds of prey here, especially the red kite, which uses its distinctive forked tail like a rudder to change direction as it searches for food.

Keep straight on after another 1km at a Ruta de la Plata *miliario* placed here by the villagers of Villanueva de Campeán. You'll start to see more vines now, which grow well and need little irrigation in the region's sandy soil. Pass a small weather station and soon see the village ahead with the grand ruins of the Monesterio de Nuestra Señora del Soto away to the right. With binoculars, you can see decapitated stone statues on the building's second storey. Pass another modern

*miliario*, then cross a narrow tarmac road and enter **Villanueva de Campeán** on a paved road, passing a Vía de la Plata route map and another *miliario*. The buildings have lovely wooden doors with thick stone lintels, but in 2003 there were no facilities here. Pass a Camino de Santiago stone plaque on an abandoned building on the right. These plaques are a common sight in the province of Zamora and are inscribed with glowing prose about places along the route and the purpose of the camino.

Cross a tarmac road and leave the village on a dirt track. Fork right 100m later and pass a *miliario*, then keep straight on 500m later at another *miliario* and cross a stream via a concrete bridge. Walk through patchworked fields with vines and sunflowers lining the way. The camino is still following the Cañada Real, which is marked by white arrows pointing back the way you've come.

After 3km, as the village of San Marcial appears ahead, turn right at a crossroads with another dirt track, heading uphill slightly. Turn left 400m later, then in 1km turn left at a T-junction with a dirt road. Be careful here as the route isn't obvious. Turn right just 10m later up a grassy track at the edge of a field, heading uphill.

As you near the top of the hill, you'll see the village of Perdigón just off the camino on the right. At the top of the ridge 500m later there are great views of Zamora in the distance, its compact centre perched on a small hill and its suburbs sprawling unchecked out on to the *meseta*. Turn left at a T-junction with a broad dirt road here, then turn right 50m later to follow a tarmac road.

Turn left off this road a little under 1km later at a right-hand bend to walk once more on a dirt track. Cross a narrow road in 400m and keep straight on along a track which occasionally narrows to a thin path between reeds and long grasses, and can get boggy for short stretches. Keep straight on at a crossroads 1km or so after crossing the road to walk on a broad dirt track heading towards a concrete farm building. Turn left in 500m on to a dirt stone road, then in another 500m turn right on to another dirt road.

In a little under 1km, cross a stream and turn right at a crossroads immediately afterwards. Pass an industrial estate away to your left, and cross a tarmac road that leads to the estate 2km after the last junction. Keep straight on along a dirt track through wasteland, then turn right a little more than 1km later at a T-junction with a dirt road. Keep straight on 200m later as the road veers right, then pass a modern house 500m later and a concrete factory in another 1km.

From here, there are great views of Zamora's cathedral and imposing city walls across the Río Duero. Cross a tarmac road and walk downhill into the **Barrio de San Frontis** (🖳🛒), a suburb of Zamora, and towards the river along Calle de Fermoselle. Keep straight along the road as it reaches the Río Duero and veers right to shadow the river. In the water, you'll see the stone stumps of an old bridge and a beautiful weir. Zamora's houses are built right down to the river's edge, and one of them still has a water wheel. Pass the Convento de San Francisco on the right then turn left to cross the Puente de Piedra into town. Turn right into Calle Puente, then turn left at the museum in

Plaza Santa Lucía. Turn right behind the Iglesia de Santa Lucía then turn left into Calle Herreros to walk uphill to the Plaza Mayor.

---

# Zamora
🄷✕🖳€🛈🛒 (416km)

A small city on the Río Duero, Zamora's walls pack in splendid Romanesque monuments and meandering streets lined with tall, narrow houses. Zamorans come out in force for the Sunday afternoon *paseo* when the streets are crowded with well-groomed locals walking off their heavy Sunday lunch.

Once known as *el bien cercada* (the well-enclosed), Zamora once had seven city walls to defend its vital position on the Río Duero; in 939, Abderrahman III is said to have lost 40,000 men trying to capture the town from the Christians. The Moors eventually did manage to conquer Zamora in 985 under Almanzor, but they couldn't hold on for long. Zamora was rebuilt after 1065 by Fernando I, and the city benefited from a royal patronage that saw a frenzy of Romanesque church building.

At the top of town, within a ruined citadel, the **cathedral**'s Romanesque origins are hidden behind a Renaissance façade. The cathedral has a Byzantine-influenced dome with distinctive fish-scale tiling and corner turrets and a tall defensive belltower. Inside, there's a statue of Santiago Peregrino in a niche to the right of the chancel, and the choir stalls are carved with saucy images of nuns and monks blatantly disregarding the laws of celibacy. The cathedral museum contains sumptuous fifteenth- and sixteenth-century Flemish tapestries depicting scenes such as the Trojan War and Hannibal's epic

**Map 17** (key page 214)

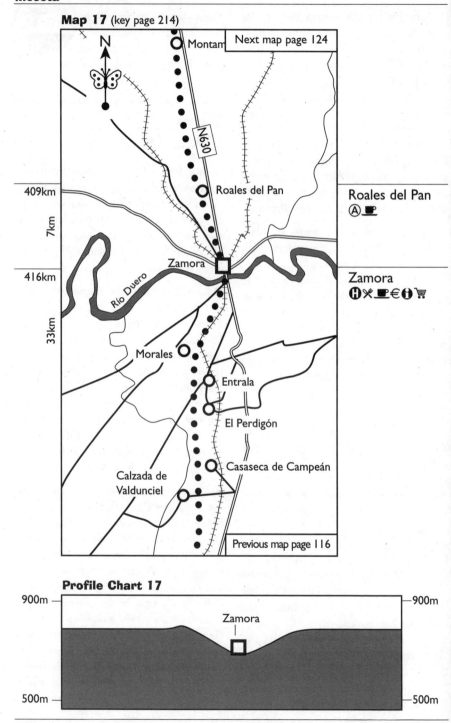

N630

Next map page 124

Montam

Roales del Pan

409km

7km

Zamora

Río Duero

416km

33km

Morales

Entrala

El Perdigón

Casaseca de Campeán

Calzada de
Valdunciel

Previous map page 116

Roales del Pan
Ⓐ ☕

Zamora
🏨✕☕€ℹ️🛒

**Profile Chart 17**

900m —

Zamora

500m —

— 900m

— 500m

adventures. Pilgrims can get a *sello* at the ticket office for the museum.

Zamora's *castillo* boasts an intact moat and splendid views over the new suburbs of the city from the old **walls**. The well-preserved walls themselves include the Postigo de la Traición (Traitor's Gate), where Sancho II was stabbed by a devious soldier pretending to lead the king to an unguarded entrance.

A striking monument to **Viriatus**, the Celtic Che Guevara, can be seen in the Plaza de Viriato. He fought a guerrilla-style war here against the invading Roman legions in the second century BC, before he was betrayed and brutally murdered by three of his followers who had been bribed by the ruthless Romans.

Zamora's **churches** were built during Romanesque times, and many have characteristic multilobed arches and heavily carved portals. Some of the best include Santa María la Nueva, with eighth-century capitals, and La Magdalena, with intricately decorated arches, gorgeous Romanesque pillars, and carved griffons and other fantastical creatures in the capitals. The town also boasts two Iglesias de Santiago. The Iglesia de Santiago del Burgos is a wonderful example of Romanesque simplicity and contains a statue of Santiago and a painting of Santiago Matamoros. The south door, high central nave and barrel vaulting are some of the finest in the city. Outside the old city walls to the west, pilgrims can find the tiny Ermita de Santiago de los Caballeros.

The Museo de Semana Santa includes *posas*, statues depicting Christ's Passion that are carried through the city during Easter week.

The **turismo** (☎ 980 531 845) is on Calle Santa Clara 20. Be sure to stock up on cash as there are no cashpoints until Tábara, 66km away.

## Accommodation

Zamora has no *albergue*, but the **youth hostel** just outside the city walls on Calle Villalpando 7 is reasonably priced.

**$ Hostal la Reina**, Calle La Reina 1 (☎ 980 533 939)

**$ Hostal Sanabria**, Plaza de la Puebla (☎ 980 526 672)

**$$$ Hostería Real de Zamora**, Cuesta de Pizarro 7 (☎ 980 534 545)

**$$$$ Parador de Zamora**, Plaza de Viriato 5 (☎ 980 514 497)

---

Leave Plaza Mayor and walk down Calle la Constanilla. Turn left down Calle de la Feria, then cross Avenida de la Plata on to Calle de la Puebla de Sanabria. Veer right on to Cuesta de la Morana and keep right as the road becomes Avenida de Galicia.

Keep straight on at a roundabout 3km from the Plaza Mayor, and walk alongside the N630 through a horrible industrial section; the track that once ran alongside this road has disappeared due to road-widening works. In a little under 4km, veer left down a side road at the Nutecal factory and enter **Roales del Pan** (Ⓐ🛏, 409km), a sleepy little one-horse town. The Iglesia de Nuestra Señora de la Asunción was heavily restored in the 1970s and now has more in common with the Disco era than its sixteenth-century origins. The **albergue** is basic (floor, cold water, donation); ask for the key in the *ayuntamiento* on the town square, where there's also a fountain and a Vía de la Plata *miliario*. There's a frequently closed bar on the main road.

Keep straight on to leave town on the

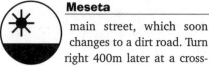 

main street, which soon changes to a dirt road. Turn right 400m later at a crossroads with another dirt road, then turn left 100m later. There are very few landmarks on the gently undulating *meseta*. There's no shade either, as you walk through huge fields of wheat and corn with the N630 away to your right, although you may see game birds such as grouse and partridge.

Pass a farm house on your right, 2km outside town. About 3km later, turn right down a dirt track, then keep straight on in a little over 1km for the village of Montamarta.

If you're after a little sustenance, turn right here to detour to the main road where the **Hotel El Asturiano ($)** has a bar, restaurant and rooms. Pass another farmhouse 500m after the junction; ignore the right-hand track here, but take the second right-hand track 100m later. Veer left at a fork in another 100m and keep straight on past a water tower to reach the village of **Montamarta** (❶✗⬛☂, 397km). Pass a camino plaque in a small well-kept park, then 50m later veer left down Calle Reblo, soon reaching Montamarta's adobe-and-stone church and its tiny *ayuntamiento*. The statue here is of El Zangarron, a mythical figure who plays a prominent part in the village's *fiesta* in the first week of January, when he chases the townsfolk through the street hitting them with a stick, a common pagan tradition in this corner of Iberia. There's a bar and shop in the village, but they are often closed.

From Montamarta, you can detour to Campillo to visit the Iglesia de San Pedro de la Nave; see page 105 for more details.

To leave Montamarta, turn left in front of the church, then turn first right at a fountain. Walk on a dirt track to head towards the Ermita de la Virgen del Castillo, which you can see ahead. This track takes you on a causeway across the bed of the Ricobayo reservoir; if the water level is high you'll need to head right and cross the reservoir via the N630 bridge instead. Go up the stairs to the right of the *ermita* and head past the graveyard. Turn left just beyond the *ermita* to walk on a dirt track, which soon merges with a broad, stony track. Pass some buildings in 500m then, in a little under 1km, cross a stream via a concrete bridge. The camino heads uphill and there's no shade until you reach a small group of holm oaks in 2km. As the main track curves left, turn right along a narrow path that heads through the trees and towards the N630.

Cross the N630 200m later, and keep straight on along a grassy track 100m later as the main track curves right, then carry straight on in another 200m as the main track curves right once more. In 500m, cross back over the N630 on to a grassy track then, in another 300m, keep straight on along a dirt track at a crossroads with another dirt road, and fork right 20m later. You can see the reservoir now as you walk downhill towards it, passing some modern houses on the right.

As you get closer and, if the water is low, you'll see ruined walls poking out of the reservoir. The water level varies throughout the year, and the route varies with it. Early in the year when the level is higher, keep on this track and turn left on reaching the N630 to cross the reservoir on the road bridge. It's simplest from here to continue on the road to Fontanillas de Castro, some 3km away. When the water is lower a longer, more convoluted but much nicer route circles the reservoir on various tracks and paths.

To follow this low-water route, veer left 100m after the houses to walk on a narrow grassy track down towards the water, and walk under the N630 bridge, a good spot to see herons. There's not much of a path on the other side, so it's easiest to go up to the road, walk along it for 100m, and then turn left down a dirt track that leads towards a house. Pass the house 200m later, and turn right to walk along a grassy track. Follow close to the edge of the reservoir until you're almost underneath the high ruined walls of Castrotorafe, then turn right to climb up a small gully towards the walls. Again, there's no definite track here and the route varies according to the water level in the reservoir; there are also very few yellow markers.

**Castrotorafe** was declared a national monument in 1931, and its walls look very impressive from a distance. This fortified medieval town was founded by the Knights of the Order of Santiago and was built to control the crossing of the Río Esla. The town was abandoned in the eighteenth century and only the walls remain; modern-day inhabitants are cattle and the occasional fisherman.

To leave the castle, follow the dirt towards the N630, then after 100m and before reaching the road turn left along a dirt track that can be muddy in wet weather. Turn right a little over 500m later on to a rocky path that soon widens to a grassy track. The mountains to the left are topped by a line of modern wind turbines, which you'll pass near Tábara,

36km away. You'll soon see the village of Fontanillas de Castro ahead, as the camino heads towards the N630. Turn right here to stop at the café-bar or turn left to follow the N630 into **Fontanillas de Castro** (⚏✕, 385km).

The village feels like a step back in time, with wooden carts and adobe-and-brick houses. The underground *bodegas* that dot the landscape in this region are carved right out of the mud. Turn left to enter the village, then turn right at the Iglesia de la Concepción de la Virgen. Keep straight on down Calle Cemeterio. As the village ends, you'll see *palomares* (dovecotes) in the field away to the right, which have been used for centuries in northwest Iberia to farm pigeons for both fertilizer and food.

As the paved road ends at the edge of Fontanillas, turn right. A couple of kilometres out of the village the camino descends a little to a shallow valley bottom with trees and a paved section of track. Fork right 200m later, then turn right in 300m to follow a narrower track. Keep straight on in another 300m past a farm building to walk on a very narrow path through a field and then alongside a building.

Turn left 50m later to walk on a sidewalk alongside the N630 into **Riego del Camino** (Ⓐ⚏, 381km), a tiny hamlet with the sixteenth-century Iglesia de San Cristóbal. There's also a basic **albergue** (mattresses, hot shower, donation) in the old people's home; be warned that the shower on the ground floor is also the old folks' only bathroom and you'll have to vacate in a hurry if someone needs a pee. If you're flagging, there's also a bar on the main road.

**Map 18** (key page 214)

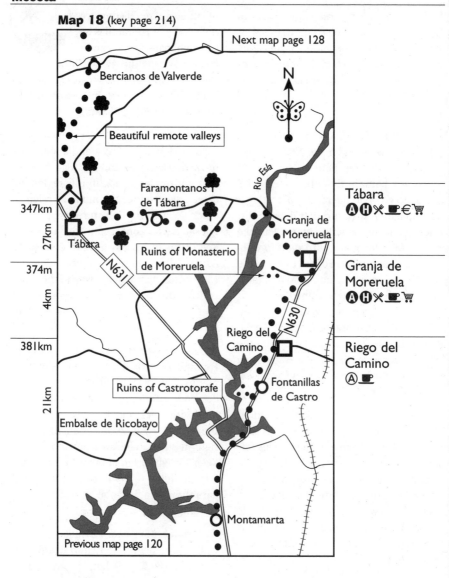

Next map page 128

N

Bercianos de Valverde

Beautiful remote valleys

Rio Esla

Faramontanos de Tábara

347km

27km

Tábara

N631

374m

4km

Granja de Moreruela

Ruins of Monasterio de Moreruela

381km

N630

Riego del Camino

21km

Ruins of Castrotorafe

Fontanillas de Castro

Embalse de Ricobayo

Montamarta

Previous map page 120

**Tábara**
Ⓐ Ⓗ ✕ 💺 € 🛒

**Granja de Moreruela**
Ⓐ Ⓗ ✕ 💺 🛒

**Riego del Camino**
Ⓐ 💺

**Profile Chart 18**

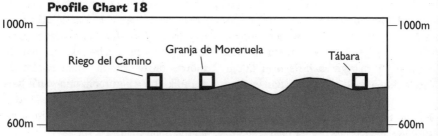

1000m — — 1000m

Riego del Camino

Granja de Moreruela

Tábara

600m — — 600m

Just 50m after joining the N630 in Riego del Camino, turn left off it once more. The paved road through the village ends in 100m, as does the tiny village itself. Turn right here, with views of the village church on the right, and walk towards a plain, whitewashed *palomar*. Keep straight on 20m after passing the *palomar* and begin walking slowly uphill. Keep straight on in another 3km, ignoring the junction to the left, and see Granja de Moreruela up ahead.

Pass some farm buildings on the left 2km later and get good views of the houses on the hill ahead and *bodegas* built into the hill. You enter Granja to camino advertising for Bar El Peregrino. Cross a minor road 400m after the farm buildings, then cross a small bridge and turn right. Turn left as you reach N630, and left again 50m later at a brick church with a camino stone. The Vía de la Plata splits here. Turn left for the route via Ourense, and go right uphill to head towards Astorga and for Bar El Peregrino, which has the key to the *albergue*.

# Granja de Moreruela
Ⓐ Ⓗ ✕ ▇▆ 🍷 (374km)

Stretched along the N630 and rising up to the edge of a small escarpment, Granja is a small, friendly village. The basic **albergue** (6 beds, cold shower, donation) is next to the N630 by a small park; get the key from Bar El Peregrino, which offers a warm welcome and tasty, home-cooked meals. Be sure to check out the bar's cellar, which features several tiny rooms perfect for a small medieval banquet.

About 3km further down the N630 is the **Hostal Oviedo** ($, ☎ 980 586 080); to rejoin the camino from the *hostal*, turn left to walk down the ZA123 all the way to Puente Quintos. There's a small shop near the church on the N630, and a *panadería* in the yellow building behind the *albergue*; neither have signs. From Granja, you can detour west to the ruined Monesterio de Moreruela, the first Cistercian convent in Spain, which dates from late eleventh century. It's 4km outside the village; to get there, turn left off the N630 just before Granja.

To continue the Vía de la Plata to Santiago de Compostela via Ourense, follow Calle Dr Gonzalez Galindo out of Granja and soon start to walk on a dirt track with lots of *bodegas* and *palomares* on your right. After just over 1km, keep straight on at a crossroads, then in 20m at a second junction turn right and start to walk uphill.

You'll soon catch sight of wind turbines on your left as the camino undulates over small hills. These turbines were erected in the spring of 2003 in an effort by Spain to increase its green power capacity. Keep straight on, going downhill into a large hollow, then climb up the other side and turn right to begin walking up a long hill. The track passes through forest and dense green bush, but the weary pilgrim is rewarded near the summit with great views of the town of Benavente, which is on the camino to Astorga over 30km to the north. Turn left at a T-junction 200m after the crest and soon clamber down a very steep 50m section which can be slippery in the wet. Once safely at the bottom, curve right and join the ZA123.

This is one of the most stunning sections of the Vía de la Plata, and although you're now walking on a paved road, your eyes are soon drawn to the majestic Río Esla. As you follow the ZA123 across the modern bridge look to your left downstream to see the five remaining arches of the old medieval bridge that still spans half the river.

Once on the far side of the modern bridge, turn immediately left to follow a narrow stone trail around a cliff face. This is a wonderful spot to stop for a rest, and the views of the tranquil river are stunning. Follow a loose trail (unsuitable for bicycles) down to the river's edge, where those brave enough can swim. The camino continues alongside the river, with good views of the medieval bridge on the far side of the Río Esla, until a large boulder blocks any more progress along the river. Turn right here to climb away from the river on a steep, well-marked trail between two trees.

Keep to the left as you approach the top of the escarpment, then veer right once the trail flattens out. Yellow markers are painted on trees, but there's no obvious single trail for over 100m, until you pass to the left of a ruined stone building and a dirt track reappears.

Follow the dirt track, then turn left 500m later, and in another 1km at a second junction, turn left again. Keep going through a mix of holm oak and scrub for another 1km, cross another dirt track and emerge from the scrub in 200m at the gates of the Finca Val de la Rosa. Turn right here and keep straight on, ignoring all junctions. Shortly after crossing a paved road, turn left at a crossroads, and you'll soon see Faramontanos de Tábara

and Tábara ahead across the valley. The approach to Faramontanos de Tábara winds this way and that, appearing to pass parallel to the village before finally turning right for an arrow-straight, kilometre-long approach.

Enter **Faramontanos de Tábara** (⬛) on Calle Benavente, a street lined with *bodegas*, some of which have collapsed through neglect. At the first *plaza* bear right then take the first right past a bar. Keep straight on past the church and leave town on Calle Pozo. At a modern *ermita*, bear right and emerge at the edge of the village. Turn left and walk down the paved road, passing a dual-purpose football pitch and basketball court on your right. At a crossroads soon afterwards, keep straight on over the ZA123.

Follow this shadeless dirt track for a little more than 2km, then at a crossroads, turn left and cross a stream. Along this stretch, there are good views of the Sierra de la Culebra to the south and of the wind turbines on the nearby hills. Shortly afterwards and about 100m before the track reaches the ZA123, turn right down a very wide dirt track. Follow this track for over 1km, then keep straight on along a grassy path as the track bends left under some power pylons. You're now walking between a wall on your left and a wire fence on your right towards the village of Tábara, which you see ahead. Above the fields that surround the village, look for sparrowhawks and buzzards.

You'll soon see Tábara's distinctive church tower, as the path widens to a dirt track. The track seems to wind its way past Tábara before joining a larger dirt track just below the tower. Turn left for Tábara and cross the main road to arrive at the village square, or turn right to bypass the village and continue along the Vía de la Plata.

# Tábara

**Ⓐ Ⓗ ✕ ⬛ € 🛒** (347km)

The unusual, square tower of the Iglesia de San Salvador dominates the skyline and is the most visible remains of the Monasterio de San Salvador, founded by Abbot Froila in the eleventh century. Magio and his disciple Emeterio illustrated the famous *Beato de Tábara* manuscript here, which is now in the Archivo Histórico Nacional de Madrid. There's an excellent new **albergue** (20 beds, hot water, kitchen, donation), about 500m from the town square; ask in the *ayuntamiento* or the shop beside the church for the key. Outside the *albergue* there's an old *lavadero*, where you can wash your clothes in the way the Spaniards have for hundreds of years. Alternatively, you can stay at the **Hostal Restaurante Galicia** ($, ☎ 980 590 136), 1km out of town on the N630; turn left at the church to get here. There are plenty of shops and bars in the village but pilgrims looking for a substantial meal will have to head to the *hostal*.

---

If you stayed in Tábara, retrace your steps to the dirt track just below the church tower. Head down the track, aiming for the wind turbines on the far hills. After just under 2km, turn left at a second junction under some phone wires, then cross a paved road and keep straight on. Just 300m later, turn right at a crossroads, looking carefully for yellow arrows that may be obscured due to track widening for fire prevention. Slowly begin to climb to the saddle of the hill to the left

of the giant turbines; if you stop walking you can hear the thumping sound they make as they rotate. Spain is one of the three largest producers of wind power in the world, after Germany and the US. Each wind turbine will replace 2700 tons of carbon dioxide, 14 tons of sulphur dioxide and nine tons of nitrogen oxide per year, and such is the pace of construction of these striking monoliths that Galicia alone already has 56 wind farms.

Once at the saddle, turn right at a junction, then turn left 50m later just before a paved road. Follow a wide dirt track downhill, then at a fork in 100m keep right. The landscape is a little wilder here with scattered fields and trees as you descend into a large bowl, and it's not uncommon to see foxes skulking in the field edges. Keep on the same track as it slowly curves to the left around a hill, crossing a stream on a concrete bridge. As the trail begins a long climb, keep right at a junction. This region is home to wolves and wild boar, and local bars along this section of the Vía de la Plata often advertise upcoming hunts, display photos of hunters with their prey and mount stuffed heads of favourite kills. Make sure you stay on the track on Sunday mornings, a popular time for locals to head out hunting, sometimes immediately following a Saturday-night drinking spree.

At the crest of the hill you'll see the mountains of Galicia ahead, a sure sign that in a few days you'll be leaving Castilla y León. You can also see the village of Villanueva de las Peras, which you bypass, as the camino's route is further east along the Rio Castrón valley.

**Map 19** (key page 214)

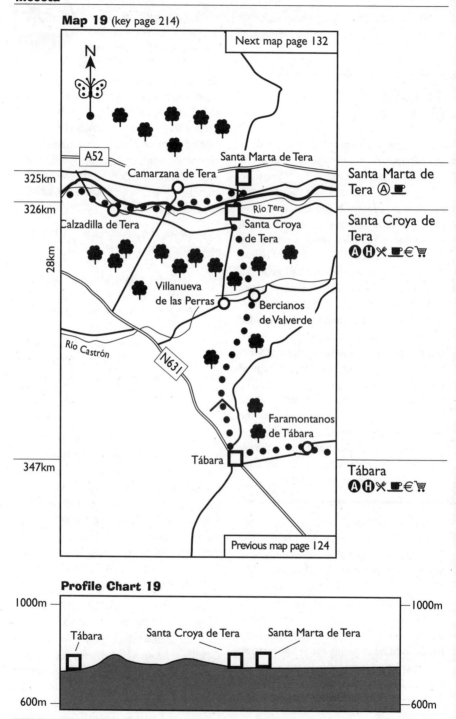

N

Next map page 132

A52

325km

326km

28km

Camarzana de Tera

Santa Marta de Tera

Santa Marta de
Tera Ⓐ 🍽

Río Tera

Calzadilla de Tera

Santa Croya
de Tera

Santa Croya de
Tera
Ⓐ Ⓗ ✕ 🍽 € 🛒

Villanueva
de las Perras

Bercianos
de Valverde

Río Castrón

N631

Faramontanos
de Tábara

347km

Tábara

Tábara
Ⓐ Ⓗ ✕ 🍽 € 🛒

Previous map page 124

**Profile Chart 19**

1000m — — 1000m

Tábara        Santa Croya de Tera        Santa Marta de Tera

600m — — 600m

Head downhill and once at the bottom turn right, then veer left at a fork soon afterwards towards Villanueva de las Peras. At a crossroads next to a lone white house turn right, walking past fields of vines with lots of colourful scarecrows. In 500m, turn left and walk through head-high cistus bushes, their heady-scented monotony broken by pockets of sweet chestnuts.

Once out of the scrub, you're able to see **Bercianos de Valverde** (🍴) ahead. Cross the paved road and then turn right into the village, following Calle Mayor to the main square. The tiny village bar is off to your right. The camino leaves the square by the road on the left. Soon after leaving the village, cross the Río Castrón via a concrete bridge.

The camino zigzags here, mostly to skirt poplar plantations. First turn left at a crossroads, then turn right 100m later and left again. Finally, turn right and pass some *bodegas* carved into the hillside and begin a short, steep climb.

At the top of the climb, there's a small bench under the trees that makes a good rest stop. Keep straight on for 4km through scrub and holm oaks, passing adobe walls that are slowly collapsing from neglect. The land here was once farmed intensively, but as rural people migrate to the cities, fields are being left fallow.

Emerge from the scrub to spectacular views of the mountains of Galicia up ahead. Walk downhill past *bodegas*, some of which are thought to be 300 years old, and see Santa Croya de Tera. The innocuous looking corrugated metal building to your left sits on top of a delicious natural

spring; sample the water from a pipe at its bottom right corner. Join a paved road and follow it into town.

# Santa Croya de Tera
🅐🅗✗🍴€🛒 (326km)

Stretched along the Río Tera, Santa Croya is a lovely village, well stocked with shops, including one of the best butchers along the camino. **Casa Anita** on the far side of the village has rooms (**$$**, ☎ 980 645 244) on the first floor and a gorgeous private **albergue** (20 beds, hot showers, €8) on the ground floor. If you stay for dinner, the friendly owners will serve wine from their *bodega*, one of the cluster of underground cellars that you passed on your way into the village.

Walk out of Santa Croya de Tera on the road along the river. On leaving the village, cross a series of three bridges over the Río Tera; be careful on the last one as it's only wide enough for a single truck. Almost immediately, you come to the Plaza Mayor in **Santa Marta de Tera** (🅐🍴, 325km), where you'll find a twelfth-century Romanesque church, built over an earlier Mozarabic building. The church, which has echoes of the Iglesia de San Isidro in León, has a square apse and lovely capitals. The floor plan is based on a Latin cross with three equal arms, and there's a statue of Santiago Peregrino in the south porch. The adjacent garden is a tranquil spot for a rest. The **albergue** (floor, hot showers, donation) is also in the Plaza Mayor; ask at the village bar for the keys.

Santa Marta de Tera marks the spot where the Vía de la Plata starts to head almost due west, following the banks of the beautiful Río Tera all the way upstream to Puebla de Sanabria. Three separate dams have altered the Valle de Sanabria dramatically since medieval times, and many of the villages in the valley are named after the river. Leave the Plaza Mayor via a narrow street on your right as you face the church. If you've come over the bridge from Santa Croya de Tera, turn sharp left to double back on yourself.

The road soon becomes a dirt track through poplar plantations. Turn left off this track after a little under 1km to walk down a pretty, narrower track. For the next few kilometres, you'll wind your way along various tracks lined with poplars and other deciduous trees. Keep an eye out for yellow markers, as there are many small junctions. Turn left at a T-junction in 500m, then left at another T-junction 300m later. Cross a bridge in 100m, then fork right immediately afterwards to head through fields of corn and poplar plantations that are alternately being planted and chopped down.

Turn right at a T-junction 1km later, then keep straight on in 500m past a white building, ignoring a trail to the right. The camino heads further up the Río Tera as it approaches the mountains. Keep straight on along a grassy track 300m later as the main track curves right. Turn right 1km later at a minor road, then turn left in 30m to follow a wider road across the Río Tera, past a recreation area, La Barca, on the right.

Turn right immediately after the bridge to walk on a path through the recreation area on the far bank. Turn right at a T-junction just under 2km later, then turn left 300m later on to a narrow path that winds through trees. It's difficult to see the yellow arrows at first but the path widens to a grassy track at the edge of a poplar plantation in less than 100m. Another 100m later, you'll find yourself walking alongside a water channel and next to some cornfields. In about 400m, turn right on to a grassy track; this is a beautiful walk, shaded and vibrantly green. At a T-junction with a broad dirt track 200m later, turn left then, in another 200m, turn right on to a paved road.

Turn right off the road a little over 500m later to walk on a dirt track, passing a fountain with delicious water in 200m. Cross a small bridge, passing *bodegas* in the hill to the left, and see **Calzadilla de la Tera** (▆) ahead. This is a place that seems to have remained in a time warp. Here, people and animals enter wooden doors into the adobe houses with straw roofs and the women all appear to be widows, dressed in black and mourning their late husbands. Don't rush past the gorgeous but sadly abandoned Iglesia de Santa Justa y Rufina at the edge of town. Even though this small church is slipping into ruin, it's fascinating to poke about in its bowels like some kind of forensic architect. Walk into the village, then turn right at a junction to leave it. Alternatively, if you want to take your chances and see if the village bar is open, carry straight on at this junction.

Cross a concrete bridge over a canal and turn left immediately afterwards to follow the canal along a grassy track. The fields are much smaller here, often worked by hand, and it's common to see older women with donkeys and carts farming the land. The path itself is narrow and grassy and lined with flowers in spring and summer. Keep straight on 500m later as the path crosses a dirt track, just across the canal from a large square adobe *palomar*.

In a little under 1km, pass a canal lock, turn left to cross a concrete bridge over the canal, and walk into the village of **Olleros de Tera** (■▜). Take the second right in the village then veer left almost immediately. There are a couple of bars just off the camino to your right and a small shop in an unmarked house near the church, although you'll have to wait until late morning for the *pan* van to show up.

On leaving the village you reach a tarmac road. From here, there are two alternative routes, both described below.

The first option heads down to the Río Tera. The riverside path can be overgrown in spring and is better later in the year when the route is more well worn and water levels are lower. At the road, turn right, then turn left 10m later to walk along a quiet tarmac road that changes to a dirt track edged with vines 1km later. Pass the Santuario de Agavanzal and walk behind it to follow a track next to a house. Just 100m later, fork left on to another dirt track. Turn left at a T-junction 500m later to head away from the river, where a sign warns of the dangers of suddenly rising water levels. In just 20m, turn right on to a grassy path that winds through cistus. Keep straight on at a second *peligro* (danger) sign, this time paying no heed to the dangers that may come. The overgrown path is beautiful and passes very close to the

river, then climbs steeply uphill to meet an old tarmac road. Turn left here, walking uphill, and reach the dam in 500m.

The second option is longer and not well marked but may be better early in the year or after heavy rain. This is also the best route for cyclists. Turn left out of the village, then turn right 200m later, following a line of telephone poles. Follow a narrow tarmac road and keep on this road, for once ignoring yellow arrows that direct you left (this is a much longer bicycle route, but even cyclists should avoid it.) A large antenna acts as a beacon to guide you to the dam. About 200m from the dam, join a paved road and turn right.

Whichever route you take, you'll wind up at the dam, with a vast, calm reservoir to your left and a narrow river on the other side. Walk across the road along the top of the dam, then at the end of the dam, turn left and follow a paved road. In 50m, turn left down a narrower paved road that hugs the edge of the reservoir. There are some sheltered spots for a picnic and some good places to paddle, although signs warn against swimming too close to the dam.

In 2km, cross a trickle of a stream via a concrete bridge and veer away from the reservoir. Turn left 100m later on meeting another road, and soon enter **Villar de Farfón**, a tiny village of adobe-and-stone houses. Turn right at a T-junction to leave the village, or left to visit the church, where the weary can snatch a brief *siesta* on a covered bench. Follow the main street out of the village, as the tarmac road changes to a walled grassy lane. The walls soon end but the lane

**Map 20** (key page 214)

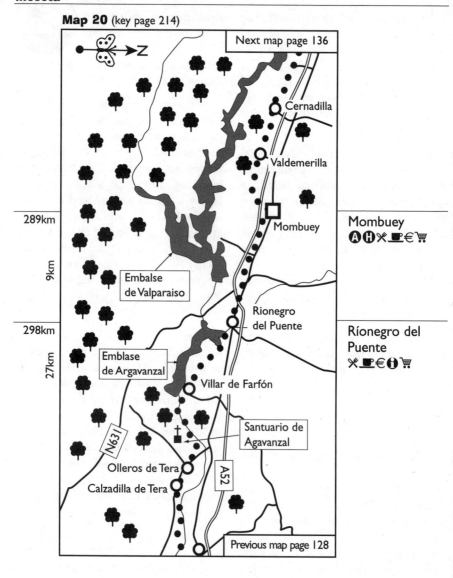

Next map page 136

Z

Cernadilla

Valdemerilla

289km

Mombuey

9km

Embalse
de Valparaiso

Rionegro
del Puente

298km

Emblase
de Argavanzal

Villar de Farfón

27km

Santuario de
Agavanzal

N631

A52

Olleros de Tera

Calzadilla de Tera

Previous map page 128

Mombuey
🅐🅗✕☕€🛒

Ríonegro del
Puente
✕☕€ℹ🛒

**Profile Chart 20**

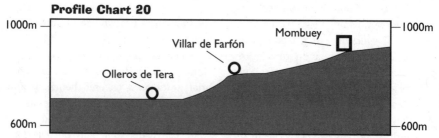

1000m

Mombuey

Villar de Farfón

Olleros de Tera

600m

1000m

600m

continues through a pastoral scene of fields, holm oaks and great views of the approaching Sierra de la Cabrera, its highest peak Vizcodillo standing tall at 2122m.

The vegetation slowly changes to scrub. Look out for piles of frantically dug earth left by wild boar as they snuff through the soil for roots and mushrooms. This remote corner of Spain is also home to wolves, although the chance of seeing one is slight as these animals are too smart to trouble a pilgrim. Climb slightly, then get great views of the mountains as the path narrows and you head downhill through a scrubland of holm oak, cistus and lavender.

Veer left some 4km from Villar de Farfón to cross a concrete bridge. Pass a group of modern houses 200m later, now following a dirt-and-stone road alongside the main road. Pass the now-closed Hostal Maxim. Just before Rionegro del Puente, keep straight on to ford the Río Negro via a concrete causeway. Turn right at the end of the causeway and walk under the road via a tunnel and turn immediately left. Turn left again 30m later to go under the road once more via another tunnel, then climb up a short rise to reach Ríonegro del Puente.

# Ríonegro del Puente
✗🚍€🛈🍽 (298km)

The Santuario de Nuestra Señora de la Carballeda in Ríonegro is run by the Cofradía de los Falifos, one of the oldest pilgrim organizations in existence; the bar opposite offers *sellos* and *bocadillos*. On the other side of the main road, a former pilgrim hospital is being restored. The only remnant of the Iglesia de Santiago is a tower that now looms over the town cemetery; there's still an image of Santiago at the base of the tower. The village's most famous son is Losada, who founded the city of Caracas, capital of Venezuela.

Pilgrims lucky enough to pass through here at the end of October may be able to join in the annual wild mushroom festival. There's a small *turismo* next to the library, near the *ayuntamiento*.

To leave Ríonegro, walk around the *santuario*, cross the main road and veer left up a paved street. Just before reaching the main road again in about 300m, turn right next to a ruined house to go down a narrow path. This widens to a track, which curves left just before the motorway. Take the second tunnel under the motorway, then turn immediately left to walk on a broad dirt road at the other side of the motorway. At a junction for Zamora, curve right and veer away from the motorway as the track becomes grassy. Pass a gas plant on the left a little over 1km after passing under the motorway then, 300m later, cross a road and walk on a narrower grassy path.

The camino heads through open grassland with great views of the mountains to the right. After a little more than 1km, the track becomes a more definite path through scrub. Keep straight on in about 300m as the main track veers left towards the road. Again, you'll find yourself walking across open grassland with very few yellow arrows. In about 2km the track widens as you see Mombuey ahead. Turn left 300m later on meeting a broad dirt road, heading towards Hostal La Ruta on the outskirts of town. Walk behind the hotel on a paved road, then join the main road 1km later and head along it into Mombuey.

# Mombuey
**ⒶⒽ✕💼€🛒** (289km)

Mombuey is famous for its thirteenth-century **Iglesia de Nuestra Señora de la Asunción**, a remarkable church built by the Templar Knights at the height of their power in the region. The distinctive fortified tower has an external staircase and rounded roof. Inside, the gorgeous painted wooden ceiling is a rare and wonderfully preserved example of this type of art. The lovely Romanesque Virgin was uncovered during restoration work and the image of the crucifixion was brought here from the Rhine.

Although almost everyone in Mombuey is friendly and helpful, the *albergue* key is grumpily guarded by the town mayor, who also runs the Hostal Rapiña on the main road. The tiny **albergue** (2 beds, mattresses, hot showers, donation) itself is on Calle Iglesia, the side street opposite the bar. It has thick stone walls and a massive wooden table, ideal for communal eating. Alternative rooms and meals are available at the **Hostal Rapiña** ($, ☎ 980 652 120) and the **Hostal La Ruta** ($$, ☎ 980 642 730). Pilgrims will find Mombuey well stocked with shops and bars.

To leave Mombuey, turn right down Calle Rodrigo, just in front of the Iglesia de Nuestra Señora de la Asunción. Turn right again 100m later as the paved road changes to a dirt track that parallels the main road. Cross a side road 500m later, and immediately veer left to walk on a dirt track, initially parallel to the main road. Pass a farm 1km later and walk through trees; the oaks and broom block the sight if not the sound of traffic from the busy road. In 1km, cross the motorway via a bridge. Turn right down a minor forestry track 300m later and see **Valdemerilla** ahead, then turn left 1km later to enter the village on a paved road. At the village fountain, turn right down Calle Principe de Asturias and keep right 50m later. Turn left in another 50m to leave the village on a gravel road.

The camino heads through more open country now although there are still lots of holm oaks. Some 2km from Valdemerilla, reach a shallow valley bottom, a lovely spot with mostly abandoned fields bordered by dry stone walls. A little over 1km later, enter **Cernadilla** (💼🛒, 281km), passing the simple stone Ermita del Cristo on the right. Fork left to continue on the camino, or detour right for the village's bar/shop, in front of a well some 50m away.

Walk to the right of another church, cross a bridge and veer left past a fountain, then keep straight on to leave the village on a walled lane lined with poplars and oaks. After 1km or so, pass an *ermita* and a fountain and keep straight on. You'll soon reach **San Salvador de Palazuelos**, where you can climb the belltower of the beautiful Iglesia de Santiago for great views of the surrounding countryside and the village itself, and to see the huge bells close up. Veer left to leave the village, walking downhill on a paved road that changes to a dirt track as it heads down into a gorgeous valley.

Climb steeply up the other side of the valley, then keep straight on just over 1km later, ignoring the track to your right. Continue straight on in another 300m, then turn right at a minor road next to group of chestnuts. Turn left 300m later on to paved minor road. Pass a *cruceiro* 500m later, and enter **Entrepeñas** in another 200m. Walk past the church and a fountain then, as the village peters out some 400m later, veer left down a dirt track. Take the left-hand fork 500m later down a lovely walled lane, and keep straight on in another 1km to cross the motorway via a bridge.

Keep straight on at a crossroads with another dirt track in 300m, then turn left down a path 150m later, keeping an eye out for yellow arrows painted on low stones. You'll soon see the church in Asturianos ahead as the path widens. Veer left to cross a stream 150m later, walk uphill past a football field, then walk to the right of a church graveyard as the track becomes paved. A picnic table in front of the impressive Iglesia de la Asuncíon is an inviting spot for a rest. Veer right just past the church and reach the main road in 100m. Cross the road to continue the camino, or turn right for **Asturianos** (✗◼☕, 272km), where there's good food at the village bars.

To continue along the camino, turn left at a paved road 100m after the main road, then in 300m turn right to walk along the main road. Turn right just 200m later down a narrower road as views open up of the mountains ahead. In 300m, turn left down a grassy track, a beautiful section that winds downhill through oaks. Turn right at an old paved road in 500m, then 20m later turn right

on to a grassy path that quickly becomes more rocky and broadens as it heads uphill. The track can be muddy in patches but it's a wonderful route and there are great views.

About 1km further on, join a wider track coming from the left and soon see the village of **Palacios de Sanabria** to the left. Cross a road 200m later then curve left around the Santuario de San Cristo de la Pierdad. Turn right at a road 100m later, then go left in 10m to walk on a grassy path. After almost 2km, cross a road and continue straight on a track that's shaded by a group of chestnut trees. After 400m, cross a road and enter **Remesal**. Fork right immediately then fork left 40m later. The village has beautiful stone-and-slate houses with stone-slab external staircases and thick wooden balconies. Keep straight on past the village fountain then turn right down a narrow path and leave the village on a grassy track, following a Camino de Santiago sign.

Fork right 100m later on a track that soon narrows to a grassy path. Watch carefully for yellow arrows and then follow a dry stone wall. Veer left after 300m, following another dry stone wall at an open section where a line of pylons goes uphill. This section can be overgrown, and it's often easier to walk on the left-hand side of the wall rather than the right-hand side, where the yellow arrows lead. This confusing section soon ends and you join a broad track next to the motorway. Turn left 200m later to scoot down a small bank and cross the motorway on a bridge. Veer left immediately after the bridge to continue on a track.

**Map 21** (key page 214)

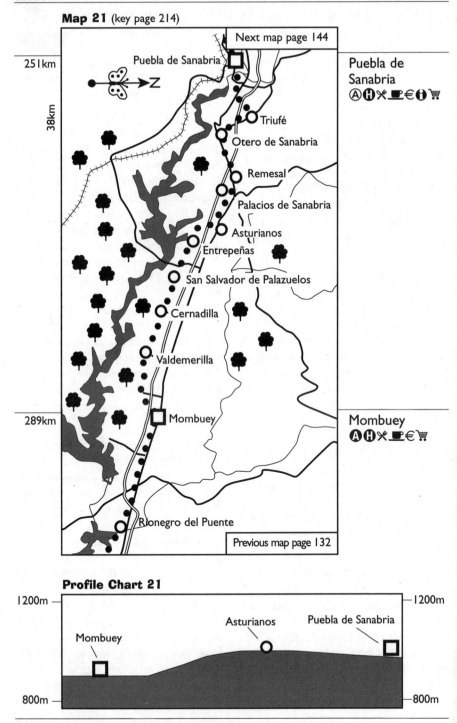

Next map page 144

Puebla de Sanabria

251km

38km

Triufé

Otero de Sanabria

Remesal

Palacios de Sanabria

Asturianos

Entrepeñas

San Salvador de Palazuelos

Cernadilla

Valdemerilla

289km

Mombuey

Rionegro del Puente

Previous map page 132

Puebla de
Sanabria
Ⓐ🅗✕💺€ⓘ🛒

Mombuey
Ⓐ🅗✕💺€🛒

**Profile Chart 21**

1200m ─                                                    ─1200m

Asturianos          Puebla de Sanabria

Mombuey

800m ─                                                     ─800m

Turn right 300m later at an often muddy section to walk on a grassy overgrown path, then head right in another 200m to follow a narrow path through fields and alongside dry stone walls. The yellow arrows can be difficult to see, but the church up ahead in **Otero de Sanabria** (■✗🛒) provides a distinctive landmark. Above the south portal, there's a stunning wooden carving of seven sinners roasting in stylized hell fires. At the end of October, there's a big *romería* (religious procession) to the nearby Santuario de la Virgen de los Remedios. Keep straight on past the church and fountain, then turn right at a very large house 200m later. Turn right in another 300m at a paved road, and follow this twisty route all the way to Triufé, passing dense scrub and heading under the motorway 500m after Otero.

Cross a bridge and soon enter **Triufé**, walking uphill into the village. Turn left down the first side road in the village, passing the simple church. Triufé is a pretty place where stone houses have external staircases and thick wooden lintels above the door. Turn left on to a paved road on leaving the village. Cross the motorway on a bridge just over 500m later, and reach the N525 in another 500m. Turn right here to walk along the main road, passing the Hotel Henri Mari 200m later, then turn left at the roundabout in 300m.

Enter Puebla de Sanabria 500m later, then cross a bridge over the Río Tera in another 500m or so. Turn left at the end of the bridge and enter the centre of town. To reach the *ayuntamiento* in the Plaza Mayor, turn right up Calle Costanilla and keep heading uphill into the old town.

**Regional Map** (key page 214)

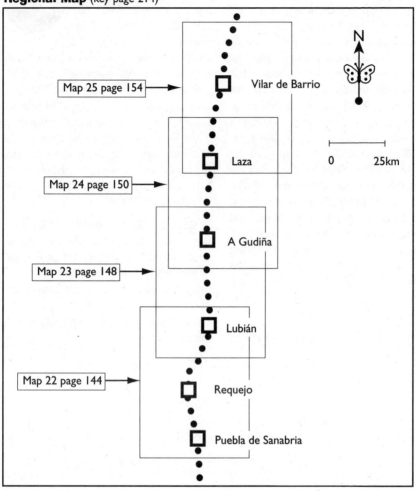

Map 25 page 154

Vilar de Barrio

Map 24 page 150

Laza

0    25km

Map 23 page 148

A Gudiña

Lubián

Map 22 page 144

Requejo

Puebla de Sanabria

## What's the Weather Like?

|                  | Jan   | April | July | Oct   |
|------------------|-------|-------|------|-------|
| **Sun**          | 3hrs  | 5hrs  | 7hrs | 5hrs  |
| **Rainfall**     | 30cm  | 19cm  | 6cm  | 19cm  |
| **Maximum Temp** | 6°C   | 13°C  | 24°C | 14°C  |
| **Minimum Temp** | -2°C  | 3°C   | 12°C | 5°C   |

Average hours of sun, total average rainfall in cm and average temperature in degrees celsius

# Cordillera Cantábrica

## Puebla de Sanabria to Vilar de Barrio

From Puebla de Sanabria, the Vía de la Plata clambers over a couple of mountain ranges before crossing into Galicia and descending towards Ourense. Despite the region's harsh climate, there are hundreds of beautiful hamlets in incredibly isolated locations, which are gorgeous in sunshine and desolate when the weather turns bad.

 **Walking**

## Geography

High winds batter the shale mountain ranges whatever the season and inhibit the growth of all but the hardiest life, and the proximity of the Atlantic Ocean means that heavy rain or even snowstorms can move in without warning at almost any time of year. On the lucky occasions when the weather's good enough for panoramic views, you'll see wave upon wave of rippling, barren mountains sliced by steep valleys carved out by rivers. The almost constant rain causes the soil to be leeched of its nutrients, making it hard for trees to grow;

farming in this part of the country is marginal at best.

A growing awareness of wind power has resulted in huge wind farms being built on the mountain ridges. These massive white turbines are set to become more common in the coming years as Spain is determined to increase its green-energy production capacity.

## Trails

Trail marking is usually very good, with abundant yellow arrows. As you enter Galicia, you'll start to see a variety of stone markers. Some record the distance remaining to Santiago to the nearest metre, whereas others are beautifully carved with camino imagery. There are a couple of steep climbs, and you'll often head uphill on ancient stone paths shaded by woodland that can be slippery in wet weather and more like a stream than a path during a heavy downpour. Elsewhere, you're forced to follow minor roads, as there's often only one possible route through narrow valleys or over mountain passes

From A Gudiña, the Vía de la Plata splits into two routes. The lower route via Verín is longer and mostly shadows main roads, so we describe the shorter, higher and more isolated route via the beautiful town of Laza.

## When to Go

The route through the mountains is an exposed one that can be misty all year. Visibility is often poor and there's also a fair chance of rain whatever the season. Summers are sunniest, but the area's smaller *albergues* can get very crowded as you near Santiago.

In winter, storms soak the region and it's not uncommon for snow to cover sections of the camino. You're unlikely to see anyone else on the route, and only a few of the *albergues* boast heating to warm up chilly pilgrims. If you decide to brave the winter, try to time your passage through Laza to coincide with Carnaval, the town's crazy celebrations before the beginning of Lent. Spring and autumn are a gamble, as the weather can swing from snow to sun and all things in between in a few hours.

## Flora & Fauna

Exposed mountain moorland consists of hardy, low-growing plants such as heather, broom and wild thyme; out of the wind you'll also see ancient holly and yew trees.

Rocky upland areas are circled by magnificent Bonelli's, booted and golden **eagles**; you may also see a chough, rock thrush or blue rock thrush. Out of the wind, the area has some of the most extensive and unspoilt oak forests of the Iberian peninsula, and chestnuts, alder, ash and willow grow lower down in the valleys.

The **wolf** is at the apex of the food chain here and, despite years of persecution by hunters, there are thought to be a couple of thousand animals left in Spain and nearby Portugal. Wolves need open space to roam, as they can cover anything from 20 to 40km in a single day, smell prey or a potential mate 2km away and, incredibly, hear sounds from up to 10km away. Whereas the wolf feeds mainly on wild boar and roe deer, the smaller beech marten, which looks like a large, stocky weasel, patrols mature woodlands looking for voles, shrews and mice.

## People & Culture

Living in the mountains is a tough experience that fosters immensely hardy people and a deep community spirit. Given the rough weather, it's surprising to see so many tiny villages in the region. These places are often tucked into valleys, isolated from surrounding communities by the steep slopes that encircle them, but you'll also find hamlets on the slopes themselves, exposed to the region's bitter weather and preserving a way of life that may not survive the death of the last of their elderly inhabitants. Most of the region's people make a living from farming or simply survive by being self-sufficient in food, and even the most inhospitable slopes are planted with fruits and vegetables or beautified with flowers.

Winters are so tough that locals

invented fantastic **festivals** to celebrate the beginning of spring, most notably in the riotous Carnaval at Laza (see Events & Festivals).

You'll also see lots of water mills and stone water channels, ingenious and often beautiful ways to make use of the region's abundant **rainfall**. Older villages will also have a forge and a communal bread oven, although most of these have fallen into ruin. Traditional houses are two-storeyed; animals are kept on the ground floor, and the upper floor is accessed by an external stone or wooden staircase and fronted by a heavy stone balcony.

# Food & Drink

Even before you've officially crossed into Galicia, you'll begin to taste some of the region's food and wine; on every *menú* you'll see *caldo gallego*, Galicia's thick, hearty soup, best mopped up with dense, heavy local bread. You'll also find dishes peculiar to the region around Puebla de Sanabria. Try *habones con chorizo*, made with the area's indigenous fat white beans that only grow above 1000m, a hearty treat on a cold evening. If you're getting sick of meat-dominated Spanish *menús*, go for *trucha* (trout), either grilled simply or cooked with prawns and garlic.

The valleys and forests on the lower mountain slopes are rife with **mushrooms** in autumn, and the people around Puebla de Sanabria take their fungi so seriously that they organize a two-week festival to celebrate local delicacies such as chanterelles and morels. If you're in the area at the end of October or at the beginning of November, you can watch demonstrations, or better still attend a tasting and sample hundreds of delicious mushroom-based meals.

# *i* Tourist Information

## Tourist Offices

The *turismo* in Puebla de Sanabria offers information on the town and the region; for more information see the town description.

## Transport

Puebla de Sanabria is the transportation hub of the mountain region. You can catch a train here from Zamora, Valladolid and Madrid, or buses from across Spain.

## Money

There are banks and cashpoints in Puebla de Sanabria and Laza.

## Accommodation

You're spoilt for accommodation in the mountains, and there's a string of wonderful, fully equipped *albergues* in Lubián, A Gudiña and Laza; some of them even have heating! There are plenty of hotels in Puebla de Sanabria, but the hordes of tourists who descend on the town in summer tend to bump up prices; budget-conscious pilgrims can sleep on the floor of the *ayuntamiento*.

## Shopping

It can be difficult to find fresh fruit and vegetables, as most locals are self-reliant and grow their own. Many smaller villages don't have any kind of shop, and you'll have to flag down the fruit and vegetable or bread delivery vans whenever you see them.

## Events & Festivals

The region's most fabulous festival is Laza's **Carnaval**, which takes places in the days before Lent. On the Sunday, *Peliqueiros*, dressed in crazy frilled costumes with massive tricorn hats, oversized grinning masks and cowbells around their waists behave with abandon. They carry sticks to hit onlookers, who are forbidden from retaliating, and can demand food and drink from any house in the village. The evening is a riot of drinking, dancing and cross-dressing where anything goes; crimes short of manslaughter that take place during Carnaval are pardoned. The next day sees running battles with flour, water and live ants. Carnaval ends on the Tuesday with the burning of an effigy and the reading of the "donkey's will," an epic poem that exposes the scandals and vanities of Laza's inhabitants during the past year.

Although the festival follows the Christian calendar, its roots lie in pagan traditions of throwing off winter and welcoming the spring. During Franco's rule, such celebrations were banned as the dictator believed that masks could hide criminals and rebels.

 # Rest Days & Detours

The **Lago de Sanabria**, 12km northwest of Puebla de Sanabria, is a popular nature park in the Sierra de la Cabrera centred around sulphur springs and the largest glacial lake in Spain. Visit San Martín de Castañeda, on the lake's northern edge, to see the remains of a tenth-century Benedictine monastery.

From Puebla de Sanabria, it's a short hop south to **Portugal** and a visit to the town of Bragança, whose tiny centre is encircled by stone walls, or to the lovely Parque Natural de Montesinho, just across the border.

# Puebla de Sanabria
Ⓐ❶✖💼€❶🍷 (251km)

Puebla de Sanabria's gorgeous old town is perched on a steep hill, a magnificent defensive position but a tough approach up steep cobbled streets for the weary pilgrim. There are stunning views all around, particularly at sunset when the walls and the *castillo* are lit up. The fifteenth-century **castillo** dominates the hill, and the views from the upper floors of the multi-storeyed keep are stunning. The twelfth-century **Iglesia de Santa María del Azoque** has a fantastic Romanesque portal and is decorated with bulbous gargoyles and heads that seem to be peering out over the landscape to get a better view. Inside, there's a Gothic vault and a late thirteenth-century font.

The galleried fifteenth-century *ayuntamiento* is across the Plaza Mayor from the church, and the old town is completed by lovely *casas consistorial* with interesting façades. These attractions, together with the popular Lago de Sanabria nearby, make Puebla de Sanabria a tourist magnet, and restaurants and accommodation can be expensive. Crowded from June to September, the place is a bit of ghost town in low season, when many of the hotels and other facilities close. The town celebrates the Fiesta de Nuestra Señora de las Victorias at the beginning of September with *gigantes* (big-headed giant puppets) and fireworks in the plaza.

The **turismo** (☎ 980 620 002), just off the Plaza Mayor, has limited opening hours.

### Accommodation

Puebla de Sanabria has no official **albergue** (mattresses, toilet, sink, no showers, donation) the floor of the *ayuntamiento*. Get the key from the *turismo* around the corner or, when closed, ask at the library, which is idyllically located in the castle at the top of town.

**$$ Hostal La Trucha**, just before the bridge into town (☎ 980 620 060)

**$$$ Hotel Victoria**, Calle Arrabal 29 (☎ 980 620 012)

**$$$ Hospedería La Carteria**, Calle Rúa 16 (☎ 980 620 312)

**$$$$ Parador de Puebla de Sanabria**, Avenida Lago de Sanabria 18 (☎ 980 620 001)

---

From the Plaza Mayor and with your back to the *ayuntamiento*, turn left in front of the Iglesia de Santa María del Azoque to walk down some steps. Turn right at the bottom of the steps down Calle San Bernardo, and turn left then right to walk steeply downhill past a graveyard. The street changes to a grassy track here, and you can admire and appreciate Puebla de Sanabria's old walls and enviable defensive position. Turn left after 300m to walk on a narrow track past a house, then left again in 50m to walk along the road. Cross the Río Castro, passing a side road to Castro de Sanabria on the right. After 1km turn left at a T-junction to walk along the N525.

Follow this road, which isn't as busy as you would expect thanks to the construction of the nearby A52 motorway. Pass a bar on the right in just over 500m, then keep straight on past the junction with the A52 in another 500m. Ignore any tracks to the left; yellow arrows that once led you off the road have been erased, as the route is very boggy and often blocked by fences or hedges.

Some 5km after the A52 junction, turn right on to a narrow paved road that very quickly becomes a grassy track, and walk gradually uphill. It's a gorgeous walk through pines, birch and oak, and even the motorway to the right can't spoil the tranquility. In 500m, turn left at a T-junction with a gravel road and soon reach the Romanesque Iglesia de Santiago de Terroso, which has scallop shells carved into the façade and the solid wooden door. You can climb the external bell tower, a typical feature of the region's churches, but mind your head on the low stone lintel.

Leave the church on a tarmac road, turn left at a paved road 100m later, then turn right in 20m down another paved

## Map 22 (key page 214)

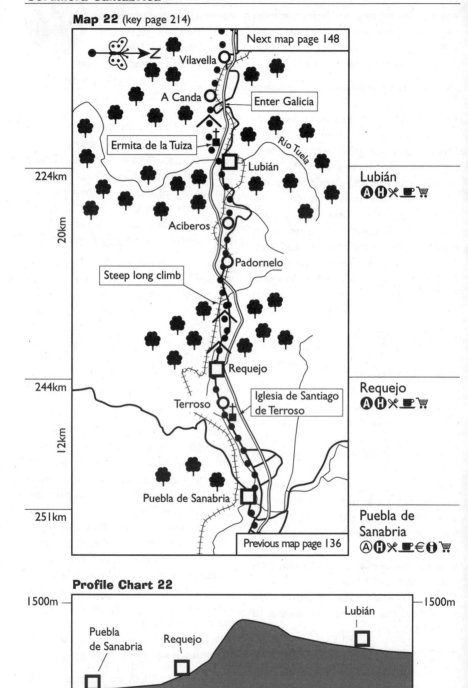

Next map page 148

Vilavella

A Canda

Enter Galicia

Ermita de la Tuiza

Río Tuela

Lubián

224km

20km

Lubián
🅐🅗✕🍴💻🛒

Aciberos

Padornelo

Steep long climb

Requejo

244km

Terroso

Iglesia de Santiago de Terroso

Requejo
🅐🅗✕🍴💻🛒

12km

Puebla de Sanabria

251km

Puebla de Sanabria
🅐🅗✕🍴💻€ℹ🛒

Previous map page 136

### Profile Chart 22

1500m — — 1500m

Lubián

Puebla de Sanabria

Requejo

900m — — 900m

road. Enter Terroso some 200m later, then veer left once in the village, soon leaving it on a dirt track, heading uphill. Cross the motorway via a bridge 400m later, from where there are great views of the mountains, and continue on a dirt track, walking uphill through oaks and ferns. Turn left to join a broader track 100m later, then turn left in another 100m down a narrower dirt track shaded by walls and a beautiful wood. Cross a collapsed dry stone wall 50m later and head downhill.

Broom and bracken sometimes intrude on to this path, but it's a beautiful, vivid green stretch, alive with wildflowers in spring and summer. Cross a stream via stepping stones 500m later and walk across an overgrown field. Turn left at a dirt road just 100m later, cross the motorway again and see Requejo ahead.

In another 300m, turn right down a narrow dirt track at a Camino de Santiago sign, ignoring the yellow arrows that lead straight on. Enter Requejo at a fountain, cross a tiny canal and soon reach the N525.

# Requejo
**ⒶⒽ✕🛏️🛒** (244km)

Requejo has the feel of a Galician village, even though you're still some way from entering the region. The upper storeys of the town's low, gorgeous houses are reached by thick stone or wooden staircases, and the walls are made of thick, irregular stone slabs. It's a very friendly place, and an excellent stop before the long haul up to Padornelo.

You can stay at the town's **albergue** (ask in the *ayuntamiento* for the key), the

**Hostal Mar Rojo** ($, ☎ 980 622 446) or the **Hostal Tu Casa** ($, ☎ 980 622 468), which is just outside town.

---

Cross the N525 and turn right at the Ermita de Guadalupe down Calle Carrera, passing a fountain with delicious water on your left as you leave town. Continue along this street as the town ends, and pass a cemetery 1km later. Keep straight on here as the road curves right, to walk up a steep dirt track, then fork left 100m later on the lower of two tracks, heading up the Valle de Sanabria through scrub and broom. Walk steeply downhill soon afterwards to cross a bridge. Pass a house in 500m and join the road that leads to it, then turn left at a Camino de Santiago sign 50m later along a dirt track.

It's a serene and lovely route, enveloped by oaks, bracken and dry stone walls. Pass a group of beehives away to your right as you walk past sword fern, moss and ivy. The path is sometimes rocky, sometimes muddy, and veers to and from the Río Castro to your left. You'll be accompanied by the wonderful sound of rushing water, the screech of a jay and the melody of songbirds. In drier spots, you'll pass heather and gorse, and if you're lucky, you may glimpse one of the deer that live in the area. Ignore the large yellow arrow leading left off the main track after a few kilometres. In another 500m, you can take a short, steep and unmarked detour to the right to avoid the worst of a particularly muddy patch.

You'll see the railway to your left on the other side of the river here, although it soon disappears into a tunnel. Just as this happens, turn right to follow a broad track coming from the ruined building up ahead, doubling back on yourself and climbing steeply.

Cross a bridge 300m later, then walk past a concrete plant in about 1km. Turn left here on to the old, disused N525 and keep on it, ignoring the gravel road to the right in 50m. There are lovely views down into the Valle de Sanabria behind you. The current N525 is just to your right, and you'll veer very close to it in about 1km. Shortly afterwards, veer right to go uphill as you see two road viaducts ahead. Walk under the viaducts and fork left 300m later, continuing uphill. The camino takes you in a large U-shape around a valley to cross a bridge in 500m and then duck under the viaducts on the other side of the valley. Be careful as you head under the motorway as there can be lots of water runoff. Turn left 200m later as the old N525 reappears. There are incredible views here down into the Valle de Sanabria as you climb steeply, yellow arrows encouraging you to go steeper still to cut off a couple of hairpin bends.

Climb for another 1km, then veer left at a small grey building, an inauspicious spot that marks the high point of the camino. Head downhill on a narrow paved road, turn right down a dirt road 200m later then turn left on to the N525 and keep on it as it crosses the motorway via a bridge. Turn left just after the bridge down a paved road heading downhill into Padornelo. Fork right 100m later then sharp left in 50m and sharp right immediately afterwards. **Padornelo** (⬤✕🛒🍴, 232km) is a lovely hillside village of thick-walled

stone houses with slate roofs. Typical two-storeyed houses have outside stone steps, and seemingly dwarf-like single-storeyed houses stretch downhill on their far side. You'll need to detour right here for the village's two mediocre bars, both on the N525; one of the bars also has a small shop. Otherwise, fork right uphill in 100m and keep straight on 50m later to join the N525 as Padornelo ends.

Turn left to follow the road, passing the **Hotel/Restaurante Padornelo** (**$$**, ☎ 980 620 106) on the left. In a little over 1km, veer right to continue on the road, then 300m later, turn left down a grassy track. This beautifully green and shady route parallels an irrigation channel and, at times, can seem more like a stream than a path. If you'd like to keep your feet dry, then stay on the road, a windy route that will add a few kilometres to your journey. Otherwise, follow the track for a couple of kilometres as it begins to descend more steeply.

Turn left on meeting a paved road, and enter the tiny village of **Aciberos**, a maze of intricate nooks and crannies and lovely houses with ornate stone balconies. Pass a church, turn right, and pass a fountain and a working water wheel that makes use of the region's abundant water supply.

Leave Aciberos down a grassy, rocky track, and keep straight on 300m later on a dirt path as the track curves left, walking on a beautiful stone-slab path between moss covered walls. Cross a pretty stone bridge 500m later and head uphill. Fork left in another 100m, still heading uphill, then turn left on meeting a track and walk through a tunnel under a railway. Fork left in 50m, then turn sharp left 200m later to walk downhill, curving right 50m later. Cross another bridge in 1km or so, and walk uphill into Lubián.

# Lubián

Ⓐ Ⓗ ✕ ☕ 🛒 (224km)

Nestled in a damp valley and squeezed on all sides by mountains, Lubián is a timeless place in a stunning location. Strung out along the camino, many of its stone houses are split vertically, with people on top and livestock on the ground floor.

Lubián's **albergue** (8 beds, hot showers, heaters, kitchen, donation) is at the start of the village; a notice on the *albergue* door will let you know who has the key. You can also stay at the **La Casa de Irene** ($$$, ☎ 902 315 513), 50m further on, or just eat huge helpings of Irene's delicious food — you'll need to order your meal in advance. There's alternative accommodation at the **Casa Rural La Pachaca** ($$, ☎ 980 624 127) in the centre of Lubián, almost 1km away; you'll find a supermarket along the camino and a couple of bars and a *panadería* just off the route on the main road.

Walk past the *albergue* and La Casa de Irene, then turn left to walk through the village, passing enchanting houses with overhanging stone balconies so solid and heavy that they seem in danger of toppling the houses over. At a modern camino sculpture the Vía de la Plata splits. Cyclists should turn right to follow the old main road all the way to the Puerto da Canda. Turn left to continue the camino on foot, and head downhill out of the village, passing fields on either side. In 500m, turn right, following the signs for Santuario de la Tuiza. Cross a

concrete bridge and arrive at an open park alongside the Río Tuela, passing under a motorway bridge. You'll soon reach the Santuario de la Virgen de la Tuiza, a Baroque church that holds a big *romería* on the last Sunday in September. Climb up a steep hill, then once at the top, follow the paved road alongside the motorway, passing picnic benches and a smaller *ermita* at the top of the hill.

Soon, the camino dips downhill again. At a fork at the bottom of the hill, turn left and cross a bridge over the river, then curve left and begin to climb uphill. In 150m, fork right and continue to climb. Once again, you're following an old cart track, part of an intricate network of routes that string together these small *pueblos* (villages) like pearls on a necklace.

This is the beginning of a long, steep haul where you'll climb 400m over 5km, so be sure to pace yourself. It's a beautiful walk shaded by oak and chestnuts; look out for toads and salamanders, particularly after one of the region's frequent damp spells. Near the saddle of the pass, turn right on to a larger, newer dirt track, arriving at the Puerto da Canda in 200m. The views back to Portilla de Padornelo are spectacular, despite the motorway running through it. A simple, modern sculpture and a camino marker signify your arrival at the Galician border.

Turn left here to begin a well-deserved descent, soon passing a camino marker stone. These concrete stones will lead you all the way to Santiago, and tell you, to the nearest metre, how far you have to go. Rather confusingly, there are two different distances marked, reflecting the split in the Vía de la Plata at A Gudiña:

## Map 23 (key page 214)

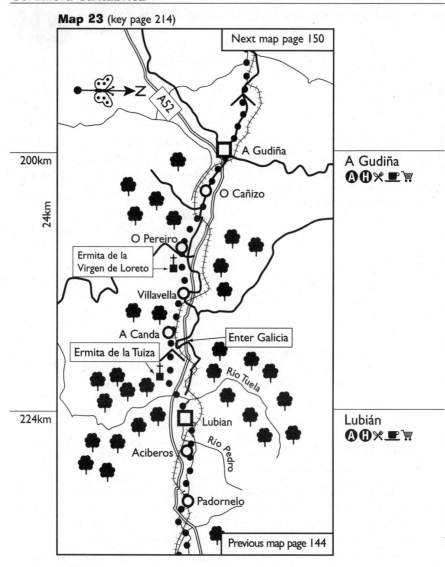

Next map page 150

A52

200km

24km

A Gudiña

O Cañizo

O Perejiro

Ermita de la
Virgen de Loreto →

Villavella

A Canda

Enter Galicia

Ermita de la Tuiza

Río Tuela

224km

Lubian

Río Pedro

Aciberos

Padornelo

Previous map page 144

A Gudiña
Ⓐ Ⓗ ✕ 💻 🛒

Lubián
Ⓐ Ⓗ ✕ 💻 🛒

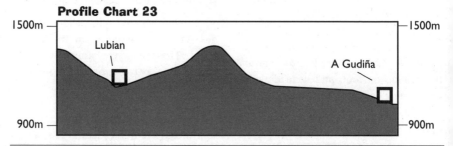

### Profile Chart 23

1500m — ——————————————— 1500m

Lubian

A Gudiña

900m — ——————————————— 900m

one measures the route via Verín, the other the route via Laza. Keep heading downhill through scrubby bushes and thick grass, ignoring turnings off the main track, then walk through the tiny hamlet of **A Canda,** which has narrow twisting streets, walled lanes and sagging balconies, on a paved road in a couple of kilometres. Shortly afterwards, keep an eye out for yellow markers, as the camino veers left off the road just after camino marker km211.4.

The route crosses a new stone bridge over a stream, then soon follows the old road once more. Pass a fountain and head through a tunnel under railway tracks. Keep heading downhill and eventually cross a stone bridge before heading uphill towards Vilavella.

Take the left-hand fork just before the village to enter **Vilavella** (🅷💺🛒, 213km); to visit the bar, which serves excellent *bocadillos*, or to stay at the **Hostal Porta Galega** (**$**, ☎ 988 425 593), walk up to the main road, about 500m off the camino. The village church has some splendid carved reliefs in the door; look out for basking lizards and a huge scallop shell.

Leave Vilavella via an old walled lane. Cross a bridge in about 1km, then keep right at a fork near a farm. You soon enter a beautiful section of the camino that follows the Arroyo de los Santos on raised stepping stones. This way of keeping feet dry is common throughout Galicia, and in very wet weather, you'll be very grateful to those who moved these gigantic stones into place. At the end of the stepping stones there's a new pilgrim's fountain, with a handy cup attached. Pass the fascinating Ermita de la Virgen de Loreto, which has a window

that allows the devoted to offer a donation by sticking their hand into the *ermita* and dropping a tribute in a slot.

Cross a bridge and curve into the small hamlet of **O Pereiro**. On the far side of the village there's a gigantic stone bridge, almost megalithic in scale, just before the camino begins to climb once more. This area suffered heavily from fire in 2003, when much of the vegetation was lost. About 3km from O Pereiro watch out, as the camino veers suddenly left off the dirt track to cross another massive stone slab bridge. In another 1km join a paved road and turn right to cross a bridge over some train tracks. The camino veers left but soon curves back and crosses over the paved road.

Keep heading straight on and just before **O Cañizo** when the dirt track heads right, turn left on a shortcut into the village. Head through the village and not long afterwards pass a *cruceiro* carved with an unusually simple depiction of Jesus.

Cross the N525 to follow a path through head-high broom, then just before a bridge over the motorway rejoin the N525 and follow it into A Gudiña. About 1km before town, pass a camino centre on the right next to the Cruz Roja (Red Cross), from which you can get a key for the town's *albergue*. Watch out for the occasional camino shortcut that cuts off a corner of this busy road.

Once in A Gudiña, follow the main street then turn right, following the road to Viana do Bolo. To continue along the camino, turn left almost immediately to follow a side street or, to stay at the *albergue*, turn right in 50m just after the

**Map 24** (key page 214)

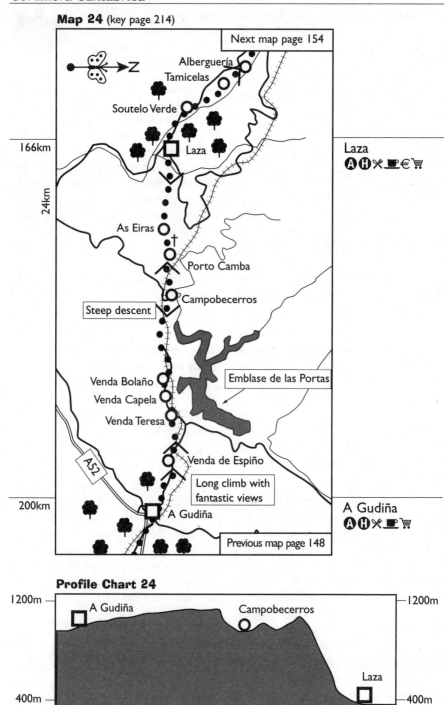

Next map page 154

Alberguería
Tamicelas
Soutelo Verde

166km

24km

Laza

Laza
Ⓐ Ⓗ ✕ 💻 € 🛒

As Eiras
Porto Camba
Campobecerros

Steep descent

Venda Bolaño
Venda Capela
Venda Teresa

Emblase de las Portas

AS2

Venda de Espiño

Long climb with
fantastic views

200km

A Gudiña

Previous map page 148

A Gudiña
Ⓐ Ⓗ ✕ 💻 🛒

**Profile Chart 24**

1200m — A Gudiña                Campobecerros          1200m

Laza

400m —                                                 400m

railway bridge. The *albergue* is the large building on your left after about 30m.

# A Gudiña

Ⓐ Ⓗ ✗ ▰ ☕ (200km)

A Gudiña is a faded town with a tired look to its modern main street. Just a few metres away, however, the older, parallel street looks more like an isolated village, with chickens and other animals still kept on the ground floor of the houses.

The town's modern **albergue** (20 beds, hot showers, kitchen, donation) has everything a pilgrim needs. A Gudiña's main street is lined with restaurants and hotels, such as **Hostal Oscar** ($, ☎ 988 421 014) or **Hostal El Relojero** ($$, ☎ 988 421 001).

Follow the camino along the side road until you come to a *cruceiro* in a few hundred metres, where the camino splits. The left-hand route goes to Ourense via Verín, a lower, flatter route that shadows the main road. We describe the right-hand route over the mountains to Ourense via the lovely town of Laza, a shorter, more dramatic and quieter option.

Climb out of A Gudiña, passing a fountain on the left. Just outside town, fork left and soon afterwards join a narrow paved road. This route can be exposed in bad weather; keep well to the side of the road, particularly in the frequent fog that cloaks the area. The landscape looks very much like the highlands of Scotland with mountains carpeted with heather, blackberry and broom. Follow a ridge uphill and after almost 5km turn right off the main road to pass

through **Venda do Espiño**, the first of a series of tiny hamlets.

Join the main road on the other side of the hamlet. In another 1km, veer left to walk through the hamlet of Venda Teresa. Perched on a ridge, **Venda Teresa** is by turns idyllic and inhospitable, depending on the weather that smacks straight into it. Many of Venda Teresa's basic houses lack electricity and running water; residents huddle together with animals to keep warm, and vegetable and flower gardens cling to the steep mountainside. The fortitude of the few remaining residents, almost all of whom are past retirement age, is awe-inspiring.

Keep climbing, and you'll soon reach **Venda Capela**, another beautiful village with fabulous views across the mountains of Galicia. There are no facilities, although if you time your visit for mid-morning on certain days of the week you'll bump into the grocery delivery van. Near a group of identical abandoned houses, likely built for railway workers, pass the old train station below you on the right, and you'll soon glimpse the Embalse de las Portas further away. Keep heading uphill and arrive at **Venda Bolaño**, the last and highest of this string of small hamlets, some 13km from A Gudiña.

The route flattens as it curves around the side of a mountain, descends a little then, 3km later, heads left off the paved road up a stone track. Sadly, the magnificent green valleys that are visible all around are sometimes marred by clearcutting. In bad weather, stick to the road here, a longer but safer route. As you reach the top of a small hill, you'll see

Campobecerros in the valley below. Loose rocks can make the very steep descent difficult. In bad weather, look for two stone cairns which guide you towards the road. Turn left on reaching the road and head into the village.

**Campobecerros** (⬛✕☕, 180km) is a charming village rising up a steep slope of the Río Camba valley. The upper storeys of many of the village's beautiful houses straddle the very narrow streets. Campobecerros has two bars; the lower one also has a shop, and the upper one serves meals. Climb out of the village on a paved road with good views of the Río Camba below you, then descend into the hamlet of **Porto Camba**, where a fountain at the end of the village has delicious water.

Climb again out of Porto Camba and reach a wooden cross in about 1km, where the camino finally leaves the paved road. Turn left here and follow a dirt track through pine trees, or turn right to detour to the Santuarío de Nuestra Señora de Pena Tellada near Cerdedelo, from which you can follow the road into Laza. The Río Tuela has carved out a steep valley on the right and offers great views.

Some 5km from Porto Camba, curve into the gorgeous hamlet of **As Eiras**, a collection of ruined and standing buildings. Just after the small church there's a ruined building where you can see an old stone oven. At the end of the hamlet there's a tranquil rest area with a fountain and picnic benches. The route down to Laza is almost entirely on paved road, although the route is often shady and the views can be spectacular; there's a fountain about halfway down. At a bend in the road almost at the bottom of the hill turn right off the paved road to zigzag down to the Río Tuela. Cross the river over a concrete bridge and join another paved road in about 400m. Turn left here and walk into Laza, forking right at the edge of town.

# Laza
**ⒶⒽ✕⬛€☕** (166km)

Laza is a small, very friendly town, known throughout Spain for its Carnaval, which takes place in the days before Lent. The most memorable sight is that of the town's *Peliqueiros*, costumed locals with massive tea-cosy-like headgear with a licence to hit bystanders with sticks. See page 142 for more on Laza's riotous celebrations. At other, less festive times of year, you'll have to make do with Laza's attractive *cruceiro* and the sixteenth-century Gothic Iglesia de San Xoán. Still, it's a lovely, fascinating town where many of the older residents still speak only Galician.

Laza's modern, glass-walled **albergue** (32 beds, hot showers, kitchen, donation) is a model of comfort and style, with small four-bed dormitories, a big lounge and dining area, kitchen and bathrooms. It also has rooms and a bathroom designed for disabled pilgrims and a peculiar, high-tech lighting system, partly automatic and partly operated by a single switch for all the dormitories. To reach the *albergue*, keep heading right towards the *Protección Civil*. They'll stamp your *credencial* and drive you to the *albergue*, even though it's only about 500m away. You can also stay at **Hostal Blanco Conde** (**$, ☎ 988 422 061**). Don't leave town without stopping at Laza's excellent *panadería*, which has a fine selection of artisan bread.

To leave Laza, keep straight on through the village (return to the Protección Civil if you stayed in the *albergue*); there are very few yellow arrows. Turn left to walk past the village shop and the *cruceiro*, then turn right to walk along the main road, soon passing the *panadería*. The fields that border the quiet road are separated by distinctive slate slab fences looking spookily like worn tombstones; you'll see these throughout Galicia. About 1km later, yellow arrows direct you right along a rough paved road signposted Villareal and Castro. This detour merely brings you back to the road 150m later via an old stone bridge, and it's simpler to continue on the road.

In a little more than 1km, turn left off the road just before reaching the village of **Soutelo Verde** (🍴), then fork right 30m later along the lower of two tracks, following a Camino de Santiago sign. You'll soon reach the delightful village itself, where balconies ripe with hundreds of hanging ears of corn enliven the streets in autumn. Pass the village fountain, cross a stone bridge then walk over a concrete bridge, passing an *ermita* on the right. The town's bar is on the main road, which you rejoin at the end of the village.

Turn right 100m later down a dirt road, following it past fields into **Tamicelas**, about 3km away, where there's a pretty picnic area to the right. Fork left as you enter the village, then turn left 30m later and turn left again in 50m at the Ermita de la Asunción, heading uphill on a dirt track.

The route climbs steadily through pine forest, forking right after 500m. Soon afterwards, it becomes a more rocky track and heads uphill more steeply through gorse, heather and low pines. After almost 1km of breathless uphill the track flattens out a little and for the next couple of kilometres alternates between very steep sections and catch-your-breath flatter parts; it can be prickly with gorse in places. The views behind you are spectacular; you can clearly see your route down into Laza and, behind it, wave upon wave of glorious mountains. As you approach the road once more, pass a chestnut grove to your left, then reach the road some 3km after leaving Tamicelas.

Turn right at the road, getting instant views of the mountains to your left and the village of Alberguería ahead. Enter **Alberguería**, turning left 100m after the village sign to walk past its lovely houses. The stone balconies that adorn some of the older buildings are incredible, seemingly insupportable horizontal boulders held up by massive vertical ones. Turn left at the village well to walk past the church.

Veer left at the end of the village to leave on a walled lane and keep straight on 100m later along a grassy track as the lane curves right. Huge stone slabs help to keep your feet well above the sometimes mucky path, and the countryside varies from walled fields to more open scrubland. Once, all this would have been farmland, but now many of the fields have been given up to encroaching gorse and the walls are collapsing, choked with brambles.

In just over 1km, cross a narrow paved road and keep straight on along a good track through vibrant heather and gorse. After another 1km, keep straight on across the main road and walk on a

**Map 25** (key page 214)

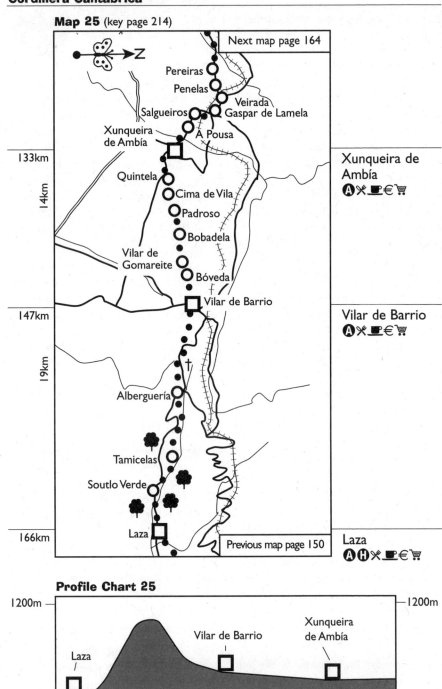

Next map page 164

Pereiras
Penelas
Veirada
Gaspar de Lamela
Salgueiros
Xunqueira de Ambía
A Pousa
Quintela
Cima de Vila
Padroso
Bobadela
Vilar de Gomareite
Bóveda
Vilar de Barrio
Alberguería
Tamicelas
Soutlo Verde
Laza
Previous map page 150

133km
14km
147km
19km
166km

Xunqueira de Ambía

Vilar de Barrio

Laza

**Profile Chart 25**

1200m
Laza
Vilar de Barrio
Xunqueira de Ambía
400m

broad dirt road up to a large wooden cross. The cross is said to have been placed here in honour of pilgrims and itinerant Galician workers who travelled this way en route to the cornfields of Castilla. From here, you can see down into Vilar de Barrio and the gorgeous plains and hills ahead; it's much flatter, greener and more populated on this side of the mountains.

Walk downhill through oak and ferns on a path that can be muddy in places. Turn right at a paved road after a 1km descent, and get excellent views of the plain of Limia ahead. Turn left off the road down a dirt track in 500m, keeping straight on almost immediately at a crossroads with another dirt track, then going steeply downhill through pines and scrub.

Turn right after 1km when you reach a dry stone wall and walk along a flattish lane shaded by oaks and surrounded by fields. It can be very muddy, and you'll have to squash yourself up against the wall to walk along large stone slabs. In 200m, turn left to walk along a narrow paved road, then turn right in another 200m down a grassy track. In another 500m, turn right on meeting the main road and pass a sign for Vilar de Barrio 500m later.

Turn right down a side street shortly afterwards, passing a ramshackle *hórreo*, an elevated building used to store corn that's a distinctive part of Galician rural architecture. Turn right after 500m as you encounter the road once more. There are shops and bars here and, in 100m, a busier road and a village green of sorts. Turn left here for the tiny petrol station, where you'll get keys to the *albergue* and a *sello*, then turn right for the *albergue* itself, just 50m up the road.

**Regional Map** (key page 214)

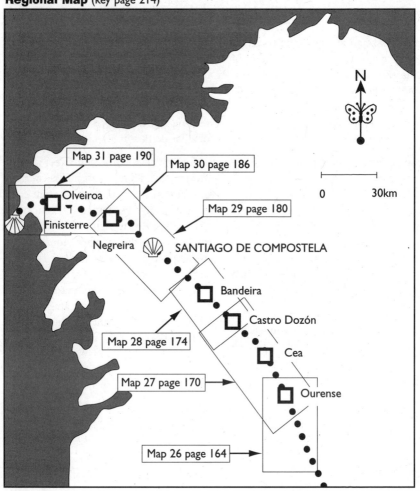

Map 31 page 190

Map 30 page 186

Map 29 page 180

N

0    30km

Olveiroa

Finisterre

Negreira

SANTIAGO DE COMPOSTELA

Bandeira

Castro Dozón

Map 28 page 174

Cea

Map 27 page 170

Ourense

Map 26 page 164

## What's the Weather Like?

|  | **Jan** | **April** | **July** | **Oct** |
|---|---|---|---|---|
| **Sun** | 3hrs | 6hrs | 8hrs | 5hrs |
| **Rainfall** | 27cm | 15cm | 3cm | 19cm |
| **Maximum Temp** | 11°C | 15°C | 22°C | 17°C |
| **Minimum Temp** | 3°C | 6°C | 12°C | 7°C |

Average hours of sun, total average rainfall in cm and average temperature in degrees celsius

# Galicia
## Vilar de Barrio to Finisterre via Santiago

Once you're in Galicia, it's a winding, up-and-down route through tiny farms and one-house hamlets and alongside rain-drenched fields and rivers. Soon, you'll reach Santiago, where you give thanks to St James in a series of historic rituals. But don't stop there; if you follow the old Celtic route to the sea at Finisterre, you'll reach the end of the known Celtic world via the solitude of quiet lanes and ancient ways.

 **Walking**

### Geography

Soggy storms clip this corner of Iberia as they fly along the Gulf Stream, dumping bucketsful of water almost all year round: in an average year, Galicia gets rain on one day in two.

The foggy Costa da Morte is a jagged mix of cliffs and long estuaries that penetrate deep inland, and the coast is a legendary wrecker of countless ships, blown on to the rocks by storms. It was off this coast that the oil tanker *Prestige* sank in late 2002, causing untold damage to the environment and to the local fishing industry. This maritime carnage may explain the name Costa da Morte (coast of death), but the coast may also be named for the nightly death of the sun as it sets on Spain's westernmost shore.

The inland landscape is one of rolling hills and steep river valleys, eroded by aeons of rainfall. Lush vegetation and mild winters make Galicia stand out from other, more arid parts of the Vía de la Plata, but for those who know the wilder parts of Ireland, the scenery will seem very familiar.

The mountains that rise up to the south and east can be dusted with snow as late as May and as early as October, and clouds seem to permanently shroud their peaks. The proximity of the sea means that the weather here is very fickle, and you can experience all the seasons on any day of the year without warning.

### Trails

The Galician government put a lot of money into trail maintenance and signage to celebrate the 1999 Holy Year and, as a result, the Vía de la Plata is extremely well marked. At junctions and at regular intervals, you'll find concrete camino bollards that show the distance to Santiago to the metre, or lovely stone monoliths depicting an abstract pilgrim.

The route can be waterlogged in parts, but big granite stepping stones or handy thick stone walls provide a means to keep your feet dry. Many of the trails are still used by locals, as they are often the quickest way to get between villages. After Santiago, the camino bollards continue, although the distance engraved is sometimes to Muxía and sometimes to Finisterre, and it's never really clear which is which.

## When to go

The old saying, "Be prepared for rain and pray for sunshine" rings true in Galicia. The winter brings almost constant storms and the sun may not shine for weeks, although it's unlikely to snow as the temperature rarely dips below freezing. In spring and autumn the weather is unpredictable, but if you're lucky you can catch a week or two of constant sunshine. Summer brings the most settled good weather but is also the busiest time of year, when *albergues* may occasionally be full.

# Flora & Fauna

Historically, the **oak** forest of Galicia was a national treasure, and its sturdy wood was used to build Spain's mighty naval armada. By the early sixteenth century, in an attempt to preserve the forest for state use, a royal decree forbade anyone from felling the huge trees without a licence.

In the nineteenth century, **eucalyptus** was brought to Spain under the mistaken belief that it would be good for construction. Eucalyptus can grow by as much as 40 feet in three years, much faster than the local oak, making it popular as a source of both pulp and firewood, but foresters soon discovered that the eucalyptus tree twists as it grows and cracks once harvested. In 1941, Franco introduced the badly misnamed State Forest Heritage Act, under which oak was widely chopped down and eucalyptus was planted in its place to feed the fledgling pulp industry, and the non-native species now accounts for 27 percent of the forest in Galicia.

When you're out walking, take a look at the undergrowth of oak and eucalyptus woods. In eucalyptus forests, there's limited plant life and very few animals; birds find little food to eat here and the tree's sticky gum can clog up a bird's throat and kill it. In stark contrast, an old oak wood is a multi-layered canopy of green. Oak forests develop slowly, the soil growing rich with decaying leaves and acorns. Ferns, foxgloves and small shrubs provide shelter and food for a variety of animals, and the trees themselves are covered in moss and lichen, a miniature ecosystem in their own right. Black woodpeckers nest in the hollows of old trees, whereas thrushes and wrens hunt for beetles and grubs among the shrubs. The stubby bullfinch, with its rosy breast and black cap, is often seen darting through thickets.

Galician **farming** practices are less intensive and pesticide-reliant than those in the more productive *meseta*. As a result, meadows burst with wildflowers in spring and early summer, and the local cows use the lush grasses to produce a rich, creamy milk that's turned into a wide variety of delicious cheeses.

Without the region's persistent **rain**, Galicia would be devoid of damp-loving plants such as the purple large-flowered butterwort and pink bog pimpernel. In the hours after a heavy rainstorm, it's common to see large green Iberian wall lizards drying themselves on slabs of rock or on walls. Fire salamanders are most easily spotted during heavy rain when they crawl out of damp crevices and go hunting: look for their bulging eyes in wet mountain regions.

 ## People & Culture

Galicians have a reputation for being more reserved than other Spaniards, but these people are some of the kindest and most open you'll meet along the Vía de la Plata.

Communication may be difficult, however. In the 1991 census, a massive 91 percent of inhabitants said they were able to speak **Galego**, the region's Portuguese-like language. *Galego* tends to be heard more in rural areas and it's still thought of as an old person's language, but there are sections of the camino where you'll meet people who speak nothing else. After Galicia was granted autonomous government in 1981, the study of the language took off, and modern writers like Manolo Rivas have led to a new interest in *Galego*.

The region has always been poor. The last feudal holding was only abolished in 1973, and the average worker earns about half that of workers in Germany. Since the 1950s, there's been a massive exodus of people from the countryside, initially to South America but nowadays to industrialized cities like A Coruña.

The historic poverty of the region may go some way to explaining why traditional **farming** methods remain popular. As you walk through tiny hamlets it's common to see *palleiros* (haylofts), *pallozas* (straw-covered huts), *bronas* (outdoor ovens for cooking corn bread) and beautiful *hórreos* used to dry and store the corn. *Hórreo* designs and materials change from village to village, from simple, sturdy concrete blocks to intricate wood-and-slate designs that belie their practical function.

Galician **music** is firmly Celtic, and perhaps nothing shows the links between northern Celtic nations and Galicia better than the *gaita* (Galician bagpipe). There seems to be a type of music for every occasion. The most widespread and well-known are the Danzas de Espadas and Danzas de Arcos, which are linked to local celebrations, but more specific music includes *alboradas*, which celebrate the rising of the sun, *pasacorredoiras* (parade tunes) and *pasarruas* (marching music). If you're lucky, you might hear farmers and field workers singing traditional *jotas* (work songs) in rural areas between Santiago and Finisterre.

 ## Food & Drink

Galician cooking is simple, hearty and fantastic. Almost every meal begins with traditional **caldo gallego**, the thick soup made from meat, potatoes, greens and beans. *Empanada gallega de raxó* is a shallow, pie-like feast made with Galician pork and peppers.

Eat seafood every chance you get, as it's certain to be fresh and delicious. Try *vieiras de Santiago*, scallops with onions and cured ham.

Galicia's trademark downpours make for happy cows, and their milk is often turned into a soft and creamy teat-shaped cheese named *tetilla* (nipple). Eat the cheese with the region's fabulous, dense bread, a real treat after the bland white loaves on the rest of the Vía de la Plata. The best comes from Cea, just northwest of Ourense, and you shouldn't leave this small town without a hunk of it in your backpack.

Those with a sweet tooth will love *torta de Santiago*, a type of almond cake decorated with the shape of the cross of Santiago and dusted with sugar. You'll see the cake all over Galicia, but particularly in the Holy City itself, where bakers tempt customers into their shops and cafés by offering free samples.

Unlike the red-wine-producing rest of Spain, Galicia's climate is better suited to white grapes. **Albariño** is a straw-coloured, firm wine with a distinctive peach flavour that's slowly becoming respected outside Spain. **Ribeiro**, its lesser-known cousin, is young, fresh, cloudy and perfect with seafood. In more traditional bars it's poured straight out of the barrel into wide, shallow clay cups. Ribeiro rarely makes it outside Galicia as EU bureaucrats insist that the bottled version be clarified, so drink your fill while you're here. Galician beer is mostly as bland as any in Spain, but the draught version is poured from gorgeous ceramic beer taps. Galicia is also the only place along the camino where you'll regularly come across draught cider.

Made from grape skins, **orujo** is a clear firewater that'll put hairs on your chest. *Orujo* is found all across Spain, but the Galicians make the best *orujo* and drink far more of it than other Spaniards. *Orujo blanco* comes straight up, whereas *orujo con hierbas* is a green, slightly calmer version flavoured with herbs. Ask for *orujo casero* to get a meaty, home-made alternative: in true moonshine style, you'll find under-the-counter *orujo casero* in unmarked bottles in bakeries and grocers, as well as in bars and cafés.

# Tourist Information

## Tourist offices

There are *turismos* in Ourense and Santiago. See under individual towns for details.

## Transport

Local buses link Vilar de Barrio, Ourense and Cea, but services can be sporadic. It's easy to catch a train from Santiago to many large centres in Spain, and the railways also link Santiago to Bandeira, Estacion de Lalín and Ourense. For more information on getting home from Santiago, see Getting There & Back on page 30.

Eight buses a day connect Santiago and Finisterre, but sometimes require a change at Vimianzo. The journey takes between two and three hours.

## Money

There are banks and cash machines in Vilar de Barrio, Xunqueira de Ambía, Ourense, Tamallancos, Cea, Silleda, Bandeira, Puente Ulla, Santiago de Compostela, Negreira, Corcubión and Finisterre.

## Accommodation

Galicia's *albergues* are built in Holy Year clutches; the Galician government provides funding but leaves day-to-day upkeep to locals. These *albergues* verge on the luxurious and are usually packed with frivolous high-tech functions such as automatic lights that work when you don't want them and don't work when you do. As you near Santiago, the *albergues* suddenly stop and you'll have to stay in hotels instead. However, another spurt of Holy Year construction should see new *albergues* such as the one in Laxe, built in 2003. Unlike most of the rest of the Vía de la Plata, some *albergues* even have a *hospitalero*, a person who staffs the hostel and makes sure that everything is running smoothly. All *albergues* in Galicia rely on pilgrim donations.

## Shopping

It's easy enough to get basics in Galicia, and many villages have a small shop. Santiago is jammed full of tacky souvenir shops, and *ad hoc* markets spring up along its streets in summer. If you're in Finisterre early on a weekday, visit the docks for the fantastic fish market.

## Events & Festivals

On July 25, the **Día de Santiago** and Galicia's national day, Santiago's Plaza do Obradoiro erupts in a sound-and-light display, a tradition that stretches back to the seventeenth century. Galicia parties for twelve months during Holy Years, when July 25 falls on a Sunday (2004, 2010 and 2021). Holy Year festivities begin with the opening of the Puerta del Perdón on the east side of the cathedral as the new year begins and end when it's firmly shut at midnight on December 31; sandwiched in between are literally thousands of concerts, dances, exhibitions and lots of fireworks.

Galicia's other festivals seem to revolve around **food**. Cea's bread festival is the first Sunday in July, Ribeiro wine festivals take place all over the region in late April and early May, there's a barnacle festival in Finisterre at the beginning of August, and many other towns hold shellfish and oyster festivals throughout the year.

# Rest Days & Detours

From Xunqueira de Ambía, it's a 7km one-way detour to the lovely medieval town of **Allariz**. Spend a couple of hours visiting the Romanesque Iglesia de San Esteban and the Iglesia de Santiago, which has an unusual round apse. The nearby Convento de Santa Clara was founded in 1282 by Violante, wife of Alfonso X, who is buried in the massive Baroque cloister; several of their children's graves are also here. Allariz is slowly reviving local traditions such as the *Festa de Boi*, a Galician running of the bulls. Galicians know the town best for the legend of the werewolf of Allariz. In 1852, Manuel Blanco Romasanta, a travelling vendor, was tried for the murder of

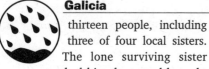
thirteen people, including three of four local sisters. The lone surviving sister tracked him down and brought him to justice, but Romasanta avoided the death penalty by claiming that he was a werewolf. If all this talk of werewolves doesn't put you off, you can stay at the **Hostal Restaurante Alarico** (**$**, ☎ 988 442 398).

Near Dornelas, pilgrims can detour 5km off the camino to the **Pazo de Oca**, a fortified manor house with its own chapel, lake and landscaped gardens. The formal French gardens alone are worth a visit, and are so impressive that the Pazo de Oca is known as the Galician Versailles.

If you're not planning on continuing on the camino to **Finisterre**, it's well worth visiting the small fishing town on a day trip, if only to dip your toes into the ocean. A tour of the wild Galician coast can also take in important places in Santiago's life. Many pilgrims visit **Padrón**, the landing place of Santiago's stone boat some 20km southwest of Compostela, where the stone pillar to which the saint's boat was moored is kept beneath the altar in the Iglesia de Santiago. Time your visit to take in lunch and try a plate of *pimientas de Padrón*, deliciously salty, oil-roasted green peppers.

Just up the coast from Finisterre, the Virgin Mary is said to have visited **Muxía** to hear Santiago preach, sailing here in a stone boat, which was clearly the transport of choice in the early first century. At the sanctuary of Nostra Señora de la Barca, you can see various bits of her boat. The hull moves whenever a person free of sin stands underneath it, and the keel is said to cure digestive problems.

# Vilar de Barrio
Ⓐ✕🛒€🍴 (147km)

Vilar de Barrio sits on the edge of a large plain nestled in the edge of the mountains. You're now firmly in Galicia, and the *hórreos* that you begin to see in Vilar de Barrio will accompany you all the way to Santiago and beyond. These elevated granaries have been used for centuries to store grain and corn away from rats and mice; many of the *hórreos* are crowned with crosses for divine protection of the crops inside. The scallop shell in the town's coat of arms shows that Vilar de Barrio has always played a role in the Camino de Santiago; the simple parish church has a chapel given by Marqués de Boveda, a Knight of Santiago, whose house still stands in the town.

The wonderful modern **albergue** (30 beds, kitchen, hot water, donation) has a good kitchen, although it's not well stocked with cooking pots; ask for the keys at the very small petrol station by the main square. Vilar de Barrio has all a pilgrim could require with two shops, a bar and a bank.

Walk out of the *albergue* past the petrol station and bar along Avenida San Sanfiz, then keep straight on 200m later on Rúa do Fonte as the main road curves left. Pass a *lavadero* (communal laundry) and some *hórreos* on your right a few hundred metres later, on the edge of town. Fork left soon afterwards, following the signs to **Bóveda** (🍴🏨) in 500m and passing a bar in the village in another 500m; there are also two fountains here. In 50m, veer right down a side street, passing a line of *hórreos* on the left. Turn right in 500m on meeting the main road again.

Bóveda ends soon afterwards, but merges seamlessly with **Vilar de Gomareite**. Just 100m after the village sign, turn left down a narrower paved road, then turn left again down a paved lane that leads into open farmland and plains. Turn right 100m later down a paved road, passing narrow strips of fields planted with corn and vegetables, then 500m later, veer left down a dirt track, walking past fields enclosed by tall stone fence posts. Pass a huge modern farm building 300m later as the fields become larger the further you move away from the village.

Follow this arrow-straight track for 3km, then turn right to walk towards the village of Bobadela, which you can see ahead. The villages in this part of Galicia are much more modern than those in the mountains, and the outskirts are almost always dominated by new monster houses built by locals returning from abroad.

In **Bobadela** (🍴🏨, 139km), turn left at a paved road then right in 30m along a side street. Turn left again in 100m then right 100m later and leave the village on a dirt walled lane, forking right 100m later uphill. Fork left in 50m, then go left in another 50m along a gorgeous walled shady lane, green with oak, moss, ivy, and ferns and dotted with foxgloves in summer and mushrooms in autumn. The oak forests here are home to green woodpeckers and, if you're lucky, you'll see goshawks swooping through the canopy of the trees.

Cross a tarmac road 1km from the village and continue on a dirt track lined with broom, gorse and oak on the either side. On meeting a road 50m later turn left and enter **Padroso**, a pretty village with great *hórreos* and some remarkable old dry stone walled houses. Veer right in 300m to keep walking through the village, passing a fountain. Turn right at the end of the village to leave on a walled grassy lane, then go left 200m later to walk uphill along a narrower lane that may be overgrown with gorse, broom and heather. The track soon broadens as the landscape becomes more open and scrub-like, with the occasional pine tree dotting the route.

Reach the top of a ridge about 1km from Padroso, from which there are fabulous views over the plains and surrounding villages. Go straight across a broad dirt track here, heading for a group of boulders which you'll reach in 50m. Follow a narrow path that threads its way through the large stones, then head steeply downhill to descend into an oak woodland. You quickly see the village of **Cima de Vila** to the left and curve left on an overgrown lane to reach it, heading past a clump of eucalyptus trees. Turn right at a paved road, skirting most of the small village, and leave it on a dirt track.

**Map 26** (key page 214)

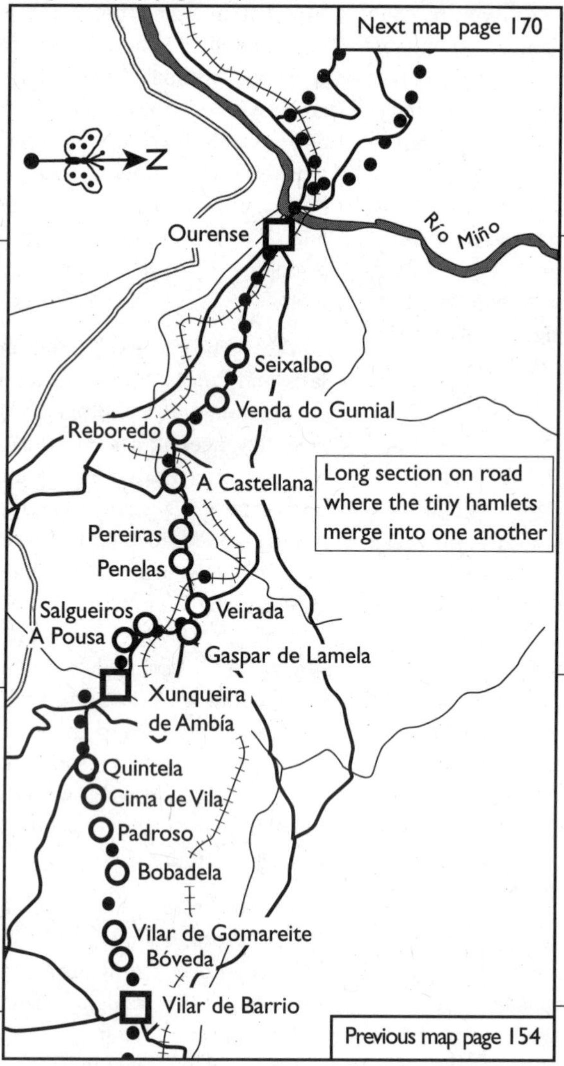
Next map page 170
Z
Río Miño
Ourense
Seixalbo
Venda do Gumial
Reboredo
A Castellana
Long section on road where the tiny hamlets merge into one another
Pereiras
Penelas
Veirada
Salgueiros
A Pousa
Gaspar de Lamela
Xunqueira de Ambía
Quintela
Cima de Vila
Padroso
Bobadela
Vilar de Gomareite
Bóveda
Vilar de Barrio
Previous map page 154

111km

22km

133km

14km

147km

Ourense

Xunqueira de Ambía

Vilar de Barrio

**Profile Chart 26**

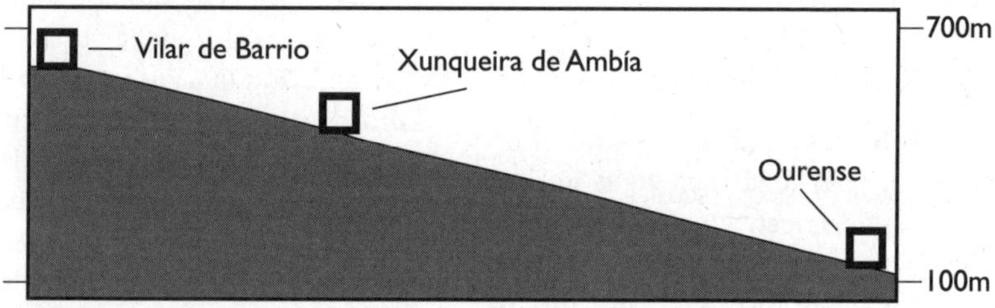
700m
Vilar de Barrio
Xunqueira de Ambía
Ourense
100m
700m
100m

Keep straight on 500m later across a dirt road, heading downhill along another lovely walled lane. Cross a road 200m later to walk on a dirt road that narrows to a walled lane through beautiful woodland and abandoned fields.

Enter **Quintela**, pass a *fuente*, then turn left to leave the village. Turn right 100m later, following signs to the *albergue* in Xunqueira de Ambía and heading downhill on a paved road. Pass the *albergue* 1km later, then turn left on reaching the main road in 200m and walk into Xunqueira de Ambía. Ignore the yellow arrows that lead off the road just as the village begins to go uphill and instead follow the road into town.

# Xunqueira de Ambía
Ⓐ ✕ ▣ € ☕ (133km)

In the fourth century, a vision of the Virgen de la Asunción in a reed bed near here led to the construction of a small chapel. As the site became more popular, control was given to the Order of San Agustín, which began work on the **Monasterio de Santa María la Real** in 1164. The monastery floor plan is based on a Latin cross and has a beautiful sixteenth-century cloister, Renaissance choir stalls and a very unusual Baroque Virgen Peregrina who looks more like Mary Poppins than a pilgrim. Outside, the garden is famous for its diverse collection of medicinal plants. In 1931 the monastery was declared a national monument.

The town is also famous for its **festivals**. During San Blas on February 2, locals club together to buy a piglet that becomes known as *el patrón*. The animal is fed and looked after by all the villagers, who then use the profits from its sale to finance the following year's festival and pay for another piglet. In more modern times, residents celebrate their Celtic past during the Festa Castrexa, during which villagers dressed as ancient Celts parade through the streets pulling floats. From Xunqueira de Ambia, you can detour to the medieval town of Allariz, 7km away; see page 161 for more details.

The **albergue municipal** (20 beds, hot showers, kitchen, donation) is just before town. Pick up the keys in the *ayuntamiento* before 2pm and in the library from 4pm to 8pm.

To leave Xunqueira de Ambía, keep straight on following the signs for Salgueiros, then turn left 50m later down a side street heading downhill. Walk to the left of the Centro de Saude towards a picnic area, then bear left to join a paved road. Keep straight on 100m later as the road curves left to walk on a grassy track past a football pitch. Cross the main road 200m later to keep on a dirt track, then turn right in 30m to join the main road.

Walk over a narrow stone bridge and begin to go uphill, then turn right 100m later up a dirt track; this soon changes to a walled lane with occasional big stone cobbled sections. After 400m, keep straight on over the road on a paved road that becomes a dirt track in 50m next to some modern houses. Turn left in 500m then turn right 50m later to walk along the road.

Enter **A Pousa** (▣ ☕) in 1km, pass some mostly disused *hórreos*, and leave the village on the same road, heading downhill. From here, you'll follow a paved road all the way to the industrial outskirts of Ourense, passing through farmland and many small villages that merge into one another.

In 1km reach **Salgueiros**, keeping to the road as it curves left through the village. In another 1km, turn left down a rough paved road to walk through the tiny village of **Gaspar de Lamela**, which you'll soon leave, turning left on returning to the road in a little under 1km. Enter **Veirada** 100m later, with views of the railway and the Río Barbaña valley to your left. Cross a stone railway bridge on the other side of the village. Pass through **Ousende**, and enter **Penelas** (■■☕) 500m later, where there are two bars, one of which doubles as a shop. In another 2km, enter **Venda do Río**, where there are lots of *hórreos*. The village merges into **Pereiras** (■■☕), a larger village with new houses.

Walk under a railway bridge 1km later, and soon enter **A Castellana** (■■☕). There's a factory ahead as you as you enter the village of **Reboredo** (■■☕) and shortly afterwards you'll be confronted with some of the ugliest scenery of the camino. Keep straight on 500m after the village at a roundabout and enter an industrial area. Turn left at a T-junction 1km later, and cross over the road here to walk on a sidewalk on the right-hand side. Veer right 300m later at a roundabout, following Rúa Don Ricardo Martín Esperanza.

Pass the bars, shops, banks and restaurants that make up **Venda do Gumial** (✕■€☕) and soon veer right off the main road uphill on a minor paved road. Pass a café-bar on the left in

500m and turn right on to the main road. Turn left off the busy N525 just 50m later to walk on a paved road downhill, passing a *cruceiro*. From here, you'll see Ourense sprawled all over the hills in front of you. Walk steeply downhill, rejoining the N525 in 1km.

Turn right here after 200m, watching closely for traffic, then turn left down a dirt track in 50m. To keep on the camino go straight across some train tracks 100m later. If you want to visit the Capilla de Santa Agueda, curve left before the train tracks to go through a train tunnel and take a path up to the Capilla. Whether you detour or not, cross the N525 in 50m to walk down Rúa de Amendo through **Seixalbo** (■■☕), a lovely village of large stone houses crammed into narrow paved streets. Turn right at a gorgeous *cruceiro* down Rúa Maior, then turn left up Rúa de Eirexa and pass the Iglesia de San Breixo.

Leave Seixalbo on a paved road with more views of Ourense. Curve left past a beautiful old *fuente* reached by a set of stone steps and go downhill, entering Ourense as you rejoin the N525. The outskirts of Ourense are a bizarre mix of car dealerships, new apartments and the occasional field of grazing goats. Keep straight on along this road, crossing a roundabout in 1km and continuing along Avenida de Zamora, which becomes Rúa do Progreso. The route is marked with ceramic blue and yellow scallop shells embedded in the sidewalk.

Just after the Mercado de Abastos, keep straight on to continue along the camino. To reach the *albergue*, turn right up Avenida Pontevedra to Plaza Mayor, past the cathedral and up Calle Juan de Austria. The *albergue* is in the Convento de San Francisco, high above the town centre on Calle Emilia Pardo.

# Ourense

Ⓐ Ⓗ ✕ 🖫 € ⓘ 🛒 (111km)

Romans called Ourense Aquae Urentes after the local hot springs, and the fountains in the Praza as Burgas still spurt out steaming waters that are also used to heat nearby houses. In the sixth and seventh centuries, the town was the seat of power of the Suevi kings but their kingdom was destroyed by the Moors in 716, and the Christians did not rebuild the city until Alfonso II came along in 900.

Although much of the town is an ugly urban sprawl, the old quarter is delightful. In the daytime, stroll through the Plaza Mayor's stylish arcades and shops, then when the sun goes down, wander through the nearby pedestrianized streets, when Ourense's many bars and restaurants come alive with the after-work crowd.

Dominating the old quarter is the massive **cathedral**. It was founded in 572, rebuilt in the twelfth and thirteenth centuries, and the façade was restored in a botch job in the sixteenth and seventeenth centuries. The highlights include Maestro Mateo's Pórtico de Paraíso, a copy of the Pórtico de la Gloria in Santiago de Compostela. The *pórtico* retains some original painting, and although the quality of the painting has been questioned by some experts, the result is both singular and vibrant. The octagonal bell tower makes the whole building appear more like a giant manor house than a place of worship.

As well as housing Ourense's *albergue*, the Convento de San Francisco above the old quarter includes a fourteenth-century clois-

ter, with 60 arches and capitals carved in the shapes of plants and humans.

Ourense's **turismo** (☎ 988 273 020) is on Rúa M. Curros Enriquez.

### Accommodation

The **albergue** (40 beds, hot showers, kitchen, donation) is in the Convento de San Francisco, and the sympathetic restoration has retained some of the monastery's huge, high ceilings.

**$ Hostal Cándido**, Calle Hermanos Villar 25 (☎ 988 229 607)

**$$ Hostal Altiana**, Calle Erveledo 14 (☎ 988 370 952)

**$$ Hotel Zarampallo**, Calle Hermanos Villar 19 (☎ 988 230 008)

**$$$$ Hotel Francisco II**, Calle Bedoya 17 (☎ 988 242 095)

---

To leave Ourense, cross the Puente Viejo, a beautiful bridge built in 1230 on Roman foundations. Although it's a pedestrianized bridge, it's still one of the main routes across the mighty Río Miño into the city. The central span is a gravity-defying 45m, and pilgrims who are wary of heights may want to focus their attention on the modern Puente del Milenium to the left, a stunning spiders' web of suspension cables. On the far side of the bridge, walk up Calle de las Caldas past the lively market.

Just 500m after the bridge, the Vía de la Plata splits. There are two routes between Ourense and Casasnovas; each is well marked, begins with a steep section and is almost the same distance. We describe both alternatives below.

## Via Mandrás

For this option, keep following Calle de

las Caldas, then in 500m keep left when it joins the much larger Rúa E Gomez Franqueira. Pass the train station on the right and an old black steam engine on the left. Keep straight on when the main road curves left to a large roundabout. Pass the Rias Balseas café on the left and in 100m cross the road and go through a small park with a play area to rejoin the main road again. Avoid the temptation to turn right and walk through the train tunnel. Keep following the main road, which can be busy with traffic, making for a very dull couple of kilometres. The only distraction is the Río Miño away to your right.

Eventually veer right into **Quintela** (✗🍴🛒), a once separate village now swallowed up as a suburb of Ourense. There are some lovely old houses among the factories that now dominate the village. Start to climb up past the huge factories and after 500m veer left off the main road on to a quiet lane downhill, following signs for Costina de Canedo and Castro de Beiro. Descend past a sawmill on your left and at the bottom of the hill go under the railway via a tunnel and enter **Cachaxuas**.

You now begin a long slog up perhaps one of the steepest hills of the entire Vía de la Plata. The route climbs more than 200m in just under 1km, but there are some great views to distract you. Once at the top, there's a stone on the left indicating only 99km left to go to Santiago. Perhaps more importantly, the village of **Cima da Costa** (🍴) has a bar where you can refuel and quench your thirst.

Keep straight on and soon you're walking through fields and oak trees on a lovely flat dirt track. In just over 1km join

a paved road and begin to head downhill. Cross a bridge and enter the hamlet of **Liñares**, then cross a road and keep heading in the same direction. There are lots of newly planted chestnut trees, and elsewhere the landscape is checkered with disused fields that are returning to scrub.

Cross a bridge and 50m later veer right off the paved road down a dirt track. Rejoin the paved road at a crossroads and keep straight on into **Reguengo**, which you'll soon leave. Climb on a dirt track through a pine forest, cross over a paved road, then soon join another paved road. Meet another paved road, then veer right 200m later. This is the beginning of a wonderful if slightly overgrown 2km section of oak forest. Descend to a beautiful humpbacked bridge over the Rio Barbantiño and into **Ponte Mandrás**, then climb out of the hamlet past a new fountain with a scallop shell to catch the water. At the top of the short climb enter **Mandrás** (🍴🛒), where there's a bar and a shop. Just 50m after the village bar keep left at a fork with a paved road.

The paved road soon ends and you'll find yourself on a walled dirt lane, another beautiful section of old fields and birch, oak and pine trees, little-changed in centuries. The dirt track is paved with huge stones worn down with generations of cartwheel traffic. Pass through a short section that suffered from fire a few years ago and is slowly regenerating.

Skirt the hamlet of **Pulledo** and walk along a paved road. At a T-junction in 500m, turn right, climbing slightly on a paved road. Ignore the turning right for Ferreiro and soon enter **Casasnovas**.

Cross over the N525, where there's a bar then join the route from Ourense via Tamallancos at marker stone km85.690.

## Via Tamallancos

Turn right 500m after the Puente Romano at a stone camino sign. Fork right in 100m, heading uphill along Calle de Santiago, and cross a railway bridge 500m later. There are lots of shops and bars here, and ceramic camino signs are embedded into the sidewalk at every junction. Just over 1km from the junction, turn right at a petrol station down a narrow paved road, fork right 150m later, then turn right in another 100m at a rough paved road.

The landscape quickly becomes more rural, with fields breaking up the outskirts of Ourense. In another 200m, keep straight on across the busy main road, then turn left 150m later in **Soutelo** (🍴), heading uphill on a stone slab road that becomes very steep. In less than 1km, pass a church, in front of which is a fountain and a *cruceiro* bearing an image of Santiago. Cross another busy road and keep heading steeply uphill, then turn right 100m later up Camiño da Costa.

The route is lined with older stone houses interspersed with modern monstrosities. Pass the Ermita de San Marcos da Costa in 500m. It's worth clambering up to this modern church with gardens and a picnic table for panoramic views of Ourense, although the city is somewhat obscured by hillside pines. Walk past some pretty stones houses and pass a *lavadero* as the route changes to tarmac.

You're now firmly in the countryside, walking through oak, ferns, scrub and still climbing steeply. As the road curves right to **Povoadura** 400m after the houses, keep straight on along a dirt track, passing a picnic table and continuing to climb. Turn left at a T-junction with a broad dirt gravel road in 200m, as the route finally flattens out. Keep straight on 1km later, ignoring a side road to Gusei, where there's a twelfth-century Romanesque church. Turn left 200m later at a road, then turn right just 10m later on to a dirt track. Alternatively, you can keep straight on to detour to the Convento Clarisa.

Turn left after 50m on to another dirt track, then veer right on meeting the main road 50m later. Turn right off the road in another 50m, and fork left 50m later down a grassy track, going uphill into more open scrub and heading towards a clump of boulders on a hill ahead to the left. The route becomes paved as you approach a house, and you follow this paved road as it curves left. Turn right along a paved road 400m later in **Outeiros da Forca**, a very new village of ostentatious modern houses; it has an eerie, unfinished, Stepford-wives quality, and each house is guarded by fierce dogs.

Walk out of the village on a quiet paved road with a generous dirt shoulder, passing oak and beech trees. Keep straight on across a paved road 1km later, passing some more monster houses. In 100m, the paved road becomes a dirt track. Veer right 300m later down another dirt track through pine and oak, catching good views across to the wooded hillside ahead and the barren hills in the distance, as you descend to a shaded valley of birch, beech and oak.

In 500m, you'll reach a busy stretch of

## Map 27 (key page 214)

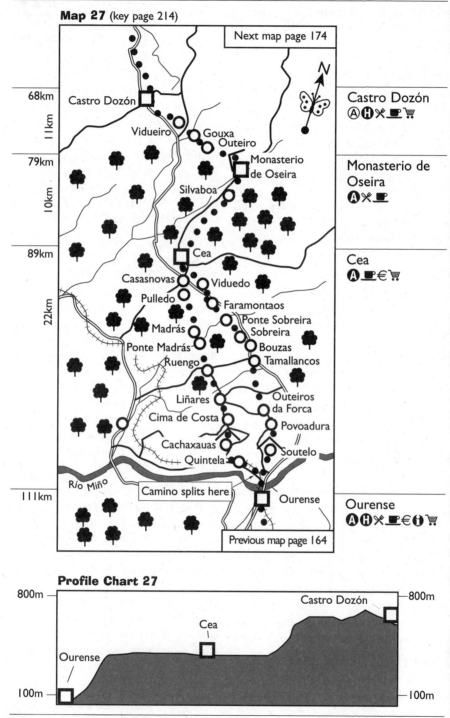

Next map page 174

Castro Dozón

68km

11km

Vidueiro

Gouxa
Outeiro

79km

Monasterio
de Oseira

Silvaboa

10km

89km

Cea

Casasnovas

Viduedo

Pulledo

Faramontaos

Madrás

Ponte Sobreira
Sobreira

Ponte Madrás

Bouzas

22km

Ruengo

Tamallancos

Liñares

Outeiros
da Forca

Cima de Costa

Povoadura

Cachaxauas

Soutelo

Quintela

Río Miño

Camino splits here

Ourense

111km

Previous map page 164

Castro Dozón
Ⓐ🅷✕🍺🛒

Monasterio de
Oseira
Ⓐ✕🍺

Cea
Ⓐ🍺€🛒

Ourense
Ⓐ🅷✕🍺€ℹ🛒

### Profile Chart 27

800m ────────────────────────── 800m

Castro Dozón

Cea

Ourense

100m ────────────────────────── 100m

the N525 lined with factories. Turn left here, then turn right off the road 100m later on to a walled lane shaded by ivy- and moss-encrusted oaks. Enter **Tamallancos** (⬛🛒€) soon after- wards. There's a fountain here, and the houses have ornate stone balconies and typical outside stone steps; if you want to visit the village bar, you'll need to detour to the main road. Just 500m after leaving Tamallancos, you'll enter **Bouzas**, pass- ing a picnic area on the right. Cross a road and continue on a dirt track through a mix of old and new houses. Turn right in the village and leave past a group of *hórreos*, turning left then right and head- ing out on a narrower paved road.

Veer left at a gate 300m later on to a dirt track, passing buildings on your right, the only blots in a landscape of birch and oaks. Cross a minor road in a little over 500m to walk along a narrow paved road, and enter **Sobreira** 500m later. Almost straight away, turn left and leave the tiny village on a paved road. As the road curves right 100m later, keep straight on down a grassy track, then 50m later cross another paved road and head downhill.

A little more than 500m later, cross a gorgeous stone bridge over the Río Barbantiño, and walk through the hamlet of **Ponte Sobreira**. Beautiful stone houses and a huge ruined *hórreo* are all that's left of this serene yet practically deserted spot.

Walk uphill on a grassy track through fields, and enter **Faramontaos** on a paved road in 500m, past a nice mix of old and new houses. Head uphill through the village, and leave on a grassy lane as the road curves right. As you climb, there are beautiful views into the valley

behind. Some 500m out of the village, keep straight on across a narrow paved road on a track through fields, pass- ing a fountain 500m later as you enter the hamlet of **Viduedo** (⬛). Turn right at a paved road in the village, passing an *ermita* 150m later. Turn left on to the main road in 50m, then turn right off it 200m later on to a grassy track. Keep straight on over a minor road about 1km later on a grassy track that can be over- grown in places. Turn left 200m later at a wider track and fork right in 20m. Keep straight on over another minor road 100m later. In 1km, turn left along a grassy lane and enter **Casasnovas**. Join the route from Ourense via Mandrás at marker stone km85.690.

The two routes are now one again.

At a fork just after the marker stone, turn left and keep heading through Casasnovas. The paved road becomes a dirt lane as you skirt around the back of some houses and a pungent pig farm. Climb through a forest of pine and ferns before passing a very lonely looking *cru- ceiro* on the right. Head downhill and in 100m cross the N525 and keep going straight. Curve left around the back of a school and pass through a tunnel, then turn left to cross an old bridge into Cea. Turn left to reach the *albergue*, or keep straight on to arrive at the distinctive Torre del Reloj in the main square.

# Cea
Ⓐ⬛🅿€🛒 (89km)

Cea is famous for *pan de Cea*, a hearty bread that's much denser and slightly darker than that found elsewhere in Spain. Baked here since the reign of Sancho IV more than 700 years ago, the bread is still made in small batches in the traditional way. In true Galician style, *pan de Cea* even has its own festival, on the first Sunday in July.

The town's other claim to fame is *Banda de Gaitas de Cea*, perhaps Galicia's best bagpipe band. The only monument of note is the rectangular Torre del Reloj, which has four arches at its base and a fountain at each corner.

Cea's **albergue** (30 beds, showers, kitchen, donation) is in a beautiful converted building and boasts a kitchen, big dining tables and unfathomable automatic lights; there's even an *hórreo* on the outside patio.

---

Leave the square in Cea, cross the main road and head uphill, passing a statue celebrating the town's bread on Calle Rúa Lodairo. Curve around the sizeable football ground, then take the track at its far side, a wide walled lane with oak trees and lots of heather. Keep to the main trail, ignoring turnings off to fields on the left and right as the oak trees slowly give way to pine plantations and fields.

Keep left at a fork in the trail then, 5km after leaving Cea, join a paved road and turn left. Fork right at a farmhouse and follow a paved road, walking through landscape charred by a recent fire.

Climb for 1km before descending into the hamlet of **Silvaboa**, passing a fountain on the right. Join a larger paved road and turn right, then bear left at a fork and follow the road for just over 2km all the way to Monasterio de Oseira. Look out for an ornate and imposing

fountain about halfway there. You'll soon see the outline of the massive monastery ahead; turn left off the road to reach it.

---

# Monasterio de Oseira
**Ⓐ ✕ ⚑** (79km)

Named for the *osos* (bears) that lived nearby, the grey, baroque façade of the Monasterio de Oseira hides a simple, Cistercian interior. The monastery was founded in 1135 but largely rebuilt after a fire in 1552. The monastery, which was almost completely ruined after the disentitlement of 1835, was lovingly restored in the late twentieth century, led by a small but dedicated group of monks. Sometimes called El Escorial Gallego for its similarity to Madrid's famous monument, the monastery is second only to the real Escorial in size. Highlights include the 1776 library, which has some original walnut cases, the grand 1647 Churrigeresque staircase leading to the upper floor of one of the monastery's three cloisters, and the fourteenth-century chapterhouse, which boasts palm vaulting and unique twisted columns.

When the monastery's twelve remaining monks aren't leading hourly guided tours, they're kept busy making delicious cream cheese and hot chocolate. There are a couple of bars outside the gates that offer refreshment. Pilgrims and those seeking religious retreat can stay at the monastery, following in the footsteps of Graham Greene, who was a regular visitor. Cells are luxurious, with single beds and sitting rooms; the monks also provide hot showers and meals.

---

Curve right 30m after the monastery gates and climb a steep concrete road, looking down on the monastery below. About 200m later, take a sudden left-hand turn up a walled lane, just before the concrete road begins to descend. Continue to climb up this overgrown lane, crossing a paved road. As you near the top of the climb, the trees disappear and the landscape becomes more agricultural. At the top of the hill, join a more well-used dirt lane and turn right. The views of the valleys ahead are a fine reward for the climb. Just before the lane heads downhill join a paved road, then turn right off it 200m later down a single-track shortcut that cuts off a corner of the road.

Rejoin the paved road just before a small hamlet and turn left downhill. Turn right off the paved road under a telephone wire and go down a very narrow stone track. Turn right soon afterwards to cross a small concrete bridge, then climb up the other side of the riverbank and fork left soon afterwards. The hillside here is fire-scarred but offers fine views. Cross a larger track and keep heading downhill. Emerge at a paved road and cross straight over past a bus shelter and into another tiny hamlet.

Climb up the paved road, winding through fields, then fork left into the hamlet of **Outeiro**. At a small farmhouse, turn sharp right uphill along a well-used lane, heading towards a saddle in the hills. Fork left at the saddle and descend, then fork left once more to cross a small river and climb up the other side through moorland. Here, you leave Ourense and enter the province of Pontevedra. Meet a paved road and turn left through the hamlet of **Gouxa** (⬛). Curve right between two farm buildings, then in 100m cross a paved road and

keep straight on. In 500m, pass a *cruceiro* next to a house and meet a paved road. Turn right 50m later down a dirt track and curve around, just clipping the edge of the hamlet of **Vidueiro**. Follow the paved lane around farmhouses then, at the edge of the hamlet near a small windmill, turn right down a dirt track.

Pass a ruined *cruceiro* that's missing its top, walk under some telephone wires and pass a pig farm, then join the busy N525 just after the large antenna that's been visible for the past few kilometres. Follow the road as it curves along the hillside down into **Castro Dozón** (Ⓐ❶✕⬛🛒, 68km). To continue on the camino, turn right off the N525 in the village next to the bar and shop. To stay in Castro Dozón, keep on the N525 for another 300m, then turn left to the town swimming pool. In this complex, you can stay at the **hostal ($)**, eat at the restaurant or stay the night in the **swimming pool** changing rooms (2 beds, mattresses, cold showers, donation).

To continue along the camino, bear right past the church on the left and a cruceiro on the right. Keep going uphill, then go downhill to a layby of the N525. Just before joining the N525, bear right to walk past a new warehouse. Follow this track downhill, then just before the track joins the N525 once again, bear right away from the busy road and turn left almost straight away down a dirt track. Fork left soon afterwards to walk parallel to the N525. At a junction with a turnoff to the new A53 motorway, cross the N525. Follow the road for 150m, turn left to follow a short section of the old road, then turn back onto the N525.

## Map 28 (key page 214)

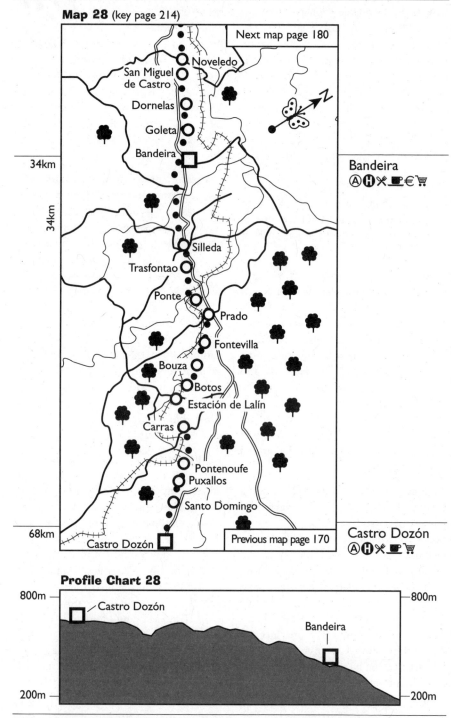

Next map page 180

Noveledo

San Miguel de Castro

Dornelas

Goleta

Bandeira

34km

34km

Silleda

Trasfontao

Ponte

Prado

Fontevilla

Bouza

Botos

Estación de Lalín

Carras

Pontenoufe

Puxallos

Santo Domingo

68km

Castro Dozón

Previous map page 170

Bandeira
Ⓐ🅗✕🍴€🛒

Castro Dozón
Ⓐ🅗✕🍴🛒

### Profile Chart 28

800m

Castro Dozón

800m

Bandeira

200m

200m

Cross the N525 and follow another section of old road before rejoining the N525 near the church in **Santo Domingo** (✗⬛), where Bar Alonso maintains the fine tradition of serving *ribeiro* wine straight from the barrel in earthenware jugs.

Keep following the N525 out of the hamlet, then at a bend in the road turn left down a dirt track. There are good views of the surrounding countryside from here. Bear left at a fork in the track and go downhill into **Puxallos**, past a posh new house decorated with a *cruceiro*, a statue of Santiago and stone lions on each gatepost. Pass an *ermita* and an older *cruceiro*, then walk out of the village and enjoy views ahead down the valley.

Cross the A53 on a bridge and curve right downhill beside the motorway. Bear left in 100m then fork left down a dirt lane under a canopy of oak and pine and follow it to the hamlet of **Pontenoufe**. Head down through the hamlet and cross a river by a concrete bridge, carrying straight on and ignoring the tunnel under the railway. Climb up a dirt road, then 300m after the village turn left on to a smaller dirt lane, heading uphill. Fork left, then turn right at a paved road, going uphill, and fork right soon afterwards to arrive at **Carras** (⬛). Keep left past the church and a new *cruceiro*, then cross the main road, where there's a bar on the right.

Descend now, keeping straight on at a crossroads before joining a paved road and turning left. Keep going downhill through chestnut groves until you reach a much busier road. Turn left here and just before a roundabout, cross the road and leave down a minor paved lane on the right. If you need sustenance, keep straight on at the roundabout for the bar-restaurant at **Estación de Lalín** (✗⬛, 56km). The town of Lalín itself is 4km off the camino.

Cross a bridge and begin to climb. Veer left at a fork next to a *lavadero* and continue to climb up the paved road. Keep straight ahead at another junction and soon enter the hamlet of **Botos**. Pass a *cruceiro* and then a little later fork left to head towards **Bouza**. At a T-junction at the top of a hill, turn left on to a dirt track through pine trees and head downhill into Bouza. You're able to see modern wind turbines on the hills opposite. Cross a paved road and keep straight on.

Walk past a large antenna on the left and a *frontón*, the first you've seen in Galicia. Reach a paved road and turn right into **Fontevilla**, passing an elaborate *cruceiro* on the right before walking past the church and heading downhill on a paved road. Fork left in 100m, then quickly fork right and keep going downhill on a dirt track. Fork right to cross a river, then climb up the other side of the valley to the motorway, where you turn left towards **Laxe** (Ⓐ). In 2003, an **albergue** was being built here.

Follow the N525 uphill past a bar, then turn left down a small paved road that becomes a sunken trail. Begin to climb, keeping a careful look out for a sudden right-hand turn uphill that leads you back to the main road. Once on the main road turn left and head into **Prado**. In the hamlet, turn off the main road once more, on to a back alley behind some houses.

From here, you can detour 2km to visit Castro de Troña, an ancient Celtic village that sits on top of a nearby hill. Visitors can still see the wonderful round buildings, some of which have been reconstructed to show what they would have looked like at the time of the Roman invasion. The whole complex is defended by a huge moat dug into the bedrock.

Leave Prado, cross a paved road and keep straight ahead, passing a very smelly pig farm. In 100m turn right at a paved road through another farm, then left at a larger paved road, heading downhill. Leave the road just before a bridge and turn left to begin a beautiful descent to an ancient bridge. Pass under a railway viaduct and then reach Ponte Taboada, a tenth-century bridge high over the Río Deza with medieval paving that dates from 912.

Start to climb again through **Ponte** and at a T-junction go left. Notice the painted yellow scallop shells someone has added to the walls here. Keep climbing until you pass through Taboada and almost join the N525 next to a church, a *cruceiro* and a statue of Santiago Peregrino. Turn left just before the rest area for car drivers and walk along a dirt lane that was once the main road. There are planted pines and eucalyptus now, rather than Galicia's native oak. Reach a paved road, turn left uphill and in 50m you'll find yourself walking once again in oak forest along a very wide walled lane. Follow this all the way to **Trasfontao**, curve through the hamlet and descend to the river on a cobbled stone lane, then begin to climb once more past a farm.

Cross over a paved road, then in 100m join another paved road next to some multistorey buildings and head into **Silleda** (⬤✖⬛€🛒, 41km), a modern town with lots of facilities but little character. It was once an important cattle centre, and the Iglesia de San Pedro de Ansemil is in Romanesque style. If you need to stay, try **Hotel Ramos** (**$$**, ☎ 986 581 212) or **Hotel Katiuska** (**$$$**, ☎ 986 592 483).

Pass a church, turn left and keep straight on through Silleda. Turn left down Rúa Escuadro Tomiz and turn right down a lane behind an industrial building. Follow the N525 for just over 500m, turn left down a walled lane, then fork right uphill to a weighbridge. Turn left next to a large factory and walk downhill on a paved road through a small hamlet. At a farm next to a football pitch, turn right then quickly left down an old dirt lane. In just under 1km, cross a paved road and keep straight on, passing a junkyard on the left. Reach a bridge in another 1km and turn left then right before crossing a larger paved road.

About 1km before Bandeira, Vía de la Plata signs lead you right with promise of an *albergue*. Unfortunately, this is more than 2km out of town and opens and closes according to the whims of the campsite owner who runs it. Keep straight on to reach the village of Bandeira, where you turn left.

# Bandeira
Ⓐ⬤✖⬛€🛒 (34km)

Bandeira has some good cafés and restaurants. The town's Fiesta de la Empañada is held on the last weekend of August to celebrate the region's flat, filled pies. As well as numerous tastings, demonstrations and competitions, there's music, dancing and general merriment.

You may be able to stay on the floor of the *polideportivo*, but this is discouraged now that the new, out-of-the-way *albergue* has been built. You can also stay at the **Hostal O Portón** ($, Rúa Camilo José Cela 12, ☎ 986 585 483), **Hostal Conde Rey** ($$, Rúa Xeral 27, ☎ 986 585 333) or **Hotel Victorino** ($$, Rúa Xeral 35, ☎ 986 585 330).

Walk through Bandeira on the main road, then once out of town take the right-hand turn for Casela and head downhill. Cross a bridge, then climb up and curve into the hamlet of **Goleta**. Walk through fields dotted with houses, and keep straight on, ignoring turnings until you approach a farm with a new *hórreo* beside a grove of trees. Curve behind the farm on to a dirt track, then fork right. Just 200m later, turn left at a T-junction. As the route begins to climb, turn right and go downhill again into open fields along a paved road. From **Dornelas**, which you'll soon reach, you can detour 5km to **Pazo de Oca**, Galicia's famous manor house; see page 162 for details. Climb out of Dornelas and join the main road, then soon afterwards go left at a fork in the road. Fork left again 1km later, then turn right in another 100m.

Follow the track then fork left through pine and eucalyptus. At **San Miguel de Castro** (🍴) reach a paved road and head straight into the village. Fork right just after the village bar then turn right 500m later, just before a large white industrial building. Pass the Ermita de Santiago and, as you enter **Noveledo**,

bear left down the other side of the ridge. Up to the right, and just before you descend towards Puente Ulla, is a *castro*; for the energetic, it's well worth a visit for the 360° views and a look at Pico Sacro, across the valley. The descent into Puente Ulla is very steep in places but it's on paved road so the footing is good. Pass the Ermita De Nuestra Señora de Gundián and its picnic area, then cross the bridge and enter Puente Ulla.

# Puente Ulla
Ⓗ ✗ 🛒 (21km)

The Romanesque Iglesia de Santa María Magdalena has a marvellous granite façade, Romanesque capitals and a representation of the miracle of San Nicolás de Bari.

There are a couple of bars, restaurants and shops, and you can stay at the **Bar Casa Rios** ($, ☎ 981 512 305) or **Mesón Río Ulla** ($, ☎ 981 512 041).

Walk through town past the church, then cross a road to a fountain and a small square with a *cruceiro*. Take the lane on the other side, heading steeply uphill beside two impressive *pozos* on a stone paved lane that can be slippery when wet. After 400m, join the main road and turn right along it, continuing uphill. You'll soon turn left off the main road along a stretch of old road that cuts off a corner. Walk along a lane parallel to the N525 for 200m, then cross the N525 and turn right up a small paved road on the other side.

In 30m, turn left through a tunnel and then left again on to a dirt track. Climb up to **Famelga**, then follow the paved road right uphill. In 500m, turn left up a wide dirt track, then at a bend in the main track keep straight on along a smaller dirt track.

Keep climbing through eucalyptus until you reach a paved road. Turn left here, following a welcome flat stretch that leads to the Capilla de Santiaguiño. Inside the chapel, there's a statue of Santiago, and across the field from the *capilla* there's a strange spectator stand, likely used to watch the local *romería*. Continue to climb through eucalyptus, the monotony briefly relieved by a small patch of recently planted oak. It's refreshing to see oak displacing eucalyptus for once, which may relieve some of the erosion problems in this area.

Keep climbing, and you'll soon pass a right-hand track that leads to the summit of **Pico Sacro** (534m), where you'll find the Ermita de San Sebastián and spectacular views. According to camino legend, Santiago's followers came here to ask Queen Lupa, pagan ruler of the surrounding area, for permission to bury Santiago's body. Queen Lupa agreed to their request but stipulated that they use local bulls to transport the body. She neglected to mention that not only were the bulls untamed and possessed by evil spirits, but also that a fierce dragon lived in the hill. Santiago's followers calmly defeated the dragon, and the bulls were so awed by Santiago's presence that they placidly allowed themselves to be hitched to a cart. Queen Lupa, understandably impressed, converted to Christianity and renamed the mountain Pico Sacro (sacred peak).

After circumnavigating Pico Sacro, turn left at a paved road and head downhill past a gym and a football pitch until you reach a *cruceiro*. Turn right here and keep going downhill. The camino soon splits; both routes are marked and meet up on the far side of Susana. You can continue straight ahead, but we describe the option that turns right. Follow the road downhill into the hamlet of **Rubial**, then at a *cruceiro* on the far side of the hamlet, turn left downhill, passing the rather ornate Casa Irene, its roof packed with antennas.

Head through tree plantations, then curve down and go through a train tunnel. Cross a river soon afterwards and walk uphill through the hamlets of **Deseiro de Abaixo** and **Pumares**. Climb up to a T-junction, where you turn left then, just before joining the main road, turn right uphill, bypassing most of the village of Susana. Reach a paved road and turn left, then join a bigger road in 100m and turn left again to cross the N525, taking the lane straight ahead between two houses.

Curve down through the outskirts of **Susana** (✕ ♨, 998km) and then go through a tunnel under the road. Climb up the other side and walk through the tiny hamlet of **Cañoteira**. The landscape here is dotted with modern houses; it's home to workers from Santiago who are keen to move out of the city centre.

Turn right uphill, then left in 100m and right again straight away over a bridge across a railway line. Fork left down into a bowl, then turn left halfway up the other side. From here, there are good views of Pico Sacro behind you, and if you continue onwards over a rise and look carefully, you'll be able to see the antenna on Monte de Gozo and below it the spires of Santiago cathedral.

At a T-junction, turn right past a *cruceiro* and into **Aldrey**, then at another T-junction turn left to walk under the railway. Turn right immediately afterwards, heading downhill into another valley. Halfway down, turn right and curve past a *cruceiro* and the Ermita de Santa Lucía, where you cross a small river. Climb uphill out of the valley and fork right past another *cruceiro*. At a bend in the paved road keep straight on, following a dirt track. Walk under a bridge, passing a makeshift scrapyard, then cross the railway for the final time on a fenced bridge and walk along Rúa do Camiño Real de Angrois. Although you're now very close to Santiago, the houses here still have a rural feel, with cows and chickens in front gardens.

Cross straight over the main road next to a *cruceiro* to walk down an old cobbled lane. Follow the lane downhill, with good views of the cathedral, and walk through **Angrois** (⬛🍴✕) on Rúa Ponte do Sar. Cross the Río Sar by an old bridge, and pass the Colegiata de Santa Maria del Sar on the left, a curious twelfth-century building on such an angle that scholars argue whether this is caused by subsidence or is a deliberate architectural feature. The gorgeous twelfth-century cloister is characterized by delicate arches and beautiful sculpture, some of the loveliest carving in Santiago de Compostela after the Pórtico de la Gloria.

Now you begin the final climb of the Vía de la Plata. Walk under a bridge and head uphill on Calle Patio de Madres. Cross a busy road and turn left through Arco de Mazarelos. Cross the Plaza de la Universidad, walk up Rúa da Calderería, turn left on to Rúa de Gelmírez, then follow Rúa da Conga to the Plaza de Platerías in front of the cathedral. To reach the Plaza de Obradoiro, turn left to skirt around Santiago's famous landmark and enter the cathedral via the Pórtico de la Gloria.

# Santiago de Compostela
🅐🅗✕⬛€🛈🛒 (0km)

It's worth planning to spend at least two days in Santiago de Compostela. The city, a UNESCO World Heritage site, is one of the most beautiful in Europe. The mostly pedestrianized old centre is a maze of narrow cobbled streets and plazas that make wandering around Santiago a dreamlike, random experience. The religious zeal of the pilgrimage is tempered by a thriving university whose students drive a wicked nightlife.

The first thing most pilgrims do on arrival in Santiago is visit the **cathedral,** give Santiago a hug and obtain their *compostela*. Medieval pilgrims would spend their first night in vigil at the cathedral and, if it was open, they would gather in front of the high altar, jostling for the best spot. This could get nasty, and in 1207 the cathedral had to be cleansed and reconsecrated because things had got so violently out of hand.

The original church was built by Alfonso II to house Santiago's tomb. Alfonso III the Greater built an even bigger church on the same spot in 899, but this was destroyed by Almanzor's Muslim army in 997. Starting from scratch, construction of the present building began in 1075 and was completed in 1211. Skilled artisans came to Galicia from all over Europe, and hunks of limestone were hefted from Triacastela in eastern

**Map 29** (key page 214)

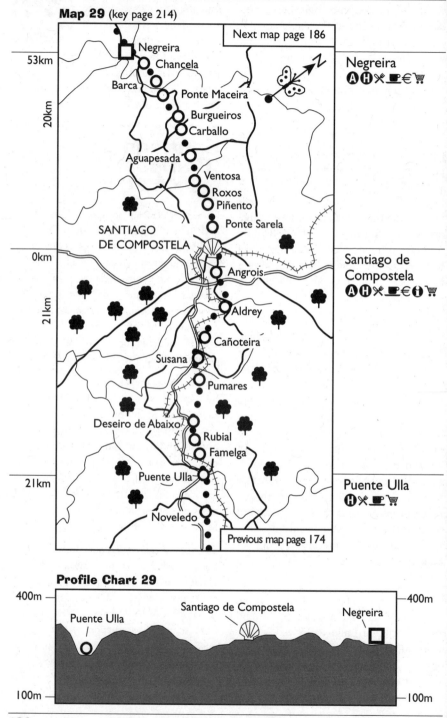

53km

20km

Negreira

Chancela

Barca

Ponte Maceira

Burgueiros

Carballo

Aguapesada

Ventosa

Roxos

Piñento

SANTIAGO
DE COMPOSTELA

Ponte Sarela

Next map page 186

0km

21km

Angrois

Aldrey

Cañoteira

Susana

Pumares

Deseiro de Abaixo

Rubial

Famelga

21km

Puente Ulla

Noveledo

Previous map page 174

Negreira
🅐🅗✕☕€🛒

Santiago de
Compostela
🅐🅗✕☕€ℹ🛒

Puente Ulla
🅗✕☕🛒

**Profile Chart 29**

400m

Puente Ulla

Santiago de Compostela

Negreira

400m

100m

100m

Galicia to Castañeda, some 40km from Santiago, where they were formed into the cathedral's stone blocks.

The cathedral is so massive and so dominates Santiago that its doors open out on to three separate city squares. The most dramatic entrance leads from the huge Plaza de Obradoiro, up an imposing double staircase to the Baroque **Obradoiro Façade**. Before you climb the stairs, walk backwards to the far side of the square so that you can take in the whole, glorious façade.

As you enter from this side, you'll suddenly reach the jaw-dropping **Pórtico de la Gloria**, built in 1168 by the Maestro Mateo, and the main entrance into the cathedral before the outer façade was built. Art historians suggest that this doorway inspired the movement from Romanesque to Gothic architecture across Europe. The *pórtico* is jammed with Christian symbolism and, like most things in the cathedral, it's worth visiting more than once. The middle pillar of the Pórtico de la Gloria depicts the Tree of Jesse, Santiago and the Virgin.

Over the years, a ritual for arriving pilgrims has developed. First, touch your right hand in the middle of the central column of the **Tree of Jesse** to give thanks for your safe arrival. Centuries of devoted hands have worn five finger grooves deep into the marble pillar, a humbling reminder of the tradition you're following. Around the back of the pillar is a small bust of **Maestro Mateo**, the architect of the Pórtico de la Gloria. Butting his head three times is said to impart some of his considerable intelligence to you.

Proceed up to the high altar. On top of it sits Santiago Matamoros shouldered by massive gold angels. On the right-hand side as you look at the altar you'll find a narrow set of stairs that lead behind the figure of

**Santiago Peregrino**. Climb up into the shrine and embrace the thirteenth-century, jewelled statue of St James from behind. The gold crown that pilgrims could place on their heads has now sadly disappeared, along with the pilgrim tradition of placing their own hats on Santiago's head.

Next, head down into the **crypt** to see the casket that's said to contain the bones of the saint and two of his disciples, Theodore and Athanasius. The tomb of Santiago was first discovered in the ninth century, enclosed in a stone mausoleum on this ancient necropolis. Santiago's bones were hidden several times over the centuries to keep them away from thieves and kings who wanted the relics for themselves. The bones were so well hidden that their exact location was forgotten, but pilgrims continued to venerate an urn on the altar that was believed to hold the saint's bones. Excavations in the late nineteenth century unearthed some bones, said to be those of Santiago when the discoverer went temporarily blind. Pope Leo XIII verified their validity a few years later, and the remains now rest in a silver coffin below the altar.

Every day at noon, there's a pilgrims' mass. The ceremony often culminates in the swinging of the **botafumeiro** (smoke belcher), a massive silver incense burner said to be the largest in the Catholic world. It takes up to eight people in a team called a *tiraboleiros* to tie the knots and set the massive silver apparatus swinging across the cathedral. This *botafumeiro* dates from 1851, after the original was stolen by Napoleon's troops when they looted the cathedral. During mass, the best place to sit is on either side of the main altar, so that the *botafumeiro* seems to skim the top of your head before it swings back to the cathedral roof.

## Galicia

If you're lucky enough to arrive in Santiago during a Holy Year, when the Día de Santiago, July 25, falls on a Sunday (2004, 2010, 2021), you can enter the cathedral through the **Puerta del Perdón**. The door is opened on the eve of a Holy Year and closed on December 31.

To receive your **compostela**, final proof that you've completed the pilgrimage, present your stamped pilgrim's passport at the Oficina del Peregrino on the second floor of the Casa del Deán, just off Plaza Platerías on the south side of the cathedral. The friendly but busy staff will record your nationality and your place of departure, to be read out at the next day's pilgrims' mass. If your motivations for the pilgrimage aren't religious or spiritual, you'll get a colourful alternative certificate instead of the traditional *compostela*. There's also a small tourist office downstairs, pointing pilgrims in the direction of accommodation and transport. You can purchase cardboard tubes to protect your document or even get your *compostela* laminated at a small trinket shop across the road from the office.

Dominating the northern side of the Plaza de Obradoiro and now a grand five-star hotel, the **Hostal de los Reyes Católicos** was originally built on the orders of Fernando and Isabel to house pilgrims and provide them with medical treatment. As part of its continuing obligation to pilgrims, the *parador* provides free meals to the first ten pilgrims to arrive at 9am, 12pm and 7pm. Arrive early as there's almost always a crowd of hungry pilgrims wanting to eat for free. To line up for your free meal, face the *parador* and turn left to walk along the front of the building to the underground parking garage and present the doorman with a photocopy of your *compostela*. You'll eat what the restaurant staff eat, washed down with a bottle or two of wine, and the food ranges from fantastic to average. Even so, it's a great experience, and you'll be led through the sumptuous, multi-courtyarded parador on your way to the staff dining room.

There's much more to see in Santiago. If you're here for a couple of days, invest in one of the many detailed guides to the city available from local bookshops. There are lots of trinket shops hoping to lure money from your wallet, and you can buy anything from tacky key chains decorated with a *flecha amarilla* (yellow arrow) to a life-size replica of the *botafumeiro*.

There are three **turismos** in Santiago: the municipal and the regional ones are on Rúa do Vilar, and the camino *turismo* on Avenida da Coruña (closed weekends) has information on the route to Finisterre.

### Accommodation

Pilgrims can stay at the **Albergue Seminario Menor**, just outside town, for a few euros, although any celebrations will be severely curtailed by the strict 11pm curfew, and some pilgrims have experienced theft.

**$$ Hostal La Estela**, Raxoi 1 (☎ 981 582 796)

**$$ Hostal Alameda**, Rúa do San Clemente 32 (☎ 981 588 100)

**$$$ Costa Vella**, Calle Puerta da Pena 17 (☎ 981 569 530)

**$$$$ Hostal de los Reyes Católicos**, Plaza de Obradoiro (☎ 981 582 200)

---

Although most pilgrims end their journey at Santiago, it's well worth lacing up your boots and continuing to the ocean. Pilgrims who walked the *camino francés* often comment on the solitude of the *camino de Fisterra*, those arriving from the Vía de la Plata may find the route busy and crowded.

The camino to Finisterre predates the medieval pilgrimage by at least a millennium. Celts and other ancient peoples travelled to the solar temple of Ara Solis, on the tip of Cabo Finisterre, to worship the sun, or they simply travelled as far west as they could without getting their feet wet. Romans thought that the westernmost tip of Spain, Finis Terrae, was the end of the world, and they would watch with concern as the sea engulfed the sun each night, hoping that it would rise again the next morning. Even medieval pilgrims often continued to the sea. Many visited Padrón and Muxía, places connected with Santiago's miraculous arrival in Spain, but pilgrim hospices and churches dedicated to the saint also lined the route to Finisterre.

The easy-to-follow *camino de Fisterra* is a lovely route through quiet countryside. If you're returning to Santiago, consider leaving some equipment at your hotel and travelling light to Finisterre.

Stand in the Plaza do Obradoiro facing the *parador*, and turn left to walk down Rúa das Hortas. In about 200m, cross a road to walk along Rúa do Cruceiro do Gaio, which changes its name, first to Rúa do Pozo de Bar and then to Rúa de San Lorenzo. Occasional faded yellow arrows are painted on the road but, apart from these, there are no signs until you reach a park in a few hundred metres. Turn right at a concrete bollard here, the first of many on a mostly well-marked trail, to head through the small park on a wide, shady, grit path. Turn left at the end of park and walk down Costa do Cano, a narrow road

edged by high walls, dripping with plants and rich with the intense smell of jasmine in spring and summer. Almost immediately, you'll find yourself in the countryside.

Cross a stone bridge at **Ponte Sarela** and turn left past some buildings to walk down a dirt track, then at a fork in 50m, take the left-hand (lower) track, which soon narrows to a path. Cross a stream, then take the left-hand fork 50m later, down a path that can be overgrown. At a small clearing in a few hundred metres, keep straight on past a concrete camino bollard.

The trail is lined with foxgloves, ferns and blackberries, and it can be a little mucky underfoot after rain. In a few hundred metres, cross an open patch of ground and walk uphill towards some modern houses, then turn left at a wider dirt track as you reach the houses, looking behind you for great views of Santiago. Turn left at a tarmac road in 50m, then turn right up a paved track in a couple of hundred metres. The route soon narrows to a stony dirt track after passing a house, and you're now walking through an oak wood that's a deep, startling green, intense and vibrant with ivy and moss.

Sadly, the oak is soon usurped by eucalyptus, and the change in light quality is instantly apparent, as is the sudden lack of undergrowth. The path flattens out near the top of a hill, then curves right at a concrete sign. Ignore minor tracks off to the right and left, and walk downhill, mostly through eucalyptus trees but also passing occasional and welcome stretches of oak. Turn right on to a smaller track just before walking under some power lines, then walk uphill again for short while before curving left to walk steeply downhill. Turn left 200m later and reach a narrow tarmac road in 50m; turn right here, then left at another road soon afterwards.

Reach **Piñeiro,** where the traditional architecture is overwhelmed by big, modern houses as Santiago's commuter belt stretches westwards. Keep straight on in a couple of hundred metres down a narrower tarmac road as the main road curves to the right. Follow this minor road as it curves to the right around a modern house in another 200m or so. The paved road changes to dirt as you walk along fields, then changes back to tarmac as the fields end. Turn right 100m later, then turn left to pass a huge *hórreo* and walk down a narrow tarmac road past the older village houses.

Leave Piñeiro on a narrow tarmac road. It's a lovely, pastoral scene, with great views back towards the village of meadows, stone houses and *hórreos.* Pass a few very grand houses, then turn right up a tarmac road, ignoring the yellow arrows that lead straight on. Note that new houses are being built here and the road may soon be paved. Follow the road as it curves to the left, then turn right just after the bend to walk on a stony path uphill through eucalyptus and deciduous woodland. This is a well-marked route through trees, and it's easy going for the most part. Ignore side tracks and emerge on a paved road at the start of a village.

Turn left at a tarmac road in a couple of hundred metres, then turn right 20m later to walk on an old narrow road. There are lovely old houses here, and vines all around this area are strung high

off the ground on parallel wires to protect the grapes from damp. Leave the village on a narrow tarmac road, then turn right in about 500m just before a small square sports centre.

Cross a bridge over the Río Roxos, then veer left 50m later, following a concrete bollard and ignoring a large white arrow painted on the road that leads right. Walk through pine and eucalyptus trees, then in about 500m, turn right to walk uphill on a tarmac road that soon changes to dirt.

Up ahead, you'll see Roxos, but turn right just before reaching it to walk along a lovely flat track through trees, passing a cluster of beehives on your right. The track soon emerges at a dirt road in **Roxos** (✗), then in about 100m reaches the main road, where there's a restaurant/bar called Meson Alto do Vento.

Turn right at the restaurant, and walk down the road for about 500m, then at a bus stop at **Ventosa,** turn right down a narrow tarmac road. Cross another tarmac road, walk through a group of houses and past a big electricity pylon as the paved road changes to stone. Turn left in a couple of hundred metres as the stone changes back to tarmac, cross a stream, then turn left at the main road to walk along the sidewalk. Pass a shop on the left and a lumber mill on the right. In front of you, the wide valley is speckled with red roofed hamlets. Walk gradually downhill to **Aguapesada** (✗🍴), a village of pretty stone houses with small square windows, passing the Meson O Cruceiro restaurant on the right.

At the bottom of the valley, turn left down a paved stone street next to a lovely, single-arched medieval bridge that's been recently restored. In a couple of hundred metres, cross a tarmac road and walk uphill on a narrower tarmac road that changes to a narrow dirt track as the houses end and you enter a eucalyptus and pine wood. This is a steep, tough climb with little shade, although occasional stone benches offer a place to rest. After about 2km, turn right at a tarmac road, next to a stone bench and a TV tower.

Climb for another 500m or so, then pass a fountain and soon reach the top. In a few hundred metres you'll arrive in **Carballo** (⛲), beautifully set amongst fields and trees, and dotted with the region's traditional red-roofed stone houses. There are lots of songbirds here, too, and gorgeous views across another beautiful valley of red-topped houses. The lower part of the village has two bars.

Leave Carballo on the main road, and soon enter **Burgueiros**, a wealthy hamlet with lots of big new houses. Almost immediately, you'll pass a sign for **Ponte Maceira** (✗⛲) and soon see the gorgeous village ahead in a brilliant green valley. Veer left towards the village's centre once you've passed the first few houses, and reach an excellent bar-restaurant. The restaurant is posh and expensive, but you can get excellent sandwiches and drinks at a modest price in its café, and it's idyllically set next to a weir on the wide Río Tambre. The bridge after which Ponte Maceira is named elegantly spans the river; from its centre you may see a heron calmly standing at the edge of the river or a kingfisher darting just above the water. Construction of the bridge began at the end of the fourteenth century, though much of what you can see

today dates from a sympathetic eighteenth-century restoration.

Turn right to cross the river, then turn left at the end of the bridge. On the other side of the river you'll see the **Capilla de San Brais** and a medieval *pazo*, a grand Galician country house, surrounded by beautiful gardens. Walk past a *cruceiro* on your left, gruesomely decorated with a carved skull and crossbones at its base. Turn left at the end of the village down a narrower tarmac road, walking through fields near the river in a beautiful green valley.

In a little under 1km, veer left off the road to walk down a dirt track towards the river through ivy-encrusted trees. Foxgloves line the route here, glorious in late spring and early summer. Pass under the arch of the "new" nineteenth-century bridge that leads to Ponte Maceira Nova, then veer away from the river along a farm track through fields.

Join the main road after about 500m and turn left to walk along it, mostly bypassing the modern, nondescript village of **Barca**. Turn left at the end of the village to walk down a minor road. You're still walking along the valley floor, and there are lovely glimpses of the tree-lined river from here. Walk uphill past a small factory, finally leaving the river behind. After a brief climb, the camino starts to go downhill into **Chancela**, passing a huge mansion called the Pazo de Chancela, and you'll soon see Negreira ahead, encroaching on and blending into Chancela.

At the main road soon afterwards, turn left to enter Negreira. Pass a couple of apartment buildings and a statue of a

**Map 30** (key page 214)

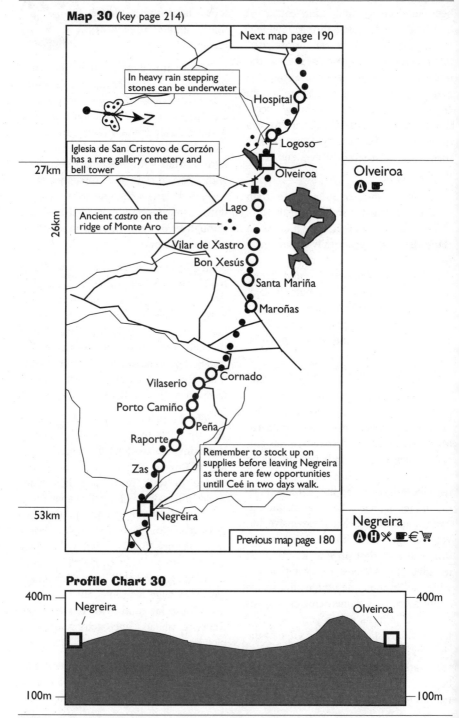

Next map page 190

In heavy rain stepping stones can be underwater

Hospital

Logoso

Iglesia de San Cristovo de Corzón has a rare gallery cemetery and bell tower

27km

Olveiroa

Olveiroa
Ⓐ☕

26km

Lago

Ancient *castro* on the ridge of Monte Aro

Vilar de Xastro

Bon Xesús

Santa Mariña

Maroñas

Vilaserio

Cornado

Porto Camiño

Peña

Raporte

Remember to stock up on supplies before leaving Negreira as there are few opportunities untill Ceé in two days walk.

Zas

53km

Negreira

Previous map page 180

Negreira
Ⓐ🅷✕☕€🛒

**Profile Chart 30**

400m — Negreira

400m

Olveiroa

100m —

100m

pilgrim on the main road into town. The *albergue* is just outside town, but there's limited signage and very few yellow arrows; to reach it, turn left a few hundred metres after the statue down the Rúa de San Mauro. In a few hundred metres, pass under the stone arch that links Pazo de Cotón with Capela de San Mauro. Cross a bridge over the Río Barcala, and turn left 100m later up a narrow tarmac road. You'll reach the *albergue* in about 1km.

# Negreira
Ⓐ Ⓗ ✗ ⬛€🛒

Negreira is a modern, well-equipped town with decadent pastry shops and excellent seafood restaurants. The town's notable monument is the fortified, medieval Pazo del Cotón. Its solid grey exterior was restored in the seventeenth century, and it's joined to the Capilla de San Mauro by an enclosed, arched walkway.

### Accommodation
The modern **albergue** (16 beds, hot showers, kitchen, donation) has the twin luxuries of single beds and modern, sex-segregated bathrooms. There are extra mattresses for summer overflow.

**$$ Hostal Residencial Tamara** (☎ 981 885 201)

**$$ Hostal-Restaurante La Mezquita** (☎ 981 885 128)

The route from Negreira to Olveiroa passes through a mix of forest and farms. The beginning is especially lovely, heading along an old trail, with fantastic views across multiple valleys. There's almost nowhere to buy supplies, so make sure you stock up on lunch and dinner supplies before leaving Negreira.

Turn right out of the *albergue* and then turn left in 100m up the road signposted "Negreira Iglesia." Go past some houses and head out of the village down a lane, looking out for good views of Negreira to the right. After a few hundred metres, the lane goes downhill; at the first bend, take the left-hand track heading through the trees. The slightly overgrown old lane leads along the side of the hill, with more good views to the right. Keep straight ahead when you join the main road, and carry on into **Zas**.

After about 1km on the main road, turn right on to a side road opposite a bus shelter. Pass a small church, then at a T-junction soon afterwards (still in the village), turn left slightly uphill and keep straight on out of Zas. At the next junction, keep left uphill on a dirt track through farmland and a eucalyptus plantation. Turn right at the next junction, then left at another junction 100m later. The camino emerges from the trees just before another hamlet, then goes right at a T-junction with a dirt track next to the hamlet's first house, and heads into trees once more. Once you reach the edge of the forest, turn left downhill to a stream and climb up the other side on a rocky track.

Cross straight over a paved road, taking the slightly overgrown trail on the far side, one of the many beautiful old walled lanes that criss-cross this part of Galicia, prettily linking fields and villages.

After 1km, descend and emerge from the forest in an area of old fields. Climb uphill from here, winding through trees towards **Rapote** and, on the far side of the hamlet, turn left downhill on a dirt track. Cross over a stream and climb up the ridge that you've seen intermittently for the last couple of kilometres; this is a lovely stretch of oak forest with ferns, ivy and big black slugs.

After 1km or so, you'll arrive at **Peña** (☕). To detour to the village bar, turn left at the sign in front of the first house in the hamlet, then turn right 100m later. There's no need to retrace your steps once you've had a drink: simply continue on the main road and you'll join up with the camino in a few hundred metres. If you're avoiding the bar, carry on through the village past a church and turn left at a *cruceiro*, then left again to join the main road, where you turn right.

You're now in **Porto Camiño**, a tiny hamlet with a smattering of houses. Keep straight on past the turning for Xallas on your left, then just after the last house in Porto Camiño, turn right on to a track. There are actually four tracks here: take the second from the right, just to the left of the water tank. Fire has destroyed much of the forest that was once here, judging from the burnt stumps, and gorse and broom has grown in place of the trees. Cross a stream and then, at a T-junction, turn left towards the main road.

At the road, turn right to follow it over the top of a saddle. Pass the sign for Landeira and after walking along the road for a couple of kilometres, descend towards Vilaserio. As the descent steepens, look out for a sharp left turn on to a dirt lane that takes you through **Vilaserio** (☕). Pass behind the village bar — or stop, as this is the last refresh-ment for 8km — and turn left on to the main road, then walk past the sign for Pesadoira and carry on along the main road until you come to **Cornado**.

Turn right into this small hamlet, then take a sharp left past the bus shelter and two stones inlaid with shells, and follow the track uphill into farmland and forest. Keep left at the next fork then, at the paved road a few hundred metres later, turn right. After about 500m, turn left at a country lane that's something of a local garbage dump. Come to a T-junction and go left uphill, then a couple of hundred metres later at the top of a rise, turn right. In another few hundred metres, keep left at a fork, heading through fields with great views of the surrounding countryside.

Keep straight on over two crossroads. The lane becomes paved and then goes up and around a small rise, then crosses a stream and leads into **Maroñas**. Turn left into the village and take a moment to notice the different style of *hórreos*: Maroñas' granaries are made entirely of stone boulders, as the rain-drenched Galician climate rots wood quickly, and stone is plentiful locally. Once through the village, keep straight on until you come to a T-junction 500m later. Turn left here, and head into Santa Mariña (☕), then veer right along a lane to the main road. Turn left at the main road, passing a couple of bars on the right.

Keep straight on the road for about 500m, then turn right up a paved road into the hamlets of Bon Xesús and Vilar de Xastro. There's an old *cruceiro* on the left just before the first hamlet. Veer left into the second hamlet, then as the houses end, go right uphill and take a sharp left soon afterwards. Some pilgrims report that parts of the route are roped off; keep a look out for yellow arrows, and duck under the ropes if you need to. You're now on a dirt track and climbing up **Monte Aro**, where there are some remains of an ancient *castro*. Keep climbing until you reach the shoulder of a hill. Zigzag first right, then left 100m later, and head down the other side of the ridge. Your climb up is rewarded with fantastic views, and there are many *rubias gallegas*, Galicia's typical rust-red cows, in the fields. About two-thirds of the way down, turn sharp left into the hamlet of Lago.

Once in **Lago**, turn left again and follow the road for about 500m, then turn right downhill on to a quieter road next to a bus shelter. There are fabulous views of wind turbines up ahead. From Lago, energetic pilgrims who need to buy provisions can detour to **A Picota** (🛒), almost 4km away, where there are good shops.

Otherwise, continue along the paved road lined with gorse and pine trees, ignoring dirt tracks off on either side. After a couple of kilometres, you emerge at the unusual Iglesia de San Cristovo de Corzón. The church is separate from its belltower, and the arched cemetery looks like a gallery of graves around the church, and the graveyard itself contains some splendid-looking crosses. Turn left 30m after the church and follow this minor road to the main road. Turn right here and cross the much-restored sixteenth-century bridge over the Río Xallas, where locals fought Napoleon's troops during the Peninsular War.

Stick to the main road for a couple of kilometres. Pass a *farmacía* on the left, and the turning for Santiago Oliveira on the right, then take the first left into Olveiroa, reaching the pretty village in few hundred metres. Turn right in the hamlet to reach the *albergue*.

**Olveiroa** (🅐🛏) is a tiny village with stunning examples of rural architecture. Village houses are made of thick stone walls, and Olveiroa's *cruceiro* is a lovely one. The **albergue** (35 beds, hot showers, kitchen, donation) has separate, beautifully restored stone buildings for sleeping, eating and hanging out. The *hospitalera* cooks fabulous *sopa de ajo* (garlic soup), and pilgrims chip in with bread, cheese and whatever else they have, then sit at a communal table in front of a roaring fire. The village bar sells *bocadillos* and bottles of wine, and a local woman sells *empañadas* from the back of her car.

The trail from Olveiroa to Finisterre can be a little confusing in places, so keep your eyes peeled, particularly around Cée, for yellow arrows. You'll also finally reach the crashing waves of the Atlantic, a distraction that may compound your route-finding difficulties. The last stretch is along a beach, and stepping off the end of the world into the ocean is a fantastic camino finale.

Keep straight ahead through Olveiroa, retracing your steps if you stayed at the *albergue*. Head downhill, then turn left at a junction next to the village *lavadero*, and walk over a concrete bridge just before the main road. Follow a track, then fork left at a junction next to a telephone pylon, looking out for a hill fort on your left. Climb up the ridge for about 100m, then turn left to walk along the side of the hill, from which there are great views of the river in the gorge

## Map 31 (key page 214)

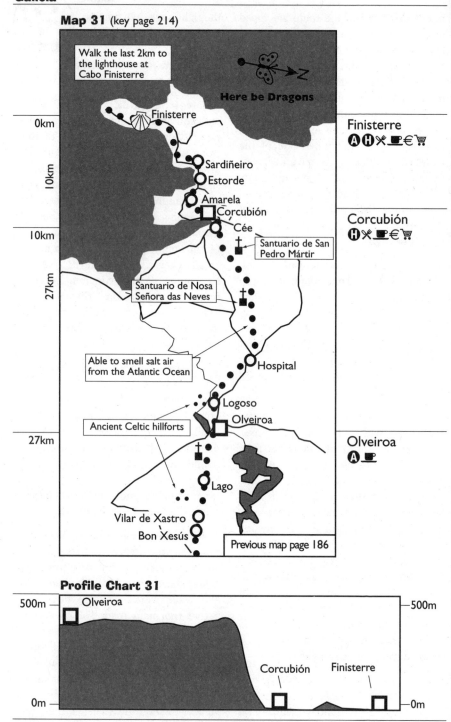

Walk the last 2km to the lighthouse at Cabo Finisterre

Here be Dragons

Finisterre

Sardiñeiro

Estorde

Amarela

Corcubión

Cée

Santuario de San Pedro Mártir

Santuario de Nosa Señora das Neves

Able to smell salt air from the Atlantic Ocean

Hospital

Logoso

Olveiroa

Ancient Celtic hillforts

Lago

Vilar de Xastro

Bon Xesús

Previous map page 186

0km

10km

10km

27km

27km

Finisterre
🅐🅗✕💻€🛒

Corcubión
🅗✕💻€🛒

Olveiroa
🅐💻

### Profile Chart 31

Olveiroa

Corcubión

Finisterre

500m

500m

0m

0m

below, and of the hills and wind turbines that surround you. Descend to the Río do Hospital, and cross it via stepping stones, a hairy adventure after heavy rain, when the stepping stones can be under a fair bit of water: a walking stick can be invaluable for balance.

Climb up the other side of the valley and follow the grassy track into **Logoso**. Walk straight through the small hamlet, then at a fork on the far side, take the track going left uphill. Keep climbing until you reach **Hospital (🍽)**, which is dominated by a massive carbide factory then, once at the hamlet, turn right then left to join the main road. Turn left here to walk along the road, and climb up past a bar that serves great *bocadillos*.

A few hundred metres later, the camino splits. The right-hand turn takes you to Muxía, a popular pilgrim destination just north of Finisterre. Turn left to continue on your way to Finisterre, walking past the carbide factory. Soon after you leave its belching fumes behind, turn right down a dirt track. Keep straight on over open ground with few trees and lots of gorse and shrubs, then pass a *cruceiro* at a paved road and keep straight on. Not long afterwards, you come to a modern stone wall. This wall has been built directly over the track, and it's difficult to see where the camino goes, but if you keep straight on, parallel to the wall, the track will reappear in about 300m.

From here onwards, you'll start to smell the salt ocean air and the track becomes sandier, although it's still another 8km or so before you reach the water. Follow the track downhill to a T-junction, turn right to head up and over a rise, then head down to the **Santuario de Nosa Señora das Neves**. Near the restored *santuario*, there's a *fonte santa* (holy fountain) said to cure all manner of ailments. Each September 8, local people arrive here for a *romería*. There's a *cruceiro* in the field below.

Turn right past the *santuario*, heading downhill briefly, then begin a long, slow, eucalyptus-lined climb that lasts for almost 3km. Eventually, you'll pass the chapel of San Pedro Mártir, whose *fonte santa* is thought to cure verrucas, rheumatism and, happily for tired pilgrims, sore feet. Keep straight on as the eucalyptus gives way to plantations of pine, heading steadily downhill, and ignoring the very tempting cobbled path off to the right. The track gets steeper as it begins the rocky descent into Cée, and you'll get your first views of the sea.

Just before you arrive at **Cée** (✗🍽€🛉), turn left at a paved road, then take the first right soon afterwards. Pass a bar, the second of the day to serve tasty *bocadillos*, then turn right on to the main road. This part of the camino isn't well marked and can be confusing. The easiest way to navigate is to ignore the yellow arrows, and head instead for the waterfront road that links Cée and Corcubión, now merged into each other.

**Corcubión (🛈✗🍽€🛉)** has some lovely manor houses, emblazoned with maritime-motif crests, and waterfront tile benches ideal for a breather. There's a range of accommodation in Corcubión, including **La Cirena** ($, ☎ 981 745 036), **Las Hortensias** ($$, ☎ 981 746 125) and **El Hórreo** ($$$, ☎ 981 745 500). As you walk around the bay, look out for a church just off the waterfront road on the right. Just before the church, as the road rises slightly, turn sharp right uphill at a junction marked by a faint yellow arrow. At a fork not long afterwards, keep left.

Keep going until you come to the Plaza de Castelao, a small square with a taxi rank, then leave the square by the left-hand corner, and head for the Iglesia de San Marcos. The thirteenth-century church has neo-Gothic towers and a fifteenth-century sculpture of the church's patron saint. At the church door, take a very sharp right up some steps, and follow the street to a small square called Campo de Rollo. Cross straight over to the tiny, high-walled lane opposite, and follow its overgrown route uphill.

Turn left once you meet another lane at the top of the hill, then turn right soon afterwards. Cross the main road, passing a basketball court and a picnic area on the left, then take the old lane that intersects two larger roads 100m later, watching for very faint yellow arrows. In 40m, turn right at a fence and follow the boundary wall behind some houses in **Amarela**. If you pass a white house, you've gone too far; retrace your steps.

In about 500m, you'll arrive at the main road again. Turn left here, then turn right at a bend about 300m later, veering right soon afterwards on to a track. In 1km or so, turn right on rejoining the main road and follow it into the village of **Estorde**.

Keep on the main road to **Sardiñeiro** (🏠✗🍴), where you can stay at the **Praia de Estorde** ($$$, ☎ 981 745 585). Just before entering the town, look on the right for a small lane just beyond the town's name sign. Follow this lane, which recrosses the main road a few hundred metres later, then rejoin the main road in another 200m, and turn left.

In a couple of hundred metres, turn right down a narrow road, then 10m later turn left down a small lane between a house and an *hórreo*. In another 100m, just before the lane veers back towards the main road, turn right and climb slowly along the old Rúa da Finisterra.

At a T-junction just out of town, turn left along a track to walk through a beautiful pine forest. Keep straight on over the main road as the camino heads down a gully towards a tiny, dramatic cove, then climbs up the other side to meet the main road once more. Take the next left along a paved road down to the beach.

To get to Finisterre, either walk along the beach to collect your scallop shell and splash about in the sea (you'll need to wade across a couple of tidal streams), or walk along a boardwalk into town. At the far end of the beach, pass a restaurant-bar and climb up to a viewpoint. Look out for the downward pointing scallop shell here, showing that your journey is almost at an end. Head down the street into Finisterre. The *albergue* is in the middle of town, one block up from the statue in the port, and next door to a supermarket.

# Finisterre
Ⓐ🏠✗🍴€🍴

Finisterre is a no-nonsense working port. There's a fifteenth-century *cruceiro* in front of the twelfth-century Romanesque-Gothic **Iglesia de Santa María de Areas**. Domenico Laffi, the Italian camino chronicler, visited the church in the seventeenth

century; the chapel next door was once a pilgrim hospice.

Finisterre shows few other signs of its camino past. Its character comes more from the sea, and it's fascinating to wander around the port, watching the primary-coloured fishing boats in the bay, or chatting with fishers as they mend gnarled nets. The town has some fancy fish restaurants, but you're better off heading down to the port and eating at one of the cluster of down-at-heel bars or at a *sardiñada*, an open-air sardine grill.

Pilgrims who walk or cycle from Santiago to Finisterre are entitled to a *fisterrana*, a certificate of completion of the pilgrimage; you can get yours from the *hospitalera* at the *albergue*.

### Accommodation

Finisterre's **albergue** (40 beds, hot showers, kitchen, donation) doesn't open until late afternoon.

**$ Hostal Cabo Finisterre** (☎ 981 740 000)

**$ Hostal Rivas** (☎ 981 740 027)

---

From Finisterre, it's a short walk to the end of the world. To continue to the *faro* (lighthouse), walk past the *albergue*, turn right in a couple of hundred metres at Plaza Ara Solis, then turn left 50m later past the Capella de Nossa Senhora del Buensuccesso. Turn left when you reach the main road in a couple of hundred metres, soon passing the Iglesia de Santa María das Areas. Follow the road all the way to Cabo Finisterre, just over 2km away, watching out for cars as there's no shoulder. There are great views out to sea when the sun's out, but the walk is also murkily wonderful in bad weather.

You'll soon reach **Cabo Finisterre** (❶✕▬), the end of the world dramatically perched on a rocky headland. The Celts believed that the surrounding ocean was the Sea of Tenesbrosum, home to monsters and the gateway to paradise. The Romans were convinced that Finis Terrae was the end of the world where the sun was engulfed by the sea each night.

There are great views from the Vista Monte do Facho, high above the lighthouse. The menhir that once stood here was the scene of Celtic fertility rites, and couples copulated against the rock to increase their chances of conception before prudish church officials tore down the menhir in the eighteenth century.

There's no trace of Ara Solis, the Celts' prehistoric temple that drew sun-worshipping Iron Age pilgrims: you'll have to make do with the solid, whitewashed *faro* (lighthouse), a hotel-restaurant and a couple of pilgrim highlights. Below the lighthouse there's a small sculpture of a pair of walking boots, where profligate pilgrims traditionally burn their shoes and clothes to celebrate their arrival at the cape. A little too enthusiastically in some cases; the boots are now charred and misshapen. Nearby, a concrete post with a downward pointing scallop shell marks the end of the camino, a familiar and fittingly poignant symbol of your journey's end.

# Pilgrim Associations

Pilgrim associations are great places to get advice and to pick up a *credencial* (pilgrim passport) before you go.

## Great Britain

The **Confraternity of Saint James** (☎ 020 7928 9988; www.csj.org.uk) is the most well established and respected English-language pilgrim association. It promotes and conducts research into the camino, publishes a newsletter, maintains a library and organizes meetings.

## US

The **Friends of the Road to Santiago** at www.geocities.com/friends_usa_santiago publishes a newsletter and runs a listserv.

## Canada

The **Little Company of Pilgrims** (www.santiago.ca) holds meetings, publishes a newsletter and offers helpful advice. It can also provide you with a *credencial* before you leave.

## Ireland

Irish pilgrims can get useful information from the **Irish Society of the Friends of St James** at www.stjamesirl.com. The web site includes an electronic notice board for announcements.

## Australia

Australian pilgrims should contact the **Australian Amigos del Camino de Santiago** at hannan@werple.net.au.

## South Africa

The **Confraternity of Saint James of South Africa** has a web site with helpful tips and useful information on getting to the camino from South Africa. It's at www.geocities.com/marievanus.

**for the camino on the Internet, see www.pilipalapress.com**

# Further Reading

This is a selection of our favourite books on the Vía de la Plata, the Camino de Santiago and about Spain in general. Visit your local independent bookshop for other suggestions, or contact one of the following (which have all given Ben a job at some point in his life):

**Wanderlust**, 1929 West 4th Avenue, Vancouver, BC, Canada, ☎ 604 739 2182, www.wanderlustore.com.

**Stanfords**, 12–14 Long Acre, London WC2E 9LP, UK, ☎ 020 7836 1321, www.stanfords.co.uk.

**The Travel Bookshop**, 13–15 Blenheim Crescent, London W11 2EE, UK, ☎ 020 7229 5260, www.thetravelbookshop.co.uk.

There's a more detailed list of retailers of who stock our titles on our web site at www.pilipalapress.com.

## General

David Gitlitz and Linda Kay Davidson's *The Pilgrimage Road to Santiago: The Complete Cultural Handbook* (St Martin's Griffin, 2000) is a hefty, detailed description of the churches, monasteries and other monuments along the *camino francés*, but its Reference Points section is a good primer for all roads to Santiago.

Nancy Frey's *Pilgrim Stories: On and Off the Road to Santiago* (University of California Press, 1998) looks at pilgrims and the pilgrimage in a refreshing, accessible and thoughtful way; its fascinating insights into pilgrims' motivations make it one of the best books on the camino.

## Pilgrim Accounts

Although all of these pilgrim accounts describe the *camino francés*, they may be of interest to pilgrims travelling the Vía de la Plata too.

The Confraternity of St James publishes *The Pilgrim's Guide: A 12th century Guide for the Pilgrim to St James of Compostella* (1992), a translation of Aymeric Picaud's fascinatingly misanthropic trip along the *camino francés* that was one of the world's first travel guides. James Hall's translation of Domenico Laffi's seventeenth-century account is out-of-print and difficult to find, but Edwin Mullins' classic 1970s account, *The Pilgrimage to Santiago* has recently been re-issued by Interlink (2001).

Personal accounts of the camino almost inevitably reveal more about the writer than the walk itself. The most popular voyages of self-discovery are Shirley Maclaine's *The Camino: A Journey of the Spirit* (Pocket Books, 2001) and Paulo Coelho's *The Pilgrimage: A Contemporary Quest for Ancient Wisdom* (HarperCollins, 1995).

# Flora & Fauna

*Wild Spain* (Interlink, 2000), *Where to Watch Birds in Southern and Western Spain* (Christopher Helm, 2001) and *Where to Watch Birds in North & East Spain* (Christopher Helm, 1999) contain good general information, although there's not much specific detail on places along the Vía de la Plata.

## People & Culture

For the best background on Spain, read John Hooper's book, *The New Spaniards* (Penguin, 1995), an erudite account of Spanish life and culture by a British journalist. Raymond Carr has collected expert historians' accounts in *Spain: A History* (Oxford University Press, 2000), while Cees Nootebooms' *Roads to Santiago: Detours and Riddles in the Land and History of Spain* (Harcourt Brace, 1997) meanders delightfully through the country without ever getting very close to Santiago. *On Bullfighting* (Yellow Jersey Press, 2000) is A.L. Kennedy's reluctant, writing-as-therapy take on Spain's iconic and brutal spectacle.

## Food & Drink

If you're itching to try some Spanish cooking before you leave, Penelope Casas' *Delicioso: The Regional Cooking of Spain* (Knopf, 1996) will have you drooling; the same author's *Paella! Spectacular Rice Dishes from Spain* is a fabulous introduction to one of the country's best culinary inventions.

# Literature

The classic of Spanish literature is, of course, Miguel de Cervantes' *Don Quixote* (Penguin, 2003), whose stomping ground lies just east of the Vía de la Plata in Castilla–La Mancha; some of Cervantes' *Exemplary Stories* are set in various places along the route itself. Read Federico García Lorca for a view of Spain before the civil war; pick up *Federico García Lorca: Collected Poems* (Farrar Straus Giroux, 2002) for an introduction to his work, or Ian Gibson's *Federico García Lorca: A Life* (Faber & Faber, 1989) for more about the poet himself, who was killed by Nationalist rebels in Granada in 1936.

Galicia's most famous poet is Rosalía de Castro, who chronicled famine and hardship in mid-nineteenth-century Galicia; none of the English translations of her work are currently in-print. Manolo Rivas, who writes in his native *Galego*, has done more than any other modern writer to revive Galician literature; his works, including *The Carpenter's Pencil*, have been widely translated. Julián Rios' *Loves That Bind* (Vintage, 1999) is a prize-winning novel from an up-and-coming Galician writer. Born in Galicia but writing in Spanish, Nobel-prize winner Camilo José Cela's works include *Boxwood* (New Directions, 2002) and *Mazurka for Two Dead Men* (New Directions, 1994). For light relief and a cracking story, try Arturo Peréz-Reverte's stylish thrillers, particularly *The Seville Communion* (Harcourt Brace, 1998).

# Language

## Castellano (Spanish)

| | | | |
|---|---|---|---|
| yes | *sí* | please | *por favor* |
| no | *no* | thank you | *gracias* |
| hello | *hola* [h is silent] | good morning | *buenos días* |
| goodbye | *adios* | good afternoon (after *siesta*) | *buenas tardes* |

| | |
|---|---|
| Do you speak English/Spanish? | *¿Habla inglés/castellano?* |
| I don't speak Spanish | *No hablo castellano* |
| I (don't) understand | *(No) entiendo* |
| How much? | *¿Cuanto cuesta?* |
| Where is ...? | *¿Donde está?* |
| I'd like ... | *Quería* |
| What time does the ... open? | *¿A que hora se abre ...?* |
| Are there any rooms? | *¿Hay habitaciónes?* |

### Useful walking phrases

| | |
|---|---|
| What will the weather be like today? | *¿Qué tiempo hay hoy?* |
| How do I get to ...? | *¿Cómo se va a ....?* |
| What is this village called? | *¿Cómo se llama este pueblo?* |
| How many kilometres to ...? | *¿Cuantos kilómetros hay hasta ...?* |
| Where does this road/path lead? | *¿A dónde se va este sendero/esta carretera?* |

## More useful walking phrases

| | | | |
|---|---|---|---|
| I'm lost | *estoy perdido* | rain | *la lluvia* |
| I'm wet | *estoy mojado* | snow | *la nieve* |
| Let's go! | *¡Vamos!* | cloudy | *nubloso* |
| right | *derecha* | fog | *la niebla* |
| left | *izquierdo/a* | wind | *el viento* |
| straight on | *todo recto* | stormy | *tempestuoso* |
| near | *cerca* | sun | *el sol* |
| far | *lejos* | blister | *el ampollo* |
| open | *abierto* | key | *la llave* |
| closed | *cerrado* | supermarket | *el supermercado* |
| (it's) cold | *(hace) frío* | toilets | *los baños* |
| (I'm) hot | *(estoy) calor* | | *los servicios* |

## Days, months & seasons

| | | | |
|---|---|---|---|
| today | *hoy* | January | *enero* |
| tonight | *esta noche* | February | *febrero* |
| tomorrow | *mañana* | March | *marzo* |
| yesterday | *ayer* | April | *abril* |
| last night | *anoche* | May | *mayo* |
| weekend | *la fin de semana* | June | *junio* |
| | | July | *julio* |
| Monday | *lunes* | August | *agosto* |
| Tuesday | *martes* | September | *septiembre* |
| Wednesday | *miércoles* | October | *octubre* |
| Thursday | *jueves* | November | *noviembre* |
| Friday | *viernes* | December | *diciembre* |
| Saturday | *sábado* | | |
| Sunday | *domingo* | | |

| | | | |
|---|---|---|---|
| spring | *primavera* | autumn/fall | *otoño* |
| summer | *verano* | winter | *invierno* |

## Numbers

| | | | |
|---|---|---|---|
| 1 | *uno/una* | 17 | *diecisiete* |
| 2 | *dos* | 18 | *dieciocho* |
| 3 | *tres* | 19 | *diecinueve* |
| 4 | *cuatro* | 20 | *veinte* |
| 5 | *cinco* | 21 | *veinte y uno* |
| 6 | *seis* | 30 | *treinta* |
| 7 | *siete* | 40 | *cuarenta* |
| 8 | *ocho* | 50 | *cincuenta* |
| 9 | *nueve* | 60 | *sesenta* |
| 10 | *diez* | 70 | *setenta* |
| 11 | *once* | 80 | *ochenta* |
| 12 | *doce* | 90 | *noventa* |
| 13 | *trece* | 100 | *cien* |
| 14 | *catorce* | 200 | *doscientos* |
| 15 | *quince* | 300 | *trescientos* |
| 16 | *dieciséis* | 1000 | *mil* |

# Galego (Galician)

| | | | |
|---|---|---|---|
| yes | *sí* | please | *por favor* |
| no | *non* | thank you | *gracias* |
| hello | *hola* | good morning | *bos días* |
| goodbye | *adeus* | good afternoon | *boas tardes* |

# Glossary

Some Spanish words used in *Walking the Via de la Plata*, or words you're likely to see along the camino. We've also included English and other words when they may be unfamiliar.

**albergue** pilgrim hostel, see also *refugio*

**alcalde** mayor

**¡Animo!** Come on! (a term of encouragement amongst pilgrims)

**arroyo** stream

**autovía** motorway, highway

**ayuntamiento** town hall. You can usually get a *sello* here, and often the key to the *albergue*

**bocadillo** sandwich

**bodega** wine cellar

**bollard** concrete post

**bordón** staff. Many pilgrims like to walk with a traditional pilgrim staff

**calle** street

**camino francés** Camino de Santiago across the Pyrenees and northern Spain

**Cañada Real** Drove road used to move animals between summer and winter pastures

**capilla** chapel

**carnaval** carnival; a big festival held on Shrove Tuesday, the day before Lent

**carretera** main road, highway

**casa rural** small rural hotel, often a bed-and-breakfast

**cashpoint** bank machine

**Castellano** Spanish language

**castro** hill fort, usually Celtic

**chorizo** spicy cooked sausage

**comida casera** home cooking

**cordillera** range, chain of mountains

**costa** coast

**credencial** pilgrim passport, needed to stay at *albergues*

**cruceiro** stone crucifix

**dolmen** megalithic tomb

**donativo** donation. Most *albergues* on the Vía de la Plata rely on pilgrim donations to stay open

**drove road** wide track to move animals between summer and winter pastures

**embalse** dam, reservoir

**ermita** hermitage; small chapel, usually in isolated area

**farmacía** pharmacy

**faro** lighthouse

**finca** farm

**frontón** court on which *pelota* (*jai alai*) is played

**Galego** Galician language

**Galego/a** native of Galicia

**guardia civil** police. Often, the *guardia civil* will have the key to the local *albergue*

**hórreo** granary, usually made from stone and wood and raised on stilts; found mostly in Galicia

**hospital** medieval hospice, which functioned as hospital, *albergue* and hotel

**hospitalero/a** person who runs an *albergue*, usually a volunteer. There are very few *hospitaleros* on the Vía de la Plata. Be nice to them.

**iglesia** church

**lavadero** communal village laundry

**menhir** prehistoric monumental stone

**menú** set 3-course meal, usually the cheapest way to eat out; also called *menú del día*

**meseta** flat plains of north-central Spain

**miliario** milestone, usually Roman

**monasterio** monastery

**museo** museum

**palomar** dovecote (building for nesting doves or pigeons)

**panadería** bakery

**parador** national chain of luxury hotels

**paseo** ritual evening stroll through city streets

**pazo** Large country house in Galicia

**pelota** popular ball sport, also called *jai alai*; played on a *frontón*

**peregrino** pilgrim

**policía local** local police. Often, the *policía local* will have the key to the local *albergue*

**pozo** well

**puente** bridge

**pulpo** octopus, a Galician delicacy served at street stalls or in a *pulpería*

**reconquista** Christian reconquest of Spain from the Muslims from the eighth century onwards

**refugio** pilgrim hostel; see also *albergue*

**reliquary** small box containing relics (possessions or body parts of Saints or other holy persons)

**retablo** altarpiece

**río** river

**romería** religious procession to a local shrine, usually made annually

**Santiago** St James

**Santiago Matamoros** Santiago as a Moor-slayer

**Santiago Peregrino** Santiago as a pilgrim

**santuario** sanctuary or shrine

**sello** stamp for *credencial*, received at *albergues*, churches and even cafés; *sellos* are evidence that you've walked the camino

**Semana Santa** Holy Week, Easter week

**sidewalk** US English for pavement. If we used pavement, North Americans would be walking in the road

**tapas** snack-sized portions of food

**tarmac road** asphalt road

**turismo** tourist office

# Camino Log

Keep track of where you are, where you've been and where you're going...

**date**      **start/end**      **thoughts**

_____
_____
_____
_____
_____
_____
_____
_____
_____
_____
_____
_____
_____
_____
_____
_____
_____
_____
_____
_____
_____
_____
_____
_____
_____
_____

**date**       **start/end**       **thoughts**

# Keep in Touch

You'll meet a lot of people along the Vía de la Plata. You could scribble their addresses on a scrap of paper, but why not write them down somewhere safe?

| name | address | phone | e-mail |
|------|---------|-------|--------|
|      |         |       |        |

# Index

major places in **bold** type

**Index**

## h

Hadrian (Roman emperor) 4, 49
Hannibal 3–4
health 34–36
   insurance 30–31
Herod Agrippa 2
Hervás 99
hiking. See walking
History 10–12. See *also* under specific
   periods, events and people
   Andalucía 40–41
   books 196
   Extremadura 61
   *meseta* 102–103
hitching 32
holm oak 19
Holy Years 3, 5, 10, 161, 182
hoopoe 25, 102
Hospital 191
hot chocolate 17
hotels 33
hunting 8, 60, 127

## i

Iberian lynx 8, 22, 40
Iberian wall lizard 24
Inquisition 12, 47, 113
insurance 30–31
Internet 37
Isabel I (queen of Castilla) 11–12, 87
Isidro (saint) 4, 41, 57
Italica 11, 14, 44, 49

## j

James (saint). See Santiago
John Paul II (pope) 4–5
Juan Carlos (king) 12

## k

kestrel 28
key 214
kings. See *under* name of individual king

## l

Lago 189
Lago de Sanabria 142
Laffi, Domenico 191, 195
language. See *Castellano, Galego*, glossary
Laxe 175
Laza 152
Liñares 168
literature 196
Logoso 191
Los Santos de Maimona 71–72
lottery. See gambling
Lubián 147

## m

Maclaine, Shirley 195
Mandrás 168
map key 214
maps 7

# Map key

| | | | |
|---|---|---|---|
| • • • • • • | camino | □ | major town or village |
| ════════ | main road | O | other town or village |
| ──────── | other road | ♣ | wood |
| +++++++++++ | railway | ⚘ | vineyard |
| ─ ─ ─ ─ | international border | ⟩ | steep climb |
| ──────── | river | † | *cruceiro* (stone crucifix) |
| ⬭ | lake or sea | ⛪ | church |
| ⚘↗ | map orientation | ⊼ | picnic area |
| | | ∴ | historical site |

# Text symbols

| | | | |
|---|---|---|---|
| **A** | *albergue* | € | bank or cashpoint |
| Ⓐ | basic *albergue* (no beds) | ❶ | *turismo* (tourist office) |
| **H** | hotel | 🛒 | shop |
| ✕ | restaurant | ☎ | phone number |
| ☕ | café-bar | | |

# Hotel prices

| | | | |
|---|---|---|---|
| $ | up to €30 | $$$ | €50–€75 |
| $$ | €30–€50 | $$$$ | more than €75 |